CHRISTIAN SACRAMENTS
and
CHRISTIAN PERSONALITY

CHRISTIAN SACRAMENTS
and
CHRISTIAN PERSONALITY

—————

BERNARD J. COOKE, S.J.

Chairman, Department of Theology

Marquette University

HOLT, RINEHART AND WINSTON

New York   *Chicago*   *San Francisco*   *Toronto*   *London*

Imprimi potest
JOHN J. FOLEY, S.J.
Provincial, Wisconsin Province

Nihil obstat
RT. REV. JOHN A. SCHULIEN
Censor Librorum

Imprimatur
✝WILLIAM J. COUSINS
Archbishop of Milwaukee
May 25, 1965

Introductory Note

The whole world of Christian sacrament is meant
   . . . to make men holy and good in God's sight and by God's power,
   . . . to build up the body of Christ which is his Church, his people,
   . . . to show worship to God in praise and prayer.

The twentieth century is a time of religious discovery and recovery—and nowhere more than in the meaning of "sacrament" and the "sacramental life" of the Christian people to which this book is devoted. The Eucharist and all the sacraments and lesser sacramentals which depend on the Eucharist are recognized as deeds and acts. They are the deeds and acts of Christ in our midst.

Perhaps an older generation is too conscious of defective notions of sacrament and sacraments. Perhaps it is too fearful that sacramental action and observance in the Church should appear in the least mechanical, as if the meeting of God and man could be reduced to some merely automatic consequences. And an older generation is perhaps excessively worried lest rite and ritual be superficial and formal.

Yet every generation properly desires to hand on its own deepest insights to its successor. In the world of sacramental rite, as understood by Christians, this is precisely what is happening at the present moment. It is reflected in this book, which seeks to convey the profound reflections of the Church upon its own mysteries for another generation to build upon.

Without for a moment neglecting the sacraments as source of God's favor, as sacred things and channels of grace, we are now called to see them more clearly, more surely. They are the meeting place of God and man. They are occasions and celebrations. They are, in a word we are perhaps over-using, encounters with the Lord.

This encounter is a personal matter, touching the innermost reaches of the individual human spirit. The sacraments or signs are deeds of faith—understood as the most complete surrender and dedicated turning of man to God.

It may be that our present understanding of sacraments is no greater than that of the fifth century or the fifteenth century. But we have every reason to believe that it is stronger and deeper than that of a century or a generation ago. At least we have put aside every ritualistic or mechanical notion we might have had of the works of worship—in favor of genuine conversion to God, which we signify or express in the sacramental acts of the Church.

They are indeed acts of the Church, which means that they are done in the midst of the Church which is the gathering of God's people. And the most personal response of the individual to God's promise and call is at the same time effective for the good of the whole Christian family.

That is why the sacrament of Penance, whose circumstances may be most private and whose consequences are most personal, is seen more clearly as a reconciliation with the brethren, with the community which is the Church. That is why the Eucharist which we celebrate is better understood as the sign of the Church, as the symbol of the unity among the people called by God.

Pope Paul and the other bishops of the Second Vatican Council have given public witness to the faith of the Church, that faith which is seen and proclaimed in sacraments. They have found the key to the deeds by which the Church worships God in the meaning of sacraments or signs: the holiness of man before God is shown by signs which the senses perceive . . . the holiness of man is achieved in the very acts by which, with God's help, he turns to God (*Constitution on the Liturgy*, Art. 7).

This is the key, this is the point of departure, that the Church's signs—words and deeds and external things—are filled with meaning. Ideally that should make it all the easier to bridge the gap between theory and practice. In sacraments there is something we can touch or see or say. Our whole effort is directed toward making the words and deeds genuinely expressive—not form or show or sham.

We study the theory, that the practice may be real. We learn the doctrine, that our part may be sincere. We translate the abstractions and generalizations into the actions of men and women drawn together in the Christian community to fulfill God's purpose.

We are in the midst, not to say the throes, of the reform of the Church, hoping that the sacramental signs will signify more clearly, looking to fresh understanding and new depth in our Christian faith. Our task is to keep firmly within the main stream of Christian tradition—of the scriptures and of the fathers and teachers of the Church—while looking toward growth and newness.

This book stands in that stream. It grows out of the reflections of the Church over many centuries, but it turns always to the concrete reality of this moment and the great expectation of the future. It should help to bring the abstract doctrine closer to the situation of this moment in history, this moment in the life of each Christian who reads its pages. Its goal is the same as that of all Christian teaching, that we may be no less committed than Christians of the past—and indeed may come a little closer, through sacramental celebration, to the blessed hope of the Lord's coming and of our fulfillment as his people.

Frederick R. McManus

Author's Preface

Few things in the development of twentieth-century Catholicism are as important as its liturgical revitalization. With the decree of Vatican II on the liturgy, a solid basis has been laid for a continuing enrichment of the Church's sacramental life. But as the decree itself indicates, the realization of this important movement in the Church will be directly proportioned to the people's educated understanding of the sacramental actions they perform.

Though the primary purpose of this present book is to provide for college students a text that will lead them to a deeper understanding of sacramental life and of its role in the development of Christian personality, it is hoped that the book will appeal to a wider reading public. Many adult Catholics, who during their high school and college years received little explanation of liturgy, are eager for knowledge about the Mass and the other Christian sacraments. This book is intended for them also.

This volume, then, is not written for professional theologians nor for those who are seeking a technical understanding of the Church's liturgy. Rather, it is directed toward a non-professional but adult Catholic reading audience; and for this reason technical complications have been avoided as far as possible. In several places this has meant a simplification of the treatment in the sense that one of several possible explanations or opinions has been presented without any attempt to discuss or evaluate other approaches. Rather than complicate the text itself with such discussion or encumber the book with scholarly footnotes, it was decided to provide a short annotated bibliography at the end of each chapter. Hopefully, this will lead the reader to pursue the question further in the source documents used, and in other literature on the problems at issue.

Again, this book does not pretend to give a complete explanation, either historical or systematic, of the Christian sacramental system. No treatment is given to the sacrament of Anointing, and there is only a limited treatment of such important sacraments as Penance and Matrimony. Instead, the book tries to explain the basic structure of Christian sacramental living, to show its connection with the mysteries of Christian priesthood and sanctifying grace. The objective is not to provide a detailed understanding of all the aspects of sacrament but rather to explain the function of sacraments in the actual living of Christianity and in the development of the Christian person.

The biblical texts translated here are, with very few exceptions, taken from the *Revised Standard Version* (*RSV*), with kind permission of Thomas Nelson and Sons, publishers of the new Catholic edition. Grateful acknowledgment is also made to B. Herder Book Company, publishers of *The Church Teaches*, for excerpts from their translation of official Church documents.

Those to whom the author is indebted for the fact that this book has finally seen the light of day are too many to be acknowledged individually. Students to whom this material has been taught have contributed their reactions and insights. Fellow teachers who have commented and contributed by their suggestions have aided far more than they realize. However, one collaborator, Miss Pauline Turner, must be mentioned. Without her constant assistance and patient cooperation, it would have been impossible to write this book in the midst of a busy schedule of teaching and administration. Acknowledgment should also be given to Mr. Emmitt O'Connor of Holt, Rinehart and Winston for his interest in guiding this book through the process of publication.

Contents

List of Abbreviations

AAS   *Acta Apostolicae Sedis*

PG   Migne, *Patrologia Fraeca*

PL   Migne, *Patrologia Latina*

ST   St. Thomas Aquinas, *Summa Theologiae*

TCT   *The Church Teaches*

CHRISTIAN BAPTISM

•

THE BAPTISM OF JESUS

•

PRELIMINARY OBSERVATIONS

CHRIST'S CONTINUING ACTIONS

By its opening words, "In the beginning . . ." sacred scripture gives an essentially historical orientation to the inspired pages that follow, an orientation that is one of the characteristics of Christianity. While our discussion of the Christian life will not follow essentially this historical approach, but will rather take the transformation of the Christian as its center of focus, it seems appropriate to begin our consideration of the sacraments with that which is the actual beginning of each Christian's supernatural life: the sacramental act of Baptism. And since this Christian action is grounded in the historical event of Christ's own baptism at the Jordan, our theological study must logically start with this first clear instance of *Christian* sacramentalism.

Behind this choice of the baptism of Jesus as our starting point, there lies a much more profound reason than mere chronological priority. As knowledge of the sources of Catholic faith (namely, the Church's living tradition and its inspired expression in sacred scripture) grows deeper and more precise, theologians are becoming increasingly aware that the primitive Church saw the sacraments as continuations of those special acts, or signs, which Christ himself worked (cf. Jn 2:11). To put it still more graphically—and later chapters will

1

attempt to justify this in detail—in the Christian sacraments Christ himself continues the acts he began two thousand years ago in Palestine. Unless this be true, that the sacraments are still the actions of the risen Christ, the sacramental acts of the Church are no more than magic or superstition.

UNDERSTANDING THE SACRED TEXT

Three preliminary remarks may provide a foundation for understanding the New Testament account of the baptism of Christ:

1. In our study of the gospel account of Jesus' baptism by John the Baptist, the scenes of the baptism and temptation in the desert will be handled as a unity. Literary analysis of the text indicates that these two scenes were intended to be grasped as *one event*. Scripture scholars tell us that the literary unity between the two passages gives us good reason to believe that they were written down as a single fragment before being incorporated into the gospel narrative by the synoptic writers.

This literary unity of the two scenes may seem unimportant. However, it reflects the mentality of the early Church, and of the gospel writers, regarding the intrinsic unity of the baptism and temptation. This is of considerable importance in trying to understand Baptism, for it seems that both scenes were intended by the early Church as instruction regarding the significance of Christian Baptism.

2. Whenever we examine a passage of sacred scripture, whether in the Old or New Testament, our primary objective must always be to find the literal meaning of the text. This does not mean the obvious meaning of the text. The letter of Pope Pius XII on sacred scripture (*Divino Afflante Spiritu*) is very clear about the necessity of seeking this literal meaning. The Pope also explains what he understands by the "literal" meaning. It is that meaning which the human author intended. This intended meaning may be far from obvious to us who, at a distance of two thousand years, read the bible through the filter of our Greco-Roman-Teutonic heritage. It is painstaking work to try to reconstruct the mentality of writers whose way of thinking was so heavily influenced by ancient Semitic culture. Yet we must make the effort if we are to discover what scripture says, and not impose on scripture what we think it says.

3. In reading the gospel account of Christ's baptism, we should remember that the gospels were written to be records of the Church's earliest apostolic teaching, the *catechesis*. They were not intended to be biography or history in the ordinary modern sense. They were neither the apologetics nor the systematized theology we know today. Rather, they were *instruction* directed toward people who already possessed faith in Jesus as Messiah and Lord, instruction about a series of facts whose deeper understanding could come only with faith. They were a teaching meant to clarify simultaneously the meaning of Jesus and the meaning of the Christian community, teaching aimed not at erudite knowledge but at intelligent living of the Christian mystery. This is not to deny that the gospels are historical,

if by "historical" we mean that the events of Jesus' ministry, passion and resurrection did actually happen; for the very heart of the gospel catechesis is the fact that Jesus did really come as the suffering Servant of Yahweh, and did actually die and rise from the dead. But the evangelists are interested in more than the mere happening; they are interested (and this governs both their choice of the events they narrate and the manner in which they narrate them) in the *significance* of these happenings.

The following study of Christ's baptism will be divided into seven points:

1. The gospel writers depicted the baptism and temptation scenes (Mk 1:3-13; Mt 3:13-4:11; Lk 3:21-4:13) against an Old Testament background.
2. The primitive catechesis saw the baptism-temptation event as the beginning of Christian revelation.
3. Christ's baptism and temptation are portrayed as the beginning of a new Israel.
4. They are also depicted as the beginning of a new mankind, with Christ as the new Adam.
5. The baptism is viewed as the beginning of messianic fulfillment, for in this action Jesus first lays public claim to his role as Messiah.
6. Christ's action in accepting baptism constitutes an exercise of human freedom.
7. Christ's baptism constitutes a promise to institute the Eucharist.

1. OLD TESTAMENT BACKGROUND

THE COVENANT PATTERN

An analysis of any New Testament passage must always begin with an examination of the Old Testament background. Old Testament history and literature were the cultural framework in which the New Testament authors thought and wrote. This is not a matter of merely connecting isolated Old Testament texts with the gospel accounts (such as the baptism-temptation narrative), but of understanding the gospel description against the whole basic outlook and structure of Old Testament literature.

Though it is an oversimplification, we can characterize Old Testament literature as a faith-guided interpretation of the great deeds Yahweh worked for his people Israel. When we examine the way in which these "great deeds" are described in various literary forms, and especially in the characteristic "salvation history" form, we discover a five-step structure in each of the important events of the Old Testament.

In the Exodus, for example, Moses and the people are *called* out of Egypt; but they must *turn away* from their life in Egypt and toward the encounter with Yahweh in the desert before they can be definitively *elected* by God at Sinai.

This election is then solemnized in a *covenant* enacted at the foot of Sinai, and this occurrence is recalled throughout succeeding ages by a *sign*, the Sabbath.

The same basic pattern is found in the case of Abraham. He is *called* out of Ur of the Chaldees, but must *leave* his pagan homeland, and is only *chosen* by God when he arrives in the land of Canaan; in a mysterious *covenant* act the Most High binds himself to Abraham and vice versa, and circumcision is the lasting *memorial* of this event. This same pattern is found, analogously, in the origin of the Davidic kingship, in the mission of the prophets, even in the person and role of the Messiah. Without further analyzing the pattern's incidence in the Old Testament text, we can enumerate the five steps that comprise it:

   a. A calling, a vocation; God always takes the initiative.
   b. A conversion by the human beings concerned; they must turn away from their previous way of life.
   c. An election, in which God chooses the people as his, and they choose God as the divinity they will worship.
   d. A covenant action that solemnizes the election and makes it "legally binding."
   e. A commemorative sign, as a lasting reminder of the covenant agreement.

PROGRESSION OF OLD TESTAMENT EVENTS

As one event succeeds another in Old Testament salvation history, there is a clearly discernible progression. If, for the moment, we try to get behind the sacred writers' view of what happened and consider the happenings themselves, we can see that there actually was a developing process in which God fashioned the faith-understanding of his people. For instance, the prophetic mission of Ezekiel during the Babylonian exile in itself manifests a more profound religious insight than earlier missions do—e.g., that of Joshua or of Samuel. This progression in the events themselves was, in fact, also seen by the Old Testament writers, and it contributes significantly to their view of God's dealings with his people.

The meaning of the Exodus becomes progressively clearer to the people of God as they successively experience the other major events of their history. Thus, the Davidic kingship, the prophetic movement and the Babylonian exile all provide, each in its own way, a deeper understanding of the Exodus. This is what is meant by saying that each focal event is a "type" of each later focal event. Generally, too, the key figure in each event is a type of the leading figure in each of the succeeding events.

Similarly, in any focal event, each element of the five-step pattern described above is a type of its corresponding element in a later event. For instance, Abraham was called by God. Ezekiel and many others were subsequently called. And these "calls" or vocations become progressively more "spiritual."

In the Old Testament as a whole, the progressive series of leader-types culminates in the ideal of the Messiah. While the messianic expectancy is grounded in the promise made to David (2 Sam 7), and the earlier stages of messianism look only to a rather proximate scion of the Davidic family who will bring peace and prosperity, the figure of the Messiah becomes more and more idealized. It is above all in the great prophetic description of the Messiah in the "Book of Consolation" (the second part of Isaiah), where the Messiah is depicted as the Servant of Yahweh, and in the apocalyptic presentation of the messianic Son of Man in the book of Daniel (7:14), that the messianic hope reaches its deepest and most exalted expression. It is the Servant who will respond to Yahweh's call in perfect self-giving and who will establish a new covenant for all mankind; it is the Son of Man who epitomizes the vocation of the kingdom of the saints which will establish God's rule in a world beyond time.

JEWISH BAPTISM

Before analyzing the kind of baptism performed by John the Baptist, we shall examine the Jewish attitude toward ritual washing. As our information about the Palestinian world at the time of Jesus grows, we are becoming increasingly aware that baptizing was common. As a matter of fact, a whole baptizing movement was afoot. Old Testament literature, especially of the priestly tradition, gives ample witness to the importance of ritual purifications of one sort or another. The idea behind such purification was, in part, to remove a stain, whether of moral culpability or of mere ritual impurity (i.e., a stain incurred through violation of detailed ritual prescriptions). Water was also used to signify a certain healing, as if a ritual or moral fault involved a loss of wholeness in the individual or the people and the water's action served to restore this wholeness.

Rabbinic texts show that there was considerable discussion about the various situations requiring ablutions, the ways in which these ablutions were to be performed, the most effective kinds of water, and so forth. Furthermore, in many of these ritualistic uses of water, there seems to have been a connection between the action of washing and preparation for offering sacrifice.

One of the most interesting uses of baptizing is found in the initiation rites of Jewish proselytes. When these Gentiles were converted to Judaism, they were admitted to the chosen people through three successive rites: baptism, circumcision, and participation in the Pasch. Why, in addition to the two rites of circumcision and Pasch, expected of any Jew, was the proselyte compelled to undergo baptism? Rabbinic literature gives at least one answer: since the proselyte had not in his ancestry passed through the waters of the Exodus, he must now compensate for that omission by his own baptismal passage through water. We can therefore see what the attitude toward proselyte baptism is. Baptism does for a proselyte what generation and birth do for a Jew; the waters of baptism are parallel to the waters of the Exodus through which the Israelites passed when they made their decisive conversion to Yahweh.

QUMRAN BAPTISM

Somewhat different, but no less interesting, were the baptismal practices of the group of dissident priests who lived in community at Qumran, and whose existence and beliefs have become better known to us through the discovery of the Dead Sea scrolls. Among this group, ritual washings of one sort or another were important. Baptism seems to have been the heart of the solemn reception of a novice into the Qumran group. But there was also a regular repetition of this solemn baptizing—indicating that entry into the group was not the primary meaning of this ritual washing. Rather, the ceremony seems to have been a purification preparatory to worship. This would suit the priestly character of the group. Moreover, purifications fitted into the broader purpose of the Qumran community, that of preparing its members for the arrival of the messianic age.

JOHN'S BAPTISM

Whatever the relationship of John the Baptist to the Qumran community (and we do not yet know the final answer to that question), it seems quite definite that John's kind of baptism was different from theirs, and different also from proselytic baptism. The gospels tell us that John saw his baptizing as an immediate preparation for the advent of the kingdom of God, as an externalizing of the attitude of conversion possessed by those who came to be baptized. The Greek word used in the New Testament to describe the attitude connected with John's baptism is *metanoia*, which means "a change of mind." John invited people to accept his baptism in order to show that they were turning away from their previous life and committing themselves more genuinely to the kingdom of God. Contrary to Qumran practice, the person baptized by John seems to have received baptism only once. Unlike proselytic baptism, John's baptism was administered to those already Jewish by birth. Unlike many of the common Jewish ablutions, "cleansing" does not seem to have been particularly indicated by John's action. Rather, it had a unique meaning because it signified the baptized person's willingness to accept the kingdom whose imminent appearance John announces (Mt 3:2).

2. BEGINNING OF CHRISTIAN REVELATION

THE FIRST EVENT

Against this background of earlier Old Testament thought and practice, and later Jewish attitudes toward baptizing, we can better appreciate the baptism of Jesus by John in the Jordan. That the primitive Christian community considered this as the first event in the presentation of the "gospel" is abundantly clear from the four gospels and Acts. In the synoptics and in St. John, the gospel narrative proper (i.e., apart from the infancy account) begins with this event;

it is the first in the series of deeds that Jesus performed and to which his apostles were to bear witness. Shortly before Pentecost, when there was question of choosing a successor to Judas, it had to be someone who, in the words of St. Peter, had "accompanied us during all the time that the Lord Jesus went in and out among us, beginning from the baptism of John until the day when he was taken up from us . . ." (Acts 1:21-22). Christ's baptism by John was, then, a most important beginning.

Let us now analyze this action—as the origin of Christ's ministry and, to that extent, of Christianity itself. It is quite evident that Jesus, who until his baptism had lived at Nazareth, is now emerging from obscurity to give public witness to the truth he was sent to convey to men. What interested the early Church in its catechesis, and the gospel writers who recorded this catechesis for future Christians, was not simply the fact that Jesus began his public ministry at this time, but the *manner* in which he did so. To put it another way, what concerned the evangelists in recording this scene by the Jordan is the *significance* of the action, both in its essence and in its details.

To people steeped in the Old Testament and awaiting the coming of a great prophet, it was most meaningful that Jesus came to the Jordan. It was on the banks of the Jordan that the prophetic mantle had passed from Elijah to Elisha (2 Kings 2:13). Now Jesus comes to John, whom he was later to compare with Elijah (Mt 17:10-13). In a sense, it would have been inappropriate for Jesus to begin his prophetic career in any other spot. However, this was a relatively incidental aspect in the eyes of the early Christian community. What was more essential to their faith-vision was that Christ's baptism announced the beginning of a new Israel, the origin of a new mankind, the dawning of the messianic age. This was what Jesus revealed in his baptism and temptation.

3. BEGINNING OF A NEW ISRAEL

THE PEOPLE AS ISRAEL

The Old Testament writers who describe the Exodus (Israel's departure from Egypt and slavery, passage through the Red Sea, sojourn in the desert and entrance into the promised land of Canaan) view this event as the beginning of a new epoch in the history of man. Actually, it is the beginning of organized revealed religion. These happenings function as a sign, as a revelation, telling the newly formed people of Israel what kind of divinity Yahweh is, what sort of being man himself is, and what man must do to reach his destiny. Since he leads the people from a place of slavery (Egypt), this God is a saving God; since he guides them through the perils of sea and desert, he is the divinity who rules nature; since he has singled out this group of nomadic tribes as his chosen people, he is a God interested in man. During the desert years, God provides the people with food and drink—even when that requires a special action, as with the manna—thus revealing that he gives life. When he makes a blood covenant with them at Mount Sinai, he indicates, though only vaguely for the time being, that he wishes to share his own life with them. This experience of the Exodus and the knowledge of God which the Israelites gained from it, remains dominant in the thinking of the chosen people throughout the whole of the Old Testament period.

CHRIST AS ISRAEL

If we carefully examine the account of Christ's baptism as narrated in the synoptic gospels, we shall see that these writers, reflecting the mind of the primitive Church, view this action as the beginning of a new Israel. It is a parallel to, or a reliving of the beginnings of the chosen people as we have described them. There are several indications of this in the gospel texts:

a. Matthew's gospel incorporates, among the very few events concerning the infancy, the sojourn in Egypt. And the gospel mentions why this event is significant: "This was to fulfill what the Lord had spoken by the prophet, 'Out of Egypt have I called my son'" (Mt 2:15). These words, "Out of Egypt have I called my son" are a citation from the Book of Hosea (11:1). In this Old Testament passage, Yahweh calls his son, the people of Israel, out of Egypt. It is clear, then, that Matthew sees Christ being called as Israel was called. And just as Israel was called to pass through the waters of the Exodus, so Jesus is called to pass through the waters of the Jordan. Long before Christ, as far back as the time of Joshua, the waters of the Jordan were already intimately associated with the Exodus experience. At the last stage of the Exodus, the people, under the leadership of Joshua, had passed over the Jordan in order to conquer Jericho and enter the promised land.

b. Furthermore, Israel had been called by Yahweh to pass through the waters and into the desert. There the people Israel were tested, and they failed then as they were to fail again repeatedly throughout their history. In the New Testament Jesus is led by the Spirit from the waters of the Jordan into the desert to be tested by Satan. Just as the chosen people sojourned forty years in the desert, so Jesus remains in the desert forty days. The parallel, even in details of these events, is too striking to be accidental; the Synoptic writers saw and pointed to it.

c. This view of Christ, as the beginning of a new Israel at the same time that he is the fulfillment of the old Israel, becomes more profound and definite when we study the temptation of Jesus in the desert. As mentioned earlier, the baptism and temptation form a single event; a single message, or meaning, runs through both stages of the event. To understand the implications of the temptation we must see it against the background of chapters 6-8 in Deuteronomy. In these three chapters, Moses is delivering a discourse to the people. He recalls the temptations they had faced in the desert and their failure to overcome them. We know that the gospels see Jesus' temptations as related to this passage in Deuteronomy because the three responses of Jesus to the tempter are drawn from it. Reflection on the synoptic text reveals the parallels between Old and New Testament: the three tests of Jesus summarize the three key areas of temptation which Israel faced throughout her history.

Not by bread alone. Much of the spiritual danger that confronted Israel in the course of her history was due to the fact that in Egypt and Canaan the chosen people were surrounded by sedentary and agricultural civilizations. The Israelites themselves were gradually transformed from nomadic shepherds into an agricultural people. In the process, it was inevitable that Israel be attracted to the agricultural religions and deities of the surrounding civilizations—religions and deities whose chief function was to guarantee the success of crops and provide bread. Deuteronomy tells us (8:1 ff.) that God tested the people's fidelity to him by allowing them to be without bread in the desert. He then provided manna to teach them that their life was not dependent upon bread alone, but rather upon his all-powerful word. This lesson of the desert is frequently repeated in prophetic and wisdom teaching. True life is conditioned, ultimately, by one thing: willing conformity to the creative word of God as expressed in the law of the covenant. Basically, it is the lesson of the Sermon on the Mount "Seek first his kingdom and his righteousness and all these things shall be yours as well" (Mt 6:33). If men will do this, God's providence will take care of them; for Yahweh, the God of the covenant, is a father who provides for his children. Old Testament history tells us, all too clearly, that Israel did not learn this lesson. Israel neither trusted God's covenant providence, nor would she accept a God who was a father. Instead she all too frequently turned to idolatrous worship, to the gods of the fleshpots.

Satan's first temptation of Christ seems to be in this context. "If you are the Son of God" (i.e., if God has made a covenant with you), "turn these stones to bread" (Mt 4:3; cf. Lk 4:3). Christ was urged to pervert the covenant by substituting a false objective, bread, for the covenant's true objective, life. The temptation was designed to sabotage God's providential plan and to foster disbelief in the fatherhood of God. Christ replied by citing Deuteronomy 8:3: "Man does not live by bread alone," but by the word of the Lord. This was a cryptic way of saying that he understood the lesson of the desert, that he accepted wholeheartedly the God of the covenant who is also a Father, that his food was to do the will of him who sent him (cf. Jn 4:34).

Testing God. If the first temptation was to mistrust the covenant, the second was designed to promote a misguided, presumptuous trust: "If you are the Son of God, throw yourself down. . . ." (Mt 4:6, Lk 4:9). This temptation to misinterpret the covenant, twisting it in order to make it fit one's own preconceived ideas and desires, and to expect that God will fulfill such a falsified view, marks every stage of Israel's religious history. Yahweh had promised Israel salvation from her enemies, but Israel was constantly impatient with God's way of accomplishing this salvation, constantly trying to dictate to him the manner in which he should save Israel. This failure of the people is adverted to in the eighth chapter of Judith. Judith upbraids the leaders of the people because they "have fixed a time for the mercy of the Lord and . . . have appointed a day for him, according to [their] whim" (8:13). Before, in the incident at Raphidim, where the people demanded, in effect, that the Lord prove himself by giving them water and which became for Old Testament thought a classic example of Israel's sins against the covenant, the people had tried to put Yahweh's covenant fidelity to the test, laying down their own conditions (Ex 17:7). The rejection of Christ by the majority of his Jewish contemporaries was rooted in this same fault. Because of their false ideas about the coming Messiah, the people had laid down for God the conditions according to which he was to achieve their salvation.

The fact that Satan quotes from Psalm 91 makes it clear that the issue is trust in God's covenant promise of salvation and, specifically, of messianic salvation. But he attempts to have Christ impose on his Father the way in which this messianic salvation will be achieved. Christ peremptorily rejects this temptation with the words of Deuteronomy 6:16: "You shall not put the Lord your God to the test" (cf. Mt 4:7, Lk 4:12).

Power and glory. The first two temptations were designed to bring about mistrust and perversion of the new covenant; the third temptation represents an unconcealed invitation to abandon it in favor of an alliance with Satan himself. Again we encounter a basic temptation that runs through Israel's history: the temptation to seek security and power and glory by making alliances with the powers of this world, instead of trusting in the alliance with Yahweh. What had always made these foreign alliances so dangerous for Israel's religious life was the fact that they led to acceptance and idolatrous worship of foreign gods. With this came the radical rejection of the covenant with Yahweh, for the essence of Israel's acceptance of the covenant lay in its acceptance of Yahweh as the only God.

Christ, by rejecting Satan, fulfilled perfectly the first precept of the covenant law; this is indicated by his citation of Deuteronomy 6:13: "You shall fear the Lord your God, you shall serve him, and swear by his name" (cf. Mt 4:10, Lk 4:8). More important, he obeyed his Father in accepting the full truth of the revelation that God had been making for centuries, especially through the prophets: the only source of true power (*exousia*) and glory (*doxa*) is the divine power and glory working for man's salvation through the spirit and the word. Thus, he rejects the false *exousia* and *doxa* offered him by the tempter. It was in this way that Satan, utilizing the same basic temptations by which he had led Israel to sin against the covenant, was completely thwarted by the new Israel's absolute adherence to the new covenant.

It is quite clear, then, that Jesus is, in his baptism and temptation, reliving the Exodus experience of Israel. As the new Israel, he lives this experience in justice and conformity with his Father's plan, making up for the waywardness of the Old Testament people.

4. BEGINNING OF A NEW MANKIND

ADAM AND CHRIST

When the writer of the book of Genesis in somewhat poetic fashion describes the creation of the world, he pictures God as first bringing into being a chaotic mass which is thought of in terms of water. Then God speaks, and his spirit "broods over the waters" (the word used for "brooding" suggests the image of a bird hovering). By the word and spirit of God, order and life gradually emerge from this first state of chaos (Gen 1:2). Genesis then goes on to describe the making of Adam: how God placed him in a garden so that he could take care of it; how Adam, whose first condition was one of complete order, lived in peace and harmony with all the animals; how there was no death in the original Paradise; how Adam and his decision to accept or refuse God's command conditioned the destiny of the whole human race descended from Adam. Finally, Genesis describes the sin of Adam and Eve and the resultant loss of order and life. Thoroughly familiar as they were with this Old Testament picture of creation, the synoptic writers would not accidentally have incorporated into their account of Christ's baptism those elements, even though they are few, that point to Christ as a new Adam, the beginning of a new mankind.

Just as the biblical description of the origin of the world and of man poetically pictures the spirit of God brooding like a bird over the chaotic waters, so in the scene of the baptism, the Holy Spirit, symbolized by a dove, descends as Christ steps from the waters of the Jordan to begin his task of bringing life and order to the world.

Moreover, there is probably some relationship in the minds of the gospel writers between Christ's temptation by Satan and Adam's temptation by the serpent. St. Luke's gospel, in particular, indicates the link between Christ and Adam (Lk 3:21-4:13). Luke separates the two episodes of baptism and temptation by giving the genealogy of Christ and tracing it back to Adam, not just to Abraham as in the genealogy prefacing Matthew's gospel. Furthermore, just as Adam lived in peace with all the animals in Paradise, even the wild ones, so Christ, according to Mark, "was in the midst of wild animals" in the desert (cf. Mk 1:13). Thus, the scene of baptism-temptation is depicted as the beginning of a new life, of a "new humanity" with the new Adam as its head.

5. BEGINNING OF THE MESSIANIC AGE

EXPECTATION AND FULFILLMENT

About half way through the Old Testament period, and under the influence of the great literary prophets, the Israelites began to look to some future event which they called the "day of the Lord."

Initially, they expected this day to be a day of destruction, a time when God would come to punish the chosen people for their infidelity to the covenant made at Sinai. Mixed with this expectation of doom were some rays of hope, some indications (as in Hosea 2) that the punishment would be followed by a reconciliation with God. But, for the most part, early thinking with regard to the coming "day of the Lord" was filled with fear and dread. This fearful view was confirmed by the utter destruction of the northern kingdom of Israel (about 700 B.C.) and the later destruction of Jerusalem, followed by the Babylonian exile (about 600 B.C.).

After the destruction of Jerusalem, the "day of the Lord" becomes the day of expected salvation and restoration. All the later centuries of the Old Testament look forward to an event marking the triumph of Israel and God over the forces of evil. Beginning with the prophet Isaiah, who was active even before the Babylonian exile, the people of the southern kingdom of Judah had looked forward to some great Davidic king. This king would establish justice and rule wisely, as David had ruled; he would make the enemies of Israel his subjects; he would bring peace and prosperity to God's people; God would use him as the instrument to effect Israel's salvation.

Over the centuries, the expectation of the Messiah is somewhat modified. His kingly character receives less attention, and prophetic ideals are applied to him. Perhaps the most important passages referring to this messianic figure are the Servant songs found in the second part of the book of Isaiah. These songs are so named because they describe the expected human "savior" as the great servant of God. At the beginning of the first song, God addresses the listener: "Behold my servant, whom I uphold, my chosen, in whom my soul delights" (Is 42:1).

At the baptism of Jesus, the voice of the heavenly Father is heard: "This is my beloved Son, with whom I am well pleased" (Mt 3:17; cf. Mk 1:11, Lk 3:22). We cannot miss the parallel. Jesus is depicted as the servant foretold in Isaiah, and the baptism is the occasion of Christ's public acceptance of his vocation to be this kind of Messiah.

The baptism of Jesus is, then, the inauguration of the messianic age; the Messiah has appeared on the scene, heralded by John the Baptist in whom is fulfilled Malachi's prophecy: "I send my messenger to prepare the way before me . . ." (3:1). Christ's public acceptance of his messianic role is the first step in the realization of the salvation to be accomplished through him. The kingdom of heaven, meant to triumph in the "day of the Lord," is no longer a thing of the vague future. "The kingdom of heaven is at hand" (Mt 4:17).

Appearing publicly at the Jordan in his prophetic role, Jesus inaugurates the new and definitive phase of the process of revelation carried forward by God throughout all the previous Old Testament centuries. And just as Old Testament revelation had come through *signs* that God worked for his people, so Jesus continued to reveal, but through a new series of signs. Among these specially significant or symbolic actions of Jesus during his public ministry, the baptism is the first. The baptism of Jesus and the sign worked at the marriage in Cana are joined together both by St. John in his gospel and by the early Church in the liturgy of the Epiphany. The fact that Old Testament revelation is here giving way to the New is manifested by the relationship between John the Baptist and Christ. Christ himself testifies that John was the greatest of the Old Testament prophets, because the Baptist is the immediate witness to the Messiah. Yet, he fades from the picture once Jesus begins to preach. With John, the Old Testament ministry of teaching and prophecy is finished.

6. CHRIST'S BAPTISM, A FREE CHOICE

CHRIST'S PERSONAL SELF-COMMITMENT

Christ's baptism, then, established him as the new Israel, new Adam, and Messiah. Now we can see the way in which Christ here realizes the five-point covenant pattern discussed earlier in this chapter. In answer to the call issued by the Baptist to all Israel to accept the coming kingdom of God, Christ "converts" from his previous hidden life by leaving it and coming to the waters of the Jordan. At the moment when Christ manifests his free acceptance of his messianic role, the Father reciprocally announces his *election* of Christ as his chosen one. Christ's action is a pledge of the new covenant; and the lasting sign of his action is Christian Baptism.

If we view the baptism this way, as Christ and the early Church viewed it, we cannot fail to notice that Christ's action is essentially one of free choice. The religious value of this free act, its importance in the scheme of man's salvation, lies not in the externals of the action but in Christ's own internal attitude. Passive submission to the ceremony administered by John would have had no great efficacy; what really mattered was the fact that Christ was completely and unquestioningly accepting the role of suffering Messiah.

This is a basic point; it must be appreciated if we are to understand Christ's work of redemption or the work of the Christian sacraments. As a human being, Christ's highest and most dignified level of personal activity could come only in an exercise of freedom which engaged his human consciousness and affectivity. It is inconceivable that the most important thing Jesus did—redeeming mankind by worshiping his Father—should not have involved his free, human self-commitment. To assume that the force of Christ's redemptive acts or of the Christian sacraments consists essentially in externals is to reduce the whole Christian mystery to magic. If any supplementary interpretation of the baptismal scene is needed to show that it is fundamentally a free choice situation, that interpretation may be found in the conjoined temptation scene, where Jesus is urged to make choices contrary to the plan of divine wisdom.

Thus, from the very beginning of the gospel, the early Christian was told that *correct use of freedom lies at the very heart of the mystery of Christ.* This is a precious insight, which must orient our entire study of the sacraments and of the Christian life that flows from them.

a. As mentioned earlier, Christ publicly manifested his acceptance of his messianic role as Servant of Yahweh. It is important to note, however, that Jesus does not begin his acceptance at this point. It is at the Jordan that he solemnly and publicly declares this acceptance for the first time. This acceptance involved embracing the vocation his heavenly Father had given him; he was to be a Messiah who would save mankind by suffering and death. Everything Christ ever said or did, everything that happened to him in his life and in his death, was part of this vocation. Therefore, in accepting it Christ was making a choice that was total; he was choosing a whole way of life. Adam had refused to accept the way of life that God proposed to him; Israel had refused to trust in God and accept God's way for caring for his people. Now the new Adam, the new Israel, makes up for that refusal by fully accepting his vocation.

The objection is often raised that Christ could not have really exercised free choice in accepting his Father's will, since it was impossible for him as a divine person to make a sinful choice. While we do not fully understand the mystery of Christ's human freedom, it will help us to reflect on two points.

First, Christ made it clear that his death and resurrection were his own deliberate choice: "I lay down my life, that I may take it again. No one takes it from me, but I lay it down of my own accord. I have power to lay it down, and I have power to take it again" (Jn 10:17-18). Secondly, human beings are free to determine who and what they will become in proportion as they love, for love is a liberating reality. Christ's love for his Father was so all-engrossing that he could not want to do anything that would separate them. But that does not mean that Christ was less free in this regard. He was doing exactly what he wanted to do.

b. It is important to compare the baptism and temptation from the viewpoint of choice. In both scenes the choice is the same: Christ asserts that he accepts his messianic calling. However, there is this important difference: the baptism is symbolic, the temptation is nonsymbolic. It is only by examining the symbolic meanings of the baptism that we can see that Christ was there declaring himself the Servant of Yahweh. In the tempting by Satan, it is made perfectly clear and explicit that Christ is refusing to abandon the kind of messiahship determined for him by his Father. The transfiguration and last supper also show Christ symbolically accepting his messianic role.

All this has very great significance. Just as Christ externally manifested his acceptance of the Father's will in two kinds of action, symbolic and nonsymbolic, so too we are to manifest our acceptance of God's will for us by both symbolic and nonsymbolic action. The nonsymbolic manifestation is in our ordinary daily actions, done in conformity to God's will; the symbolic manifestation is found for us in the Christian sacramental system, beginning with our Baptism.

7. PROMISE OF EUCHARIST

BAPTISM AS COVENANT-PLEDGE

When viewed within the perspective of his whole public life, Christ's baptism is a solemn public promise to institute the Eucharist. Not that the people who witnessed John baptizing Jesus saw, at the time, that Jesus was committing himself to the Eucharistic action of the last supper, but rather that the apostles realized this after Christ's resurrection from the dead.

Christ, by his baptism, was publicly accepting the role of the Servant of God. In the first of the Servant songs it is also said that the Servant will establish a new covenant or, more accurately, that he will somehow *be* a new covenant between mankind and God: "I have given you as a covenant to the people, a light to the nations . . ." (Is 42:6). Therefore, in claiming to be this Servant, Jesus was pledging himself to undertake the establishment of the new covenant. At the last supper Christ took the chalice of wine and said, "This cup is the new covenant in my blood" (1 Cor 11:25). By his baptism Christ promised to enter into his public career and to end it with the Eucharist, and the fulfillment of the Eucharist in his death and resurrection.

Thus there was a very intimate link between these two great symbolic actions of Jesus. Had the institution of the Eucharist not taken place, the full meaning of the baptism would never have been realized. Without the Eucharist, the baptism of Christ would have been completely and essentially meaningless.

CHRISTIAN BAPTISM

ST. PAUL ON CHRISTIAN BAPTISM

THE PAULINE EMPHASIS

A cursory look at the teaching of St. Paul regarding the Christian sacrament of Baptism in the early Christian community is now in order. We have seen that the synoptic presentation of Christ's baptism was really a profound form of catechesis about the Christian sacrament. St. Paul instructs the early Christians more explicitly regarding the implications of the sacramental rites. Pauline teaching on Baptism is inseparably intertwined with his whole message; nevertheless a study of five basic elements will help us understand the present-day rite of Baptism.

UNION WITH CHRIST

One theme runs throughout the writings of St. Paul: the Christian is united with Christ, lives with Christ, lives in and through Christ (Col 3:3-4; Gal 3:27).

This union with Jesus is begun in the Christian rite of initiation, above all in the first step of that initiation, Baptism (Col 2:12).

Precisely because of each Christian's union with the living Christ, there exists a profound union of each Christian with all other Christians (Eph 4:4-6). They share "one Lord, one faith, one baptism" (4:5). True, the bond of communal love and the action of the Holy Spirit, who causes this love, are also forces of unity among Christians (Col 3:15), but the union of each Christian with Christ is the most essential consideration.

We would miss the full meaning of Paul's message if we failed to appreciate Paul's statement that we are baptized *into* Christ (Rom 6:3). Christ and the fulfillment of the Christian mystery are the goal of the baptismal act; Christians are meant to progressively "put on Christ" (Gal 3:27). Christ is meant to "grow on them" in a very real sense; they are to enter into the intentions and hopes and motivations of Christ himself as he works through those who are his Church.

Union with Christ's Death and Resurrection

In line with the baptismal practice of his day (in which Christians went down into the water and emerged from it), St. Paul teaches that the Christian is assimilated to Christ's death and resurrection through Baptism (Rom 6:1-11). In going down into the water, one dies and is buried with Christ. In emerging one rises with Christ to new life. It is clear that the Christian, knowing this symbolism of the baptismal ceremony, was at his Baptism publicly manifesting his belief in these mysteries of Christ. He was also, by assenting to the wisdom of Christ in accepting death and resurrection, joining his own attitude to Christ's. Thus the consciousness and will of the baptized Christian is deeply conformed to the mysteries of Christ's death and resurrection (Rom 12:1-2).

But St. Paul is also talking about something even deeper. There is a real insertion of the baptized into the historical events of Christ's death, burial and resurrection. Mysteriously, the Christian dies with Christ—dies, that is, to the old life of sin and enslavement to evil and to legalistic religion. The "old self" is buried in the waters of Baptism (Rom 6:6). Mysteriously, too, the Christian rises to begin new life in Christ, the life that is to be his unending existence (Rom 6:9-11). From this point onward he can appropriate to himself the words of the Apostle: "It is no longer I who live, but Christ who lives in me" (Gal 2:20).

Incorporation into Christ

There are several ways in which St. Paul attempts to express the extent of our union with Christ through Baptism. Perhaps the most frequent is that of incorporation into Christ. This involves the whole mystery of Christ continuing to live on throughout history in those who form his Church, the mystery that Paul calls the "mystery hidden for ages . . ." (Eph 3:9). This is the mystery to which we refer as "mystical body of Christ." In Baptism, the new Christian is made a member of this living organism, the corporate body of Christ; he begins to live with the life of Christ that courses through this body. Literally, he lives in Christ and Christ lives in him. Christ, with his members, forms the "new creation" (2 Cor 5:17; cf. Gal 3:28), the corporate reality that is the key to the understanding of the Christian era of human history. Each Christian is meant to contribute to the development of this new creation (2 Cor 5:17); at the same time, each Christian as an individual should grow to the full stature of Christ.

This new reality, Christ and his members, is the fulfillment and replacement of Israel as the people of God; the Church is the new Israel (Gal 6:16). Since the Old Testament people were already considered a priestly race (Ex 19:5-6), the new Christian enters upon a life of priesthood, he becomes a part of a sacerdotal people (as is also stated in the baptismal catechesis contained in 1 Pet 2:5). Just as faith was the prime requisite for true membership in Israel, so the Christian must accept the mystery of Christ in humble faith, and profess it in Baptism, the sacrament of faith. It is clear from such passages in Paul that the early Church saw baptism as an action of professing faith in Christ.

REDEMPTION BY CHRIST

However, Baptism is most essentially an action of Christ himself. As such, it is the continuing redemption of the individual Christian and of the entire Church.

Without attempting to distinguish between the elements that belong properly to Baptism and those that pertain germinally to the sacrament of Confirmation (a most difficult historical problem), we can point to the *signing* of the Christian to which St. Paul refers. The newly baptized person is signed with the mark of Christ. St. Paul compares this mark to the mark "paid" or "canceled" stamped on a bill one owes. In this case, the unbaptized person carries in himself the debt owed to God because of sin. In Baptism this debt is canceled; Christians are, as it were, marked "paid." Christ places this mark of cancellation through his death on Calvary (Col 2:14) for it was on Calvary that he paid the debt of our sins.

The baptized is bought back, he is redeemed; he now belongs to Christ, is possessed by him. To be possessed by Christ is not a slavery; rather, the Christian has been freed from enslavement to sin and can now begin a life of free service in the kingdom of God (Rom 7:1-6). Christ paid the debt of our sins on Calvary; Baptism, because it is an entry into the mystery of Christ's death, makes us the beneficiaries of its saving power.

"SEALING" BY THE HOLY SPIRIT

The mark connected with Baptism is, however, not only the mark of Christ; it is also the mark of the Holy Spirit. Pauline teaching on this point is complex and highly nuanced, and it is part of his treatment of the basic tension between "flesh" and "spirit." We are marked in Baptism by the Holy Spirit in the sense that the third Person of the Trinity is given to us by Christ, and his abiding presence marks us out, in most profound fashion, as belonging to Christ, "for by one Spirit we were all baptized into one body" (1 Cor 12:13). In his abiding presence, this Spirit leaves a mark on us, a transformation rendering us intrinsically Christ-like. St. Paul speaks quite definitely about the reality of this seal, as we can see from a passage in his second letter to the Corinthians: "But it is God who establishes us with you in Christ, and has commissioned us; he has put his seal upon us and given us his Spirit in our hearts as a guarantee" (1:21-22). But St. Paul does not delineate the nature of the sealing, and it took several centuries of Christian reflection before this *sphragis* was understood in detail. Actually, in St. Paul, it seems to involve elements both of grace and of the sacramental character.

CHRISTIAN BAPTISM TODAY

CONTINUITY WITH PRIMITIVE CHRISTIANITY

New Testament literature gives us an extremely valuable but tantalizingly fragmentary glimpse into early Christian sacramental practice and theology. If we were to enter into a complete scientific investigation of Baptism, we would have to trace the gradual clarification of sacramental theology through medieval theology and canon law, through the problems of the Protestant Reformation and on into modern times. We do not have space here to pursue an exhaustive historical study; instead we shall study the baptismal ritual of the present-day Church—a ritual that shows surprising continuity, even in details, with the most ancient Christian baptismal ceremony known.

ENTRY INTO THE PEOPLE

Christian Baptism is, quite definitely, an *entry into a new chosen people, the Church*. In the ordinary setting for the administration of Baptism in the early Church—the Easter Vigil—after the completion of the ceremonies in the baptistery, the catechumens were solemnly led into the Church and were received by the Christian community assembled there for the Easter celebration. Entrance into the building itself, the symbol of the spiritual temple which is the real Church, was a sign of the catechumens' desire to enter the Church. That this significance was seen by the early Christians is manifest from the prayer which the bishop said over the newly baptized immediately after entry into the church building:

We bless you, Almighty Lord God, that you have restored these as worthy to be born again, and that you pour out upon them thy Holy Spirit, so that

they are now united to the body of the Church, never to be separated by
alien works . . .

The baptismal bath was also looked upon as the womb of the Church in which
the children of God received a new birth.

In comparison with the ceremonies surrounding the sacrament of Baptism in
the early Church, our modern-day practices are considerably modified and abbre-
viated. Despite this fact, the essential meanings are retained. For example, the
significance of entry into the Church remains in today's rite, although the sign
itself is truncated. The instructions for the baptismal rite direct the priest to meet
the candidate at the door of the baptistery where the candidate must express his
desire to enter the community of faith.

REDEMPTION FROM THE POWER OF EVIL

The series of exorcisms and accompanying blessings symbolize the fact that
this individual, who is about to enter into the Christian mystery, is being freed
from that period of history when Satan, as Christ himself describes him, was
"the ruler of this world" (Jn 14:30). In the Easter Vigil ceremony described for
us by St. Cyril of Jerusalem (about 350 A.D.), the final rite before the actual
baptizing took place in the outer hall of the baptistery. Here the catechumens
would turn to the west, the region of sensible darkness symbolically standing for
the dominion of Satan, and renounce the devil, his works, pomp and service
(*Mystagogic Catechesis*). This climactic rejection of Satan had been prepared for
by the rite of exorcism which the catechumens underwent during the forty days
of Lent just before their daily catechesis. The exorcism ritual was designed to
free the soul little by little from the power the demon exercised over the catechumen, and so prepare him for Baptism.

Today's baptismal ceremony points to this same reality. First, the person being
baptized undergoes a solemn exorcism in which the priest, in God's name and by
his authority, commands the spirit of evil to withdraw from the body and the life
of the person to be baptized. Then, in an act symbolizing departure from the realm
of Satan and entry into the kingdom of God, the catechumen is led by the priest
from the entrance of the church into the house of God. For the baptized person,
this signifies an entry into the Christ-dominated age of the world, for he becomes
at this moment part of the Christian era of human history.

COMMUNICATION OF LIFE

The ceremony quite clearly indicates the fact that a *new life* is communicated
to man. In the conversation between Christ and Nicodemus, we find Christ telling Nicodemus that "unless one is born anew, he cannot see the kingdom of
God" (Jn 3:3). Throughout this entire discourse, it is stressed that what is on

the natural level, the level of flesh, cannot reach the divine level without being elevated. This elevation cannot be accomplished solely by man's power. In order to make it possible, the second Person of the Trinity descended from the divine to the human level, assumed a human nature and experienced the salvific events of death, resurrection and ascension. He did this in order to raise man to a divine level of living. John's text further explains the motivation and necessity for this: "For God so loved the world that he gave his only Son, that whoever believes in him should not perish but have eternal life" (Jn 3:16).

In Christ's own teaching, then, Baptism is described as a *new birth*. This regeneration, brought about through the action of water and the Holy Spirit, draws upon the effective salvific activity of Christ and culminates in elevation to new life for the baptized person. The idea of new life emerging from water made fecund by the Spirit of God, first introduced in the Genesis narrative of creation and deepened through understanding of Christ's own baptism, is finally transformed in the new context of Christ's resurrection. The new life to which we are called, and into which we emerge as we come from the baptismal font, is a *participation in the risen life* of the glorified Christ.

The baptismal practice of the early Church presents this symbolism more clearly than does the present-day ceremony. In earlier times, Baptism was administered at least partially by immersion—i.e., the person being baptized went down into the water. This action of descending into the waters was looked upon as a symbolic entry into the death and burial of Christ (for water can cause death). Emerging from the baptismal waters symbolized participation in the life of the resurrected Christ (for water can also cause life).

Acceptance of Vocation

Finally, the ceremonies of Baptism indicate that the baptized person is undertaking a vocation that continues Christ's own messianic role. Immediately after the actual baptizing, the baptized is anointed on the top of the head with blessed chrism (the same consecrated mixture of oil and balsam that is used by the bishop at Confirmation) to signify an initial, and very important, possession of the baptized person by the Holy Spirit. This anointing, this conferring of the Holy Spirit, this "Christ-ing" constitutes our appointment to the Christian vocation. Henceforth, the baptized is irrevocably set aside for that apostolic life which Christ as Messiah initiated, and to which he admits us in order to complete his messianic work.

With the sacrament of Confirmation comes an intensification of this Christian vocation to apostolic life, for Confirmation marks a man for a specific kind of participation in the power of the Holy Spirit. Both Baptism and Confirmation indicate ceremonially that the baptized person possesses and is possessed by the Spirit.

EXERCISE OF FREEDOM

Any treatment of Baptism must emphasize the fact that it involves choice. This is clearly demonstrated in the baptismal ceremony. After the final exorcism the neophyte is asked: "Do you renounce Satan?" The response is: "I do renounce him." An adult answers for himself, an infant through its sponsors. Then, after the anointing, the one to be baptized is solemnly asked to profess his faith in each person of the Trinity and in the Church. His profession of faith completed, the neophyte publicly expresses his decision to be baptized, answering the question, "Do you wish to be baptized?" with a clear and explicit "I do." After making this choice, characterized on the one hand as a rejection of Satan and his works, and on the other as a positive and direct choice to accept the Trinity and Church, the neophyte is washed in the baptismal waters.

What are the works of Satan the baptized chooses to reject? Christ's baptism, because it is closely linked with the diabolical trials he underwent in the desert, provides the answer. The temptations he encountered there were the same three temptations Israel faced time and time again throughout her history.

In the time of the new Israel, the Church, these temptations must be faced by every man who is summoned to the Christian vocation. In Baptism, the new Christian joins himself to Christ's own initial rejection of them. Just as the renunciation of Satan, his works and pomps was an enduring decision for Christ, so it is meant to be an enduring decision for the newly baptized Christian. Each year at the Easter Vigil he will reaffirm his baptismal promises when, during the ceremony, these questions will be put to him: "Do you renounce Satan? And all his works? And all his pomps?"

In the baptismal ceremony the neophyte is called upon not only to acknowledge his rejection of Satan and to cut himself off from the sphere of evil; he is also summoned, and this is even more important, to publicly profess his adherence to Christ. Baptism symbolizes an assimilation to the death and resurrection of Christ. This is evident from the fact that the baptized person publicly presents himself for the sacrament of Baptism and declares—before all who wish to see— that he is abandoning a secular way of life and adopting Christ's principles. He is publicly asserting his acceptance of Christ's death and resurrection. It is obvious why Baptism has always been called the sacramentum fidei, the sacrament or sign of faith: Baptism is a commitment of oneself to Christ in the mystery of the Church.

Just as Christ's acceptance of his messianic vocation was a choice involving his entire human existence, so *the Christian vocation is a total choice.* When we accept Christ as he is in the mystery of the mystical body, we are committing ourselves to principles that govern all our human acts; there is nothing in the whole of our lives that is not touched by the supernatural mystery of Christianity. The profession of belief which the baptized person makes during the baptismal ceremony implicitly affirms this.

Baptism is not an action which happens once and has no further significance for our life; rather, all the significance of this sacrament passes dynamically into the daily living of the Christian. The Church annually brings this important fact to our attention in the Easter Vigil services when she explicitly asks us to "renew the promises of our holy Baptism," to renounce Satan and all his works, to reject that spirit of the world, callous and resistant to grace, which is the enemy of supernatural living. She reminds us that in our Baptism we were buried with Christ into a death to sin and that we walk now in the newness of his risen life. Henceforth, we must in our living adhere to Jesus Christ and serve God faithfully in the holy Catholic Church.

Both in the original initiation into Christianity and in the yearly reaffirmation of our baptismal pledges, we are making a total choice. Just as Christ's acceptance of his messianic vocation was a choice involving the totality of his human life, so we, in entering upon the Christian vocation, commit the whole of our lives. When we accept Christ in the mystery of the mystical body, we pledge ourselves to principles that are to govern all our human acts. There is no free choice a human can make that is more basic than the choice involved in the sacrament of Baptism.

The choice which Christians make in Baptism involves the practical acceptance of a set of standards, an outlook on life, considerably different from the secular standards of judgment that surround them. By ordinary human reckoning, the mystery of Christ's death is completely enigmatic. St. Paul long ago said to his Corinthian converts: "We preach Christ crucified, a stumbling block to Jews and folly to Gentiles" (1 Cor 1:23). Yet when one is baptized, he says in effect that the death and resurrection of Christ alone give ultimate meaning to human life.

BEGINNING OF CHRISTIAN MATURITY

Maturity involves, first of all, a correct view of life and a clear vision of the values that should govern life. Secondly, maturity demands the straightforward acceptance and practical living out of this vision. Therefore, it involves knowledge and love, both of which converge in free choice. We can see, then, how Baptism is in a very important sense the beginning of a mature way of life. It is not just a matter of privately confronting the vision of faith which is presented to us in the mystery of Christ's death and resurrection as continuing in the Church; it is a public acceptance of that vision. By the very fact that a man professes faith, accepts Christ with all that Christ implies, he is acknowledging the practical truth and value of the insights into human life given by Christ in his death and resurrection.

In explicitly rejecting a false standard of values, symbolized by Satan and all his works and pomps, we are opening ourselves up to a full and honest acceptance of Christ. True, Baptism is but a beginning. Maturity is not yet gained; it is something which must be gradually acquired by constant effort. However, in the work of deepening Christian maturity, the vision and ideal to which we subscribe at Baptism will be the guiding norm. If a man is faithful to his Baptism, if he lives out the conformation to Christ initiated at this moment, if he develops the life of faith and hope and love which begins with baptismal grace, he will certainly attain profound and genuine maturity.

PLEDGE OF THE EUCHARIST

One of the most important practical aspects of the sacrament of Baptism is its *orientation to the Eucharist*. From the Church's earliest days, the Eucharist was looked upon as the completion of the baptismal consecration of self.

In early Christianity, it was customary to administer in one ceremony three sacraments as "sacraments of initiation" into Christianity. To some extent, this paralleled and continued the Jewish "rites of initiation" for a proselyte, i.e., baptism, circumcision, participation in the Paschal feast. The Christian sacraments of initiation were Baptism, Confirmation and the Eucharist, the new Pasch. The action begun in baptism was not thought of as fully completed until one had entered into the sacrificial action of the Mass. Documents concerning the early baptismal liturgy of the Church confirm this. St. Ambrose's *Concerning the Mysteries* is an example. Here Ambrose describes the ceremonies at the baptismal font, and the receiving of the spiritual seal after emergence from the font. He continues: "Rich with these adornments, the cleansed people hastens to the altar of Christ." This is how St. Justin (about 150 A.D.) describes the celebration of the Eucharist which immediately follows the ceremony of Baptism:

As for us, after having 'washed' him who believes and who has joined himself to those who are called brothers, we lead him to the place where these are assembled. We pray together for ourselves, for him who has just been 'enlightened,' for all others in whatever place they may be, that we may obtain, with the knowledge of the truth, the grace to practice virtue and to keep the commandments, in order to merit eternal salvation. When the prayers are over, we give each other the kiss of peace. Then bread and a chalice of wine tempered with water are brought to him who presides over the assembly of brothers. He takes them and praises and glorifies the Father of the universe in the name of the Son and of the Holy Spirit; then he celebrates a long Eucharist, in thanksgiving for having been judged worthy of these benefits. When he has finished, all the people exclaim "Amen." Amen is a Hebrew word which means: "so be it." When he who presides has celebrated the Eucharist and all the people have answered, the assistants, whom we call deacons, give the consecrated bread and the consecrated wine mixed with water to all those who are present and bear them to those who are absent.

We call this food the Eucharist, and none can partake of it if he does not believe the truth of our doctrine, if he has not received the bath of

Baptism for the redemption of sins and regeneration, and if he does not live according to Christ's precepts (Apology 1. 65-67: PG 6. 427-430).

As we saw, Baptism signifies entry into the new chosen people. Already in the Old Testament, the people were seen to be set aside for the purpose of offering true sacrifice to God. When the people are castigated by the prophets, it is most often because their sacrifice is not genuine. The *Benedictus* of Zechariah in the Gospel infancy narrative (Lk 1:68-79) indicates the extent to which the primitive Church saw that the new people of God, beginning with Christ, existed to offer genuine sacrificial worship. In joining this people, one is pledging oneself to participate in attaining the objective of the Church, namely, worship of God the Father.

Like Christ's own baptism, the Baptism of a Christian is an inchoative form of that covenant relationship to God into which he enters fully in the Eucharistic action. In the Old Testament, the notion of covenant was a controlling concept. The people thought of their relationship to God essentially in terms of such a covenant. Through the Exodus, they broke with their previous life in Egypt and pledged themselves at Mt. Sinai to a lasting service of God. This they carried out most fundamentally in their worship. In Christian times Baptism has always been looked upon as a contractual situation. It is a promise to enter fully into that new covenant which is the Eucharistic action of worship.

Christ, in his baptism, promised to go on to the action of the new covenant, the last supper. The Christian, in his Baptism, promises to fulfill his priestly role by participation in the covenant sacrifice of the Mass.

BIBLIOGRAPHY FOR CHAPTER 1

GENERAL WORKS ON SACRAMENTS

J. Jungmann, *The Early Liturgy,* Notre Dame, Notre Dame University Press, 1959. Scholarly and readable description of the earliest development of Christian rituals and creeds.

B. Leeming, *Principles of Sacramental Theology,* Westminster, Newman, 1960. Thorough textbook treatment, in more or less classical style, of the basic aspects of Christian sacraments.

Proceedings of the National Liturgical Week, Washington, National Liturgical Conference. Stretching over more than two decades, these proceedings contain many excellent talks on various aspects of sacramental life.

K. Rahner, *The Church and the Sacraments,* New York, Herder and Herder, 1963. Small but provocative essay on the intrinsic nature of sacrament; very good on relation between Church and sacrament.

———— *Theological Investigations,* vol. 2, Baltimore, Helicon, 1963. Contains several essays dealing with topics pertinent to material on grace and sacraments treated in this present volume.

E. Schillebeeckx, *Christ the Sacrament of the Encounter with God,* New York, Sheed and Ward, 1963. One of the most important books on the nature of sacraments, a work of rare insight and synthesis.

WORKS ON BAPTISM

J. Crehan, *Early Christian Baptism and the Creed,* Westminster, Newman, 1950. Careful study of the origins of Christian baptismal practice.

C. Davis, *Sacraments of Initiation,* New York, Sheed and Ward, 1964. Up-to-date and clear presentation of the origins and nature of Baptism and Confirmation.

B. Neunheuser, *Baptism and Confirmation,* New York, Herder and Herder, 1964. Careful scholarly treatment of the historical development of these two sacraments. Has excellent bibliographical helps.

P. Palmer, *Sacraments and Worship,* Westminster, Newman, 1955. Valuable collection of texts pertaining to the history of Baptism, Confirmation and the Eucharist.

D. Stanley, "The New Testament Doctrine of Baptism: An Essay in Biblical Theology," *Theological Studies* 18 (1957), pp. 169-215. Good introduction to the important studies on the NT teaching about Baptism.

2

THE SACRAMENTAL
CHARACTER OF BAPTISM

•

SEALING, ASSIMILATION, INCORPORATION

•

1. THE BASIC MEANING OF CHARACTER

SACRAMENTAL ACTION

Sacramental action is the special kind of action that actually causes, or brings into being, what is symbolized in the sacrament's external ceremonies. Schillebeeckx describes it, in his summary volume on Christ and the sacraments, as:

> . . . a divine bestowal of salvation in an outwardly perceptible form which makes the bestowal manifest; a bestowal of salvation in historical visibility.

Our next step, then, in studying the sacrament of Baptism is to examine the changes that take place in the baptized person.

LASTING SPIRITUAL REALITY

It is important to recall that a sacrament like Baptism is not just a single happening—one isolated moment in life. While the external act of Baptism is performed only once, at the very beginning of a Christian's new life, the sacrament continues to work as a permanent reality throughout his earthly existence.

Once baptized he *remains* baptized; a permanent change has been accomplished in him; the sacrament continues to work as a dynamic influence on his whole life.

In our last chapter we saw that Baptism points to the very beginning of a new life. This is achieved in the baptized person through the reality of sanctifying grace, which radically transforms his capacity for life and human activity. We saw also—and the present chapter will be devoted to deepening this point—that Baptism signifies entry into a new chosen people and orientation to the sacrificial action of the Eucharist. Both take place by means of a real modification in the baptized person. This modification, which sets the baptized apart as belonging to the Church and directs him to the Eucharist, is called the *sacramental character of Baptism.*

We must be careful not to think of this Baptismal character as something material; we can use the word "physical" in describing it, because "physical" when applied to man can embrace both material and spiritual realities. The sacramental character is a strictly spiritual reality. The Council of Trent indicates as much when it states that the character is "a kind of indelible spiritual sign whereby these sacraments (i.e., Baptism, Confirmation, Orders) cannot be repeated" (TCT 673). In his study of the sacraments, St. Thomas Aquinas clarifies still further the nature of this strictly spiritual reality:

> The character is directed toward those things which pertain to divine cult. Cult, however, is a profession of faith by means of external signs. Therefore, the character must be situated in man's power of thought, for it is in this power that the virtue of faith resides. (ST 3. 63. 4. ad 3).

However, because it is inseparably linked with the mystery of grace and the sacraments, the character is a reality that can be known only by faith and revelation. Like many other matters of revelation, the sacramental character is not explicitly treated in sacred scripture. Nevertheless, the basis of the Church's teaching on the point is founded in scripture.

SEALING BY THE SPIRIT

The sacramental character may be viewed as a *sealing* by the Holy Spirit. St. Paul, in his letter to the Ephesians, refers to this when he writes: "You also, who . . . have believed in him, were sealed with the promised Holy Spirit" (1:13); or again, "And do not grieve the Holy Spirit of God, in whom you were sealed for the day of redemption" (4:30). In 1 Corinthians, the apostle instructs the community: "But you were washed, you were sanctified, you were justified in the name of the Lord Jesus Christ and in the Spirit of our God." Paul then reminds them of their great dignity as Christians and of the conduct befitting that dignity, when he asks: "Do you not know that your bodies are members of Christ? Do you not know that your body is a temple of the Holy Spirit within you, which you have from God?" (1 Cor 6:11, 15, 19).

This sealing of the Christian, which is accomplished by the Holy Spirit at Baptism, indicates that the character is connected with a very special presence of the Spirit. It also shows that Baptism permanently marks one as Christ's "unto the day" of redemption.

Furthermore, Baptism signifies an entry into the new chosen people; and membership in this new people of God is permanently effected by the sacramental character of Baptism. Just as Yahweh, speaking through Moses, designated the chosen people of the Old Testament as "a kingdom of priests," so the letter of St. Peter speaks of the new chosen people as "a chosen generation, a kingly priesthood." Over the centuries the Church has gradually clarified this notion. In 1964, the fathers of Vatican II described it as follows:

> Christ the Lord, high Priest taken from among men (Heb 5:1-5), made the new people "a kingdom and priests to God the Father" (Apoc 1:6; 5:9-10). The baptized, by regeneration and the anointing of the Holy Spirit, are consecrated as a spiritual house and a holy priesthood, in order that through all those works appropriate to Christian man they may offer spiritual sacrifices and proclaim the power of him who has called them out of darkness into his marvelous light (cf. 1 Pet 2:4-10) . . . The ministerial priest, by the sacred power he enjoys, teaches and rules the priestly peoples; acting in the person of Christ, he makes present the eucharistic sacrifice, and offers it to God in the name of all the people. But the faithful, in virtue of their royal priesthood, join in the offering of the Eucharist. They likewise exercise that priesthood in receiving the sacraments, in prayer and thanksgiving, in the witness of a holy life, and by self-denial and active charity (*Constitution on the Church*, 2:10).

In the following pages we will further discuss the sacramental character of Baptism under the aspects of assimilation to Christ and incorporation into the Christian community.

2. CHARACTER AS ASSIMILATION TO CHRIST

PATRISTIC IMAGERY

To explain the sacramental character, the Church fathers made use of two images. They compared it, first of all, to the brand that permanently identified Roman soldiers as men dedicated to the military service of the Roman Empire. St. Cyril of Jerusalem said:

> This is in truth a serious matter, brethren, and you must approach it solemnly. You are, each of you, on the point of being presented to God, before innumerable hosts of angels; the Holy Spirit is on the point of setting a seal on your souls; you are coming for enlistment under the great King. Make ready, therefore (Catechesis 1. 3-4: PG 33. 428).

In this instruction to his catechumens, Cyril obviously sees the baptismal seal as somewhat like the military mark, inasmuch as it represents a lifelong enlistment, but in the Christian militia.

Another image used to convey an understanding of the baptismal character was that of the wax impression left by a signet ring. Just as a signet ring molds the wax to itself and leaves its own impress on the wax, so Christ molds the baptized person to himself in the sacrament of Baptism. This molding is accomplished by the humanity of Christ. Obviously, the primary and absolutely indispensable molding power can only be a divine action. But Christ's humanity is the mold which the divine Persons use as an instrument in shaping the baptized. For this reason, there is a resemblance in the spiritual order between the baptized person and Christ. It is this real, though invisible, resemblance that distinguishes or marks a man as belonging to Christ, as a *Christ*ian.

To understand another important point about the character and how it is caused, we must change our example from a signet ring placed on wax to a signet ring placed in water. In this latter case, there is a shaping of the water to the seal of the ring, but this impress, or seal, lasts only so long as the ring remains in the water. So, too, with the sacramental character. Since it is a permanent supernatural reality, it demands a constant impressing action by Christ. We know from the teaching of the Church that this character is a permanent reality remaining throughout life (TCT 673). This, if we reflect upon it, means that Christ is constantly present and working in a baptized person, even when that person is in mortal sin.

SPIRITUAL ASSIMILATION

For still greater understanding, let us change the example from material impressions produced by signet rings to instances of spiritual impression or assimilation familiar to us. Parents shape the outlooks, attitudes and values of their children. This amounts to a real assimilation of the children to their parents, an assimilation that is spiritual rather than material. Much the same sort of thing takes place in the classroom, where a teacher molds the thinking processes of his students, causing them to resemble his own. These assimilations are *strictly spiritual*.

Applying all this to the sacramental character, which is a spiritual assimilation, we can see that in Baptism Christ assimilates the baptized person to his own human attitudes and outlooks. The resemblance between the baptized person and Christ consists in a certain community of attitude. However, it is necessary to remember that the sacramental character is not in itself a fully developed attitude, already perfectly conformed to Christ's. Rather, it is the germ of that attitude, the power or ability to effectively acquire such an attitude. This is clear in the case of infant Baptism, for the infant receives the character, even though it is as yet incapable of a conscious attitude.

ASSIMILATION TO CHRIST'S REDEMPTIVE ATTITUDE

We must remember that the baptized is not assimilated in some vague and amorphous way, to some vague attitude of Christ's. The assimilation is to that precise attitude or intention by which Christ redeems mankind, the attitude of accepting his Father's will. Thus the Baptismal character is the *ability to conform one's thinking effectively to Christ's redemptive frame of mind*, the ability to share his obedience to his Father in order that men might be redeemed. We must also recall that Christ's external action of dying was not what essentially redeemed us; we are redeemed by Christ's human inner attitude, by his acceptance of death in love and obedience. A Christian is one who, by joining Christ in this attitude, joins him in the work of redemption. And it is the baptismal character that gives us the ability to do this. It is the baptismal character that makes us intrinsically Christian, that joins us to Christ, that makes it possible for Christ to act through us.

ASSIMILATION TO CHRIST'S PRIESTHOOD

Finally, since the full expression of Christ's redemptive attitude was realized in the priestly action of sacrifice—which began at the last supper and continued through the cross and resurrection—any sharing in that redemptive attitude is a sharing in the priesthood of Christ. St. Thomas Aquinas provides one of the classic explanations of the likeness to Christ imparted by the character:

> A character is properly a kind of seal, whereby something is marked as being ordained to some particular end: thus a coin is marked for use in exchange of goods, and soldiers are marked as being designated for military service. Now the faithful are designated for a twofold end. First and principally for the enjoyment of glory. And for this purpose they are marked with the seal of grace. Secondly, each of the faithful is designated to receive, or to bestow upon others, things pertaining to the worship of God. Now the entire liturgy of the Christian religion is derived from Christ's priesthood. Consequently, it is clear that the sacramental character is especially the character of Christ, to whose character the faithful are likened by reason of their sacramental characters, which are nothing else but certain participations of Christ's priesthood, flowing from Christ himself (ST 3. 63. 3).

The redemptive attitude described above is the very heart of the action of sacrifice; if we can share in this attitude of Christ's, we can share in the heart of his sacrifice. Such is the case, for the Church clearly teaches that all baptized persons are able to participate in Christ's priestly actions. They have a share in the priesthood, and this share in priestly power is the sacramental character. To be a priest means to have the ability to perform certain priestly actions; because of the character, all members of the Church have the ability to perform certain, though not all, priestly acts.

The fathers of Vatican II, in their *Constitution on the Sacred Liturgy*, stress the fact that the faithful should actively exercise their priestly role in the Eucharistic action of the Mass:

> Mother Church earnestly desires that all the faithful should be led to that full, conscious and active participation in liturgical celebrations which is demanded by the very nature of the liturgy. Such participation by the Christian people as "a chosen race, a royal priesthood, a holy nation, a redeemed people," is their right and duty by reason of their Baptism (2:14).

[The Christian people have a real share in, though not the fullness of, the priesthood of Christ.] The faithful really do offer the sacrifice of the Mass, even though their role is different from that of the ordained priest.

What, then, is meant by the "priesthood of the faithful?" There can be no doubt that there are distinct functions in the Church. Furthermore, only those who have received Holy Orders possess full priestly power. All Christians, however, possess a genuine sharing in Christ's priesthood, a sharing that comes to them with their Baptism. St. Peter refers to this in his first letter (1 Pet 2:5) when he calls the early Christians "a holy priesthood." The entire Church is meant to be a mediator for the rest of mankind. Within the Church, ordained priests are meant to be mediators between God and the faithful.

There are two sacraments, in particular, through which the faithful in the Church exercise their baptismal priesthood: Matrimony and the Eucharist. This is clear in the sacrament of Matrimony, because in the wedding ceremony the priest is only the witness; the couple themselves are the ministers of the sacrament. Their action is a priestly one in which they directly cause grace. In the Eucharistic act of the Mass, the faithful also have their proper role in offering the sacrifice; and the fundamental ability to do so comes to them with the character they receive in Baptism.

3. INCORPORATION INTO THE CHURCH

THE INDIVIDUAL IN COMMUNITY

Though the past two decades have seen a greatly increased awareness of the social dimension of Christianity, there is still need to insist that the individual is a *Christian in community*. While a Christian is very personally related to Christ and to the work of Christ, he can never be truly Christian if he remains individualistic. Christian priesthood and Christian apostolate are realities that must be found in the Christian community.

[To be a Christian means to share the life of the community, a life that is based on faith in Christ.] It is as a member of this community that the individual Christian will find his sanctification. It is as a member of this community, sharing the community's life and activity, that a man will be able to discover his identity as a Christian.

Baptism signifies the individual's initiation into this Christian community, into this faith-society. There is the external action by which the baptized indicates his desire to share in the communal life of the group, and by which the group signifies its reception of the individual into its midst. [There is also the change that is effected internally in the newly baptized by which he is inserted into the living reality of the Church. This internal change is the sacramental character of Baptism.]

We must be careful not to think of the sacramental character as a purely static entity, to consider it as a "thing" that is added to the Christian. Rather, it is a *"directedness" to fulfilling a certain function* in the faith-society that is the Church. It is a delegation to perform a portion of the Church's redemptive activity and to play a role in the Church's act of worship.

Because it is a human society, because it has a complex task to perform in the history of mankind, the Church possesses diverse functions, to be performed by different members. Sacraments like Holy Orders and Matrimony direct the Christian to certain particular and specialized roles in the Church's activity. But the fundamental "directedness" toward exercising the Church's priesthood comes to the Christian with his Baptism. It is the baptismal character that makes him an officially recognized member of the society, and that gives effectiveness to the acts he publicly performs as a member of the community.

Christian tradition has always maintained that a person, once baptized, retains the baptismal character throughout his life, even if he is unfaithful to his Christian vocation. Grave sin may deprive him of the supernatural life of grace. Apostasy may even separate him from unity with the Church as a society. Yet he retains the intrinsic orientation to the Christian priesthood which he received at Baptism. In as early a writer as St. Augustine (early fifth century) we find this clearly taught:

> A man baptized in the Church, if he be a deserter from the Church, will lack holiness of life, but will not lack the mark of the sacrament, the kingly character . . . (Sermo 71. 19. 32: PL 38. 462).

> If any one bears the military branding, whether he be a deserter, or even a private individual, is it not true that if he is discovered to be so marked, he will be punished as a deserter: Even if a man who was never in the army were to discover such a mark on his body, would he not be terrified and appeal to the clemency of the emperor; and if his prayer was granted and mercy extended, and he began to serve in the army, would that character be repeated, and not rather acknowledged and respected? Have Christian sacraments less power than this bodily mark? For we know that even apostates do not lose their Baptism, since it is not restored in their penance on returning and hence is judged incapable of being lost (Contra Ep. Parmen. 2. 13. 29: PL 43. 71).

THE CHURCH AS CHRIST'S BODY

To understand what it is that happens to a man when he is inserted into the community of the Church, we must know more accurately what kind of society the Church is. Like other human societies, it is made up of human beings joined together for the accomplishment of a common task. As such, it is necessarily visible and organized. Yet the deeper reality of this society is a strict mystery, invisible and known only by faith—i.e., the mystery of *Christ's continued presence to and activity in this community.*

Somehow, the Church is a living, organic unity in the supernatural order, a real continuation of Christ, both in his glorified humanity and in his historical role. We use the term "mystical body" to express this view of the Church. Though the idea is difficult to explain, and difficult to understand, we should not hesitate to think and speak of the Church in this way. The reason is that the concept is traceable to the language of Christ and of the primitive Church as expressed in St. Paul's letters and in the gospel of St. John.

In the fifteenth chapter of St. John's gospel, Christ describes the union between himself and his followers: "I am the vine, you are the branches. . . ." (15:5). If we examine this passage in detail and analyze the metaphor used, it becomes clear that there is:

A vital union. It is a matter of sharing life, the life that flows into the branches from the vine stalk. The branches (and Christ explicitly says that this is a reference to his followers) cannot have the Christ-life unless they remain united to the vine, Christ himself. One common vital force flows throughout the Church and has Christ for its source.

An organic union. While there is one life, there are diverse ways of expressing that life according to the various functions of the different parts of the vine. So also, among Christ's followers, there is to be diversity of function in the various roles that they play in the Church.

Ordained to productivity. The life flows through the branches so that grapes will be produced. In the Church, the life flows through those in the Church so that the work of redemption may be carried out in people's lives. Christ says that his Father takes care of "the vine" in order to insure this fruitfulness.

In St. Paul's letters, particularly in the early chapters of Ephesians, this same truth is taught through the parallel metaphor of the human body. Without going into detail, we can discern the same elements we found in Christ's metaphor of the vine: vital union, diversity of function according to different parts of the body, Christ as the source of the life of the body, the life and function of the various parts ordained to the accomplishment of the Church's work.

From these scriptural passages and the Church's teaching over the centuries, culminating in the two great encyclicals of Pius XII (*The Mystical Body of Christ, On the Sacred Liturgy*) and the decrees of the second Vatican Council, we can gather a better idea of this doctrine. Briefly, Christ lives on in those who are joined to him in his Church throughout history. The supernatural life he possesses in superabundance he shares with us; but we must remember that he does this by helping to cause our supernatural life. There is no question of our losing any of our individuality; there is no merging into Christ in the sense that our own personality is suppressed. The members of the Church, who are members of the mystical body, not only retain but intensify the unique personal characteristics proper to each of them. Yet, at the same time, the bond uniting those who belong to the Church is much different from that joining people together in a purely natural society, such as a social club or a nation or even a family. Those who are in Christ's Church really share the same supernatural life which comes to them from Christ.

At the root of this mystery of sharing in Christ's mystical body is the exceptional nature of Christ's priesthood and Christ's grace. He has that grace which we call the "grace of the head" (*gratia capitis*), which means (contrary to our own condition, in which grace is limited by our personality) that Christ's grace is unlimited and coextensive with all possible human beings and their supernatural transformation. For this reason, Christ's grace can act as the operative source, instrumental but still efficient, of the grace that is given to all human beings. The same thing is true of his priesthood, which is a priesthood or mediation coextensive with the redemptive needs of the whole human race. Because of this, that priesthood can be shared with all men.

To clarify the point, let us take as an example an artist who possesses a great creative gift, a gift which can be shared with many disciples. All the disciples receive the artistic gift from the master artist, but each receives it in his own way and expresses it in his own way. The disciple's own artistic individuality is not suppressed because he possesses this new artistic insight. It is intensified. Yet, one would certainly see the influence of the master in the works of his disciples. And, if one were to combine all the artistic gifts which the disciples share with their master, the artistic genius of the master would still surpass this.

A similar situation prevails in the matter of grace. Our own personality is in no way diminished. While we do live the life of Christ and do exercise the priesthood of Christ, each one of us lives it and exercises it in his own way. This is an integral element in the *catholicity* of Christianity.

BAPTISMAL CHARACTER AND INCORPORATION

Since Christians are joined to Christ in the mystical body so that Christ may continue to work through them for the fulfillment of his redeeming work in history, the mystical body is an active reality. Christ is able to use us as ministers in continuing his priestly action because we have received in Baptism that ability to perform priestly actions which we call the sacramental character. By causing this character in us, Christ joins us to himself in his apostolate, molding us in the way we have already described. Possession of the sacramental character of Baptism is an indispensable condition for membership in the mystical body, the Church.

Those who possess this priestly assimilation to Christ function for him as his "body." We cannot understand all that this means, for we are dealing with a strictly supernatural mystery, yet we can gain some insight into it by reflecting upon the role of the human body. The body is what situates a human person in a space-time context. Accordingly, we can say that Christ, who in his risen state is not limited by or situated in our space and time, is situated in this world by the Christian community in whose midst he dwells. Again, in each human being the human body acts as a *translation* into the visible order of an individual's spiritual aspects. His bodily visibility makes his entire person visible to us. In somewhat similar fashion, the invisible presence of the risen Christ is expressed, or translated, by the members of the Church with whom he identifies himself. Finally, our bodies function as the *instrument* through which we carry out the plans and intentions conceived in our consciousness. Similarly, Christians who comprise Christ's body are the instruments by which Christ continues, throughout the course of human history, to worship his Father and to work for the redemption of mankind.

BIBLIOGRAPHY FOR CHAPTER 2

WORKS ON THE SACRAMENTAL CHARACTER

J. Danielou, *The Bible and the Liturgy,* chap. 3 ("The Sphragis," pp. 54-69), Notre Dame, Notre Dame University Press, 1956. Interesting explanation of the patristic development of the notion of sacramental character.

J. Van Camp, "The Sacramental Character: Its Role in the Church," *Theology Digest* 1 (1953), pp. 28-31. Short but valuable essay, followed by good bibliography (up to 1953) on the topic.

WORKS ON THE CHARACTER AND THE ROLE OF THE LAYMAN

F. X. Arnold, "The Layman's Position in the Church," chap. 14 (pp. 313-326) in *Mission and Witness* (P. Burns, ed.), Westminster, Newman, 1963. Balanced and succinct exposition of the layman's role.

K. Rahner, "The Sacramental Basis of the Layman's Position in the Church," chap. 4 (pp. 83-113) in *Nature and Grace*, New York, Sheed and Ward, 1964. Basic essay by one of the leading contemporary students of the theology of the layman.

WORKS ON THE CHURCH AS THE "BODY OF CHRIST"

Basic ecclesiastical documents on this topic are the encyclical letters on the mystical body (Mystici corporis) and the liturgy (Mediator Dei) of Pope Pius XII, and the decrees of Vatican II on the liturgy and on the Church.

The Church as the Body of Christ (R. Pelton, ed.), Notre Dame, Notre Dame University Press, 1963. Collection of essays by Catholic and Protestant scholars on the scriptural teaching and theology about the Church as "body of Christ."

Mission and Witness (cited above) has two chapters dealing with this topic: chap. 3 (pp. 61-78), C. Mooney, "Paul's Vision of the Church in Ephesians"; and chap. 4 (pp. 81-96), J. Vodopivec, "The Church—The Continuation of Christ." These chapters concentrate on the biblical and patristic treatment of the topic.

3

THE GIFT OF THE SPIRIT

•

GRACE AND DIVINE FRIENDSHIP

•

GRATIA INCREATA

A Greater Gift

The vocation to Christian priesthood, conferred by Baptism and the sacramental character, is a great gift. But a still greater gift is bestowed on the new Christian. This is the gift of new life, life that is a sharing in the divine way of being. We call it *sanctifying, or habitual, grace.*

At the root of the mystery of grace lies a still greater mystery: the fact that men are offered *friendship with the three divine Persons.* Before going on to an analysis of grace (in chapter four), it might be profitable to investigate what is involved in this new personal relationship opened up to mankind. In studying this point, we are touching upon the finality of the entire plan of salvation and creation. For everything that the three divine Persons have done in the process of creating a world of men and redeeming it is controlled by this purpose: to bring created persons to familiarity with themselves.

A Personal Gift

Theologians have been accustomed to refer to this aspect of the mystery of grace as "uncreated grace" (gratia increata). Essentially, this term means that the gift of grace in question is the three divine Persons themselves. But it might be more correct to say that it is the Persons *in their graciousness* toward us, i.e., not in their eternal existence, apart from their creative knowledge and love of the world, but precisely in their loving self-giving to the human creatures who are the result of their love.

Reflection on this truth makes us aware that there is question here of the most baffling and incredible situation: divine Persons, utterly independent and fulfilled in the infinite being they possess in common, completely and unchangingly happy, have freely decided to establish a bond of intimacy with created persons, with men. In human friendship, the most important and precious thing one person can give another is the gift of himself. Other gifts, even those of understanding and concern and love, are only signs of the ultimate gift of one's own person. And in the mystery we are now discussing we find that Father, Son and Spirit offer themselves in this fashion to human beings.

Neither reason nor revelation can explain why the three divine Persons give themselves to us—other than that they love us. We encounter here a gratuity in love we cannot achieve or experience in our ordinary personal relationships. The divine loving is totally devoid of self-seeking. Fundamental to this mystery is the very nature of the Godhead. As St. John tells us, "God is love" (1 Jn 4:8).

This simple statement of John was preceded by centuries of divine action on behalf of the people of the Old Testament and by the early Christian experience of Jesus' public life and redemptive action. All these centuries, because they witnessed the "great deeds" of God for a chosen people, contain what we call "supernatural revelation"; and no element in this revelation is more basic than the truth that ultimate reality, God, is life-giving love, and that this life-giving love is the source of human existence and human fulfillment.

OLD TESTAMENT REVELATION

In the earliest stages of salvation history, when the religious sensibilities of the Old Testament people were still largely undeveloped, God's intervention on their behalf was seen almost exclusively as a matter of his guarding them from hostile elements in nature and from human enemies in war. Even at this early stage, however, the Jews seem to have been aware of some kind of blood bond linking them to their God in covenant relationship (cf. Ex 24). Insufficient as their understanding was, the earliest textual witnesses indicate that there never was question of Israel coming to know her God by way of philosophical argument or mythic projection. The Israelites knew Yahweh because they had come face to face with his historical action on their behalf.

Particularly under the impact of the prophetic teaching, the Israelites gradually came to see that the nature of the covenant relationship was one of great familiarity with their God. Yahweh was the all-powerful God of nature and of battles, but he was also the God who spoke of himself as Israel's father, as the husband who had espoused Israel to himself in unending love, as one whose tender love for his people surpassed that of a mother for her child. Though Israel's infidelities filled centuries of history, God's fidelity to his people remained firm and unchanging.

For her part, Israel was invited by God to deal with him in closest familiarity. The people were urged to approach God, to come to know him, to trust in the concern he had for them. When the people failed to do this, God's love demanded that he correct Israel by punishment in order to win back their affection and acknowledgment; but, at the same time, he also complained to them through the prophets, telling them how he had wished to bless and help them.

Despite the continuing misunderstanding and infidelity of the people, God assured them that he would not abandon them. If they proved unfaithful to the covenant he made with them at Sinai, he would make a new covenant. This covenant would be even more profound, more personal. For he would write the law on their very hearts (Jer 31:33), he would take away their hearts of stone and give them hearts of flesh that could respond to his love (Ezek 36:26). And, in the day when he would come in visitation and salvation, he would send his spirit in fullness into them and so transform them for himself (Joel 2:28-29). His own spirit poured out in abundance upon them would be the lasting pledge of his infinite love.

New Testament Revelation

Familiar and intimate as it was, Old Testament revelation did not yet tell the people about the ultimate reality—God's own inner life. Israel did not know that the divine being is possessed by three Persons whose love for one another is so total that they form an absolute identity in divine being. This mystery, that in the Godhead there are three "selves," is revealed with the coming of the Son in the incarnation.

We shall not go into all the details of the redemptive incarnation. But we can profitably note, at least, the way in which this God-becoming-man intensifies the familiarity between men and God. In this man, Jesus of Nazareth, we are now able to contact a divine Person in a way understandable to us. St. John expresses it well, in his first letter, with the words: ". . . which we have heard, which we have seen with our eyes, which we have looked upon and touched with our hands, concerning the word of life" (1 Jn 1:1). Even though we today cannot contact in ordinary visible form this Jesus of Nazareth, who now lives a risen human life, we can still properly understand what he is as man because we also are men.

The Jews of the Old Testament expressed God's nearness to them by speaking of his "dwelling" with them. For the Israelites this dwelling was associated with the Holy of Holies in the Jerusalem temple. But with the coming of Christ the idea takes on a new reality, for the Godhead really does dwell in extraordinary fashion in this man Jesus. One of the divine Persons is truly a member of the human race. Not only did he live in our midst in ordinary historical form for a period of slightly more than thirty years; he is still present and active in human history through the mystery of his risen existence. He abides in the members of his Church as he promised to do at the moment of his ascension: "And remember, I am with you always until the end of the world" (Mt 28:20).

NEED FOR HUMAN TRANSFORMATION

WHAT DIVINE FRIENDSHIP DEMANDS

Friendship cannot, because of its nature, be given by one person to another if the recipient is unable or unwilling to receive it. This is true even when it is a divine Person who offers himself in friendship. A divine Person cannot give himself as friend to man unless man is able to enter into such a relationship. For this reason, a transformation of man is necessary.

We can see this more clearly if we reflect on the fact that in a true friendship I know my friend with some kind of privileged immediacy. If I only know *about* a person, no matter how thorough and exhaustive my information, I cannot form a friendship. I must know *him*. Similarly, in order to identify myself with a friend through love, I must relate myself to him—and not simply to some idea I have about him.

But human beings, by their purely natural powers of understanding and love are incapable of such immediate contact with divine Persons. Only when a revelation of the three divine Persons has taken place are we actually in touch with divine personality as it really is. Only when our power to know is transformed and amplified by faith are we capable of receiving the revelation of the Trinity.

In the very act of giving themselves to men in friendship, the three divine Persons simultaneously transform the inner personal being and potential of the human person, so that he is capable of recognizing and responding to this self-giving on the part of God. This deepening and opening up of the human personality is what we call sanctifying grace. In a later chapter, we shall study this transformation in greater detail.

TRANSFORMATION BY DIVINE PRESENCE

PRESENCE AND COMMUNICATION

In the matter of grace, the three divine Persons are involved in a kind of causing quite different from that found in the rest of creation. Everything else is, indeed, created and sustained in being by the three Persons, but they do not exercise their causality precisely as distinct personalities. In the case of sanctifying grace, however, the Father, Son and Spirit have an effect according to their own personal way of being. This they achieve by a special kind of presence to us.

"Presence" is a notion that can be understood in different senses. An inanimate object can be present in a room by the very fact that it occupies a certain portion of quantified space: nothing else for the moment can fill the particular place where it is situated, and it is located spatially by everything that surrounds it. Insofar as he is a quantified being, a man can also be present this way; he can simply "be there." Man is able, too, to extend his presence spatially insofar as he can use some instrument to cause an effect at a distance. For example, when a rocket is sent to the moon, man makes himself present in some sense to the surface of the moon.

There is another kind of presence connected with human communication. If I am situated in a large room with people, I am at least spatially present to all of them. I am truly present only to those with whom I am engaged in conversation at a given moment. To put it another way: if I am affecting the consciousness of others I am present to them in a way quite different from my presence by mere spatial location. Influence on the consciousness of others can also be exerted at a distance through the use of some instrument, such as a telephone or letter.

One can distinguish in the area of personal presence between two chance acquaintances who engage in small talk, and two close friends who converse about things of great mutual concern. In the latter case, one person communicates his very self to the other; he opens himself up to being known as he truly is; he makes his concern and his love available to the other person. Such presence, which can only exist between friends, is a deeply transforming reality. It is clearly exemplified in the case of a husband and wife who truly love one another.

THE IMPACT OF DIVINE PRESENCE

It is personal presence that is involved in the mystery of sanctifying grace. The three divine Persons make themselves available to us, reveal their personalities to us (as Father, Son, Spirit), manifest the depths of their concern and love for us, open themselves to us so that we may intimately relate ourselves to them. If the deeply personal presence of a human friend can have such a profoundly transforming effect, can make it possible for me to find myself as a person and turn outward in friendship and genuine humanity, then the impact of the personal presence of Father, Son and Spirit should be even greater. And it is. Because of this intimate Trinitarian presence, man's very being as a person is reoriented, his entire ordination to knowing and loving is radically changed, he becomes capable of being and living divinely. This, as we shall see in greater detail later, is the reality of sanctifying grace.

Sacred scripture speaks of this interior transformation of man, but it pays much more attention to the wonder of the divine presence. This is especially true in those chapters of John's gospel that are known as "the last discourse" (Jn 13-17). Here Christ describes the relationship between man and God as one of "dwelling together," of God abiding with man. "If a man loves me, he will keep my word, and my Father will love him, and we will come to him and make our home with him" (Jn 14:23). The concept of close friendship is also quite explicit: "No longer do I call you servants . . . but I have called you friends" (Jn 15:15).

This section of John's gospel is not the only instance in which scripture treats the question of God's presence to men. St. Matthew's gospel takes as a central theme the messianic title of Jesus, Emmanuel, which means "God is with us." And the final recorded words of Jesus, spoken just before the ascension, pledge the continuance of his presence to the Church throughout its existence: "Remember, I am with you always . . ."

INDWELLING OF THE SPIRIT

THE SPIRIT AS GIFT

Since all three divine Persons are specially present to the human being transformed in grace, the question arises: Why has the Church traditionally spoken of the "indwelling of the Holy Spirit?" Is there something special the Spirit does?

What is in question is the *mission* of the Spirit. The Father and the Son are personally present to us in love. As Father and Son they express their love for us in the person of the Spirit—just as they do for one another in the Trinity. The whole mystery of uncreated grace, which we have been describing, is a mystery of the divine Persons expressing their love for men, making themselves present to men in true self-giving. But since the Father and Son express their love in the Spirit, personally give of themselves in the Spirit, they make themselves present to us in love precisely by sending the Spirit.

In human friendship, one person expresses his love for the other by giving a gift. To some extent, there is something of the giver himself in the gift that he brings. The gift is a sign of the giver's presence and self-communication. So, too, the Father and Son give us the gift of the Spirit; they are themselves uniquely present in this Gift, because all three Persons are identical in being. Therefore, the Father and Son do not send the Spirit to us as if he were totally distinct from them and of a different order of being. On the contrary, they are most intimately present to him and to us. Because Father and Son give the Spirit, faith teaches that "Gift" is a proper name for him.

As the expression of the Father's love for us, the Holy Spirit works dynamically to form us to divine sonship, thereby drawing us to the Father. As the expression of the Son's love, the Spirit teaches us the profoundest meanings of Christ, who is the Son; he molds our personalities from within according to the model of Christ's own sonship. This transformation which he is sent to accomplish by his presence to man, is what we mean by the *mission* of the Holy Spirit. Although the function of the third Person cannot be divided into parts, still, in order to clarify his "mission," we shall discuss some of his roles: his dwelling in men, inspirational power, teaching and power to sanctify.

OLD TESTAMENT: THE SPIRIT'S DWELLING WITH MEN

One of the most prominent themes in the Old Testament is that of Yahweh's special dwelling with his people. The Israelites had been warned by their law not to make graven images of Yahweh (Ex 20:4), and so reduce him to human form and the limits of the human imagination. Nevertheless, the God of the Old Testament was very real and very close to his people. He was not a God limited to this or that place, as were most of the divinities of ancient peoples. Wherever the people of God went, they found their God already waiting for them. There was no nation not subject to his governance; there was no part of creation that was not his doing; nothing that happened in the world or in the hearts of men was beyond his scrutiny. Still, for the people of God, the Israelites, he had a special providence, a special care (Ex 29:45-46). The sign of this was his special dwelling in their midst. At first, this dwelling was indicated by the ark of the covenant and the tabernacle; later, by the Jerusalem temple. But he also "dwelt with them" through the prophets and kings and priests who were the constant sign that God still loved his people and worked distinctively in their history and destiny.

At the beginning, this dwelling was thought of in rather temporal and spatial terms: Israel was the land in which God dwelt; it was his abode. It was, therefore, the Holy Place. Through the prophets, the dwelling of God in the hearts of men gradually received more attention. Jeremiah, for example, recast the central covenant idea of Old Testament thought in terms of a new covenant in which God would not work on man's life from without, but would dwell in the heart of man, transforming him from within (Jer 31:33).

Old Testament thought never arrived at the notion of a Spirit of God as a distinct person. For centuries, however, there was a developing insight into a mysterious power of God which the Israelites called Yahweh's spirit. Generally accompanying the "word," which is the instrument of God's power, the "spirit" in the Old Testament is a restless dynamic influence working in creation and in human history. According to the description of creation in the Book of Genesis, the spirit of the Lord hovers over the chaotic waters, and it is through the presence of the spirit, accompanying the "word" which God speaks in creation, that order and life emerge from the primitive chaos (Gen 1:1-3).

The spirit of God fills Moses as he puts order into Israel's life through the Law and institutions of the Old Testament. It is the spirit which comes upon all the great men, prophets, kings and priests, as they work to carry out the designs of Yahweh in the history of Israel.

This spirit, symbolized by a cloud (Is 63:9-14) or a hovering bird or a rushing wind, makes an ordinary man a charismatic leader, a king or a prophet. In the period of the judges, it was the spirit of the Lord who came upon them and changed them from ordinary individuals into men who fearlessly led the people of God against their enemies (Judg 3:9; 6:34; 11:29; 14:6; 15:14). It was the spirit of God whom Samuel called down on Saul (1 Sam 10:6-10) and on David at the inauguration of the Israelitic kingship (1 Sam 16:13).

The personal dwelling of the spirit comes to the forefront most clearly in the prophets of Israel. Elijah and Elisha are spoken of as possessing the prophetic spirit (2 Kings 2:9, 15). By the time of the great literary prophets, there was no doubt that a prophet was a man in whom the spirit of God resided. Above all, in the servant of Yahweh (Is 49), the highest ideal of the prophetic vocation, the spirit of Yahweh was to be found. Therefore, the dwelling place of God is found not only in the temple, but also in the lives of men.

New Testament: Christ's Spirit

Christ was fully aware of the fact that the Spirit dwelt in him in unique fashion. St. Luke points out that the incarnation itself took place with the Spirit overshadowing Christ's mother (Lk 1:35). Thus, Christ's life began—like the first life that came into the world—under the aegis of the Spirit (Gen 1:2). Furthermore, by depicting the Spirit hovering over the Virgin Mary at the time of the annunciation, St. Luke is calling attention to the fact that Christ had a prophetic call from the first moment of conception in his mother's womb.

Christ's possession of the Spirit is the fulfillment of the "spirit's" dwelling in the temple and in the men who were the great mediators of the Old Testament. Christ is the new Temple in which the personal Spirit of God dwells. He is the new prophet to whom the Spirit is given, and the new king who possesses through his anointing, the Spirit of the Lord. In him, the Spirit works. St. Luke tells us that Christ, having rejected Satan's temptations, left the desert in the power of the Spirit (Lk 4:14). This spirit was the source of Christ's utterances and miraculous healing power.

St. John's gospel abundantly testifies to Christ's promise to give his infant Church that Spirit which was his own in order that he might share with the Church the life he had from the Father. By sending his Spirit into the Church, Christ is fulfilling the promise made by the Lord in the Old Testament:

And you shall know that I am in the midst of Israel, and that I, the Lord, am your God. . . . And it shall come to pass afterward, that I will pour out my spirit on all flesh . . . Even upon the menservants and maidservants in those days I will pour out my spirit (Joel 2:27-29).

It was on Pentecost that the head of the mystical body poured forth into the members organically united to him and to each other this quickening and vivifying Spirit of life. It is in the Church, Christ's mystical body, and in each member of the Church that the Spirit dwells. Because of that indwelling, the Church as a whole as well as each member, is a temple. Both the Church as a whole and each of its individual members fulfill the Old Testament concept of the "sacrament" of God dwelling with his people.

What constitutes this dwelling, or special presence of the Spirit? A spirit is present by virtue of what it effects. The Holy Spirit is present in us because of what he effects in us. Therefore, in examining the following three functions of the Spirit, we are studying the manner of his presence in our midst.

THE HOLY SPIRIT AS SOURCE OF POWER AND INSPIRATION

THE SPIRIT IN ISRAEL, IN CHRIST, IN THE CHRISTIAN

The spirit of God portrayed in the Old Testament is above all a force, the power of Yahweh, a dynamic element which enters into the creation of the world and causes its transformation. It is the spirit which induces the prophet to speak (Ezek 3:24; 11:5), and moves the heroes of the Old Testament to witness to God. Under the spirit's influence, the people of God are guided by their leaders to fulfillment of the covenant which Yahweh had made with them. Because of the spirit, men who would otherwise be very ordinary, even weak and unimportant, become capable of standing up against all the forces, wiles and threats of the powerful and the great of this world. Because of the power of the spirit within them, the prophets are able to transform the history of Israel and the history of mankind—not merely in its external manifestations, but in its deeper spiritual currents.

The spirit—understood in the fuller, Christian sense as the Spirit who is a divine Person—was also the source of Christ's power. We can see this throughout the gospel account of Christ's great deeds. To complement St. Luke's remark that Christ returned from the desert "in the power of the Spirit" (Lk 4:14), the gospels describe many instances in which Christ applies that power through his word and work. When Christ was challenged by the scribes and pharisees concerning his miraculous deeds, they charged that he accomplished them through Beelzebub. Christ responded by accusing them of blasphemy, specifically accusing them of sinning against the Holy Spirit. In their folly, they identified his power with the power of evil—when it was really the power of the Spirit (Mt 12:31-32).

Such an incident shows us how aware Christ and the primitive Church were that the infinite power of the Spirit stood behind the words and acts of Christ.

The Spirit worked through the humanity of Christ for the transformation and redemption of the world into which Christ had been sent. And Christ sent his Spirit to continue the redemptive work solemnly inaugurated in the mysteries of the last supper, death and resurrection.

There is an interesting interaction of powers within the mystical body. Christ as man continues to effect the human element in the synthesis of human and divine which is the work of redemption. It is the Spirit himself who ultimately gives force and life to this human activity in the Church. But it is not simply the Spirit who works in the Church; it is the Spirit who works *as sent by the Father and Son.*

It is the power of the Holy Spirit that enables each Christian to live supernaturally and communicate his vision of faith, to transform the world by supernatural love and worship the Father in union with Christ. The Spirit works at the very heart of a Christian's being, transforming him and communicating to him a power beyond his own natural abilities. St. Paul tells us in the letter to the Galatians that it is the Spirit in us who cries out, saying, "Abba! Father!" (Gal 4:6). Without this indwelling Spirit we have no power to do what we are called to do; for our vocation is to become divinized and to be ministers of divinization for the world in which we live. This requires divine force and the divine force which we have is the Spirit of Christ who is our Spirit because we are Christ's.

THE HOLY SPIRIT AS TEACHER

WORKING IN MAN'S MIND AND HEART

Nothing gives us deeper insight into the action of the Spirit than Christ's words at the last supper, when he speaks of the Spirit as a teacher. After telling his apostles it was good that he himself leave them, he then went on to say that "the Counselor, the Holy Spirit, whom the Father will send in my name, he will teach you all things, and bring to your remembrance all that I have said to you" (Jn 14:26). With these words, Christ pointed out that his disciples would not understand the deeper meaning of his words and actions until the Spirit had come. The Spirit working within them would clarify for them the full meaning of Christ and his mission. When we examine the fourth gospel and the Holy Spirit's activity during the first decades of Christianity, we find that the Spirit functions as teacher par excellence. Christ himself is the Word who reveals the Father and fashions the faith of each individual Christian as well as the entire mystical body. But the Word is a *word of life.* And since it is a word of life, it requires the vitalizing force of the Spirit in those who receive it so that it may produce a living, conscious grasp of revelation. The Holy Spirit is sent to accomplish within us this response to the Father's Word—i.e., Christ in his redemptive work.

The Holy Spirit works within the individual to cause that supernatural receptiveness into which the revealed word of God can come and bear fruit (1 Cor 2:12-14). In the parable of the sower (Mt 13:3-23), the Church tells us that the dispositions of heart favorable to the growth of the word must await the word's coming in order to bear fruit sixtyfold or a hundredfold. The parable also teaches that such dispositions cannot be produced by what is purely natural. Supernatural power of consciousness and supernatural power of affective reaction are needed as the good soil in which this seed can bear fruit. It is the Holy Spirit who causes the supernatural powers of faith, hope and charity in us, and who provides the orientation, openness and reciprocity required by the word which the Father speaks to mankind.

A human teacher can never enter directly into the psychological dynamism of the students he teaches; he can only present words and images which, by touching the sensibilities and imagination of the student, may instrumentally influence his thought. A teacher, though he might now and then wish it were possible, cannot shape from within that psychological receptivity to which he appeals in his teaching. The entire process of thinking must take place inside the individual who reacts to stimuli from outside.

It is not so with this divine teacher who is the Spirit. As the Creator, he can actually work within the heart and mind of man, disposing, shaping and ordering man's powers of consciousness and love. He can, and does, direct these powers to their fulfillment in conscious awareness of the revealed word and conscious acceptance of the implications of God's revealed love.

To summarize more precisely: the Holy Spirit's function is to mold, directly and from within, the individual's personal life of consciousness and affectivity, according to the model of Christ.

To be a Christian means to be as Christ; it means to continue in one's own personal life those habits of thought and love which characterized and still characterize the human psychic life of Jesus Christ. The Holy Spirit molds us on the model of what Christ thought and now thinks. But there is a still deeper causal mystery, and it is this: the Holy Spirit, in molding our thought and love to Christ's, uses as his instrument the present thinking and loving of the human Christ.

An analogy gives us some insight into the mystery. In trying to shape the thinking of his students, a teacher will often employ as his instrument the recorded thought of some writer or philosopher. The teacher who uses Plato is assimilating the consciousness of his students both to his thinking and to the thinking of Plato. However, it is important to note that the teacher is using as his instrument only the recorded thought of Plato, not the very real and personal psychological processes of Plato himself. The Holy Spirit, on the other hand, uses as his instrument the present living consciousness of Christ. It is the Spirit who makes us Christlike, who shapes the very roots of our capacity to think and love like Christ.

However, the Holy Spirit also works from the outside. At the same time that he is molding psychic attitudes within the Christian, he is acting in the Church as it presents the revealed word of God to the Christian in scripture, sacrament and dogmatic teaching. It is not sufficient to have powers of knowledge. Each power must have its proper object proposed to it if the power is to develop according to its specific nature. Unless revelation be presented to the powers of faith, hope and charity, these powers cannot develop to the fullness demanded for true Christian maturity. The Holy Spirit teaches the Christian through the Church, of which he is the animating Spirit or soul. As an extension of that mystery of the Old Testament in which the spirit of God moved the prophets who conveyed the word of God (Zech 7:12), the Spirit of the Lord, Christ's own Spirit, is sent by Christ into his mystical body to be the animating principle in the Church's prophetic life. The spirit still speaks in the Church, announcing and proclaiming the word of God in scripture. The Spirit speaks in the authoritative magisterium of the Church, which officially continues Christ's own messianic teaching office. Finally, the Spirit teaches most profoundly through those sacramental actions which are simultaneously the words of Christ and of his Church.

The Christian is, then, the recipient of two teaching operations of the Holy Spirit. Working from within, the Spirit touches the very roots of his powers of consciousness in order to mold and orientate them to the mind and will of Christ. Working from without, the Spirit presents to the Christian that revelation of the meaning of Christ which can provide the specification required to give form and precision to his inner Christlife. It is this continuing process, carried on through study, sermons, reading, contemplation, and particularly through sacramental action, which leads step by step to the development of the Christian mentality and Christian affectivity.

In this way the Holy Spirit fulfills the promise made by Christ to his disciples and to all who follow in their footsteps: "the Holy Spirit, whom the Father will send in my name, he will teach you all things, and bring to your remembrance all that I have said to you" (Jn 14:26).

THE HOLY SPIRIT AS SANCTIFIER

INDIVIDUAL AND SOCIAL CONSECRATION

We have already seen that the Holy Spirit was sent by Christ to dwell in the individual Christian and in the entire Christian community. We have seen also that this dwelling is effected by the action of the Holy Spirit communicating power and life, molding both the individual and the Church to the mind of

Christ. This action of the Spirit, communicating both priesthood and sanctifying life, constitutes a dedication on both the individual and the social levels.

This dedication, this setting aside of the Christian in the Church as someone sacred, is foreshadowed in those Old Testament texts which connect anointing with the gift of the spirit. We know that anointing, whether it be of a sacred stone, altar or individual (such as a prophet or a priest), signifies that the thing or person can no longer be considered profane. He or it is now especially ordered to God, to activity in the realm of the sacred. In the context of Old Testament thought, anointing takes on its most profound significance in instances when a person is set aside for a sacred office. This involves not simply an external rite, but the communication of God's own spirit, which that rite occasions.

When a prophet was anointed, the deeper effect took place inside the anointed. The person was set apart from what was not sacred, set aside for a special function, set aside because he was possessed by God. He was ontologically differentiated because the spirit of Yahweh worked within him in ways in which it did not work within others (Is 61:1).

In a sense, the entire people of the Old Testament were the anointed ones of God (Is 44:3-4; Ezek 36:27; Joel 2:27-28; Zech 12:10; Ezek 37; Ps 51:12 ff.). The spirit was given them, to some extent, as a people (Is 32:15-20; Ezek 36:26-27). But the fullness of the spirit was promised to the messianic community, the remnant who would remain faithful and to whom the destiny of Israel was entrusted. Joel speaks of this anointing when he says, "And it shall come to pass afterward, that I will pour out my spirit on all flesh . . . your old men shall dream dreams and your young men shall see visions" (Joel 2:28). In this text we have already a hint of the fact that the spirit will someday dwell in a special way in the messianic community. It will be a period in God's dispensation truly able to be characterized as *spiritual*.

In New Testament times, St. Paul points out that this special group of anointed, and therefore dedicated, people is found in the Christian Church. And it is the Holy Spirit who, by his presence, effects this dedication. Christians are living stones that are formed into a "holy temple in the Lord . . . built into it for a dwelling place of God in the Spirit" (Eph 2:21-22). No longer is there a particular sacred space such as the Holy of Holies in the Jerusalem temple. Now all space is sacralized by the presence of those who are members of Christ's Church, because within them there dwells the sanctifying presence of the Holy Spirit. What anoints the Christian is his possession of the Spirit whom Christ sends to dwell in him. He is set apart because the Spirit works within him, transforming him through the bestowal of priesthood and grace.

"Dedication" as we use it in this context is an active concept. To dedicate a person means to set him aside for a particular function. He is chosen by God and singled out as belonging to him in order to accomplish a specific task in the work of redemption. Thus, too, dedication by the Holy Spirit, be it the dedication of an individual person or of the Christian community, is something which proclaims the orientation of that individual or community toward cooperation with Christ in the redemption of the world. Christians are set aside by the Holy Spirit, just as the prophets of old were set aside and just as Christ himself is set aside.

By examining the workings of the Spirit within Christ during his public life, we can learn much about the Spirit as he presently works in Christians. In Christ, the Spirit worked against evil in all its forms: against ignorance and error, against social injustice and physical disability, against the root of all evil which is sin in all its forms. So, too, throughout the history of the Church, the Spirit of Christ works within the Church by continuing to oppose with the infinity of his divine power the evil in men's minds and bodies. This presence of the dedicating Spirit within him should be reflected by a Christian's intelligent and conscious participation in the Church's apostolate.

BIBLIOGRAPHY FOR CHAPTER 3

SCRIPTURAL TREATMENT

B. Ahern, *New Horizons,* Notre Dame, Fides, 1963; chap. 7 (pp. 145-158), "The Spirit of Christ in the Christian," and chap. 11 (pp. 211-218), "The Spirit in the Church Today." Combined scriptural and theological treatment by one of America's leading NT scholars.

J. Guillet, *Themes of the Bible,* Notre Dame, Fides, 1960; chap. 7 (pp. 225-279), "The Breath of Yahweh." Fundamental study of the biblical teaching on the Spirit, by a master of the "thematic approach."

THEOLOGICAL TREATMENT

Y. Congar, "The Holy Spirit and the Apostolic Body, Continuators of the Work of the Church," chap. 13 (pp. 275-312) in *Mission and Witness.* Scholarly and stimulating essay on the Spirit's role in the life and mission of the Church.

C. Davis. In addition to chap. 4 in his *Sacraments of Initiation* (already cited under chap. 1), he has an excellent approach to the role of the Spirit in the Church in chap. 9 (pp. 121-138), "The Christian Mystery and the Trinity," *Theology for Today,* New York, Sheed and Ward, 1962.

J. Mouroux, *The Christian Experience,* New York, Sheed and Ward, 1954. Chapter 5 (pp. 121-158), "The Experience of the Spirit in St. Paul," discusses the Spirit's role in the Church from the point of view of the individual Christian's faith experience.

M. Scheeben, *The Mysteries of Christianity,* St. Louis, Herder, 1946. A classic on the topic; one of the most important modern influences in directing theological thought on grace and sacraments to the role of the Spirit.

4

GRACE

•

DIVINE LIFE WITHIN US

•

REBIRTH, REGENERATION, PARTICIPATION

BAPTISM AND SANCTIFYING GRACE

We have seen in preceding chapters that the Christian is introduced into the mystery of the Church by his Baptism. He makes the choice (or, in the case of infant Baptism, the community makes it for him) to accept Christ's principles and to follow the Christian path of life. Christ, in turn, admits him to the Church, both externally through the ceremony performed by a priest and internally through the mystery of the sacramental character and grace. We have also examined at some length the nature of the sacramental character in Baptism, concluding that it is essentially a share in Christ's priesthood because it enables the Christian to work along with Christ, both for his own individual redemption and for the redemption of mankind.

We saw, further, that in the transformation of the Christian which occurs in Baptism, it is the Holy Spirit—as sent by Father and Son who also work with him in us—who shapes man's personal being so that he becomes genuinely Christian. The Spirit, working in each individual Christian as well as in the Church as a community, is the animating principle making effective the priestly actions of the Church's members. The Church, whose "soul" is the Holy Spirit, is a living reality. It has a life that it shares with its head, Christ. This life is the life of grace, the organic bond of Christ's mystical body. We shall study the mystery of grace in the present chapter.

Because sanctifying grace is a strictly supernatural mystery, its very existence can be known to us only through God's supernatural revelation. But even when we know of its existence through revelation, we can never adequately understand the nature or essence of this supernatural reality. Supernatural grace is life; above all, it is life on a personal level. Like all personal life, it is essentially a very simple reality. Yet this simple reality, because of its great richness, can be understood only progressively and little by little. We shall therefore approach it from several points of view, always remembering that these are only different ways of looking at something basically quite simple and unified.

SANCTIFYING GRACE AS NEW BIRTH

> They [men] would never have been justified except through rebirth in Christ, for this rebirth bestows on them through the merit of his passion the grace by which they are justified (Trent, Session 6, TCT 559).

When studying the sacrament of Baptism, we saw that the externals of the sacrament point to the beginning of new life. In its symbolisms, Baptism recalls the beginning of that new, resurrected life, which Christ attained after his passage through death. As life came out of the primeval waters at the beginning of time, as Christ passed through death into life, so the Christian in passing through the waters of Baptism experiences a "new creation": he dies, is buried with Christ and then rises from the waters to begin a new life. Since Baptism is a sacrament, it not only points to the beginning of some new way of living, but actually causes it.

Early in his public life, Christ began to point to the sacrament of Baptism as a new birth, the start of new life. In the third chapter of St. John's gospel (which very likely records the baptismal catechesis of the early Church), the meeting between Christ and Nicodemus is described. Coming by night, because he feared to commit himself publicly, Nicodemus approached Jesus to find out if he was the messiah. Christ said to him: "Unless one is born of water and the Spirit, he cannot enter the kingdom of God" (Jn 3:5). Unquestionably, this text refers to the sacrament of Baptism, in which, through the mystery of water and the coming of the Spirit, man is introduced into new life. Christ's further explanation to Nicodemus makes it clear that this new life is of a different kind than purely bodily life. It is life which flows from the Spirit; it is, in a very profound sense, spiritual life.

Throughout the writings of St. Paul we find the same teaching: a new life has begun for the Christian in Baptism (Rom 6:3-5; Col 2:12). While he does not speak of it in terms of being reborn, St. Paul clearly points out that from Baptism onward the Christian is involved in an entirely new way of living, a way that is intimately and inseparably bound up with the mystery of the Spirit. Paul will speak often of the "new man" (Eph 2:15; Col 3:9-10), of the "new creature" (2 Cor 5:17), and will exhort the Christians of his day to grow in this new life into the fullness of the new man in Christ.

We find the same mentality in the Petrine letters. Those recently baptized are spoken of as "new born babes" (1 Pet 2:2). It seems quite clear, then, that from its very inception the early Christian community saw the mystery of Baptism as a mystery of the giving of new life, as the beginning of a new existence for the Christian. This notion continues to be found with ever-increasing frequency in the writings of the early fathers of the Church and in primitive liturgical texts.

Obviously, the process of rebirth that takes place in Baptism, and the new life involved, concerns the spiritual dimension of man's being. It concerns him in his conscious and affective being; it pertains to him precisely as a person. Already personal by reason of his human nature and natural birth, man now receives in some mysterious way an entirely new kind of personal living. The newness is so drastic that it can be described only as a second birth.

The fact that this kind of living is spiritual in nature in no way detracts from its reality as life. The forms of life are not limited to the vegetative and sensitive orders. The deepest kind of natural life which we as humans possess is that found in our intellectual and volitional activity. To just live humanly we must live consciously. Similarly, the new kind of life that begins for a Christian with Baptism is a distinctively conscious life.

Sanctifying grace is very truly a life principle. By it our nature is transformed so that we live in a new fashion; we live more profoundly, with greater fullness. Sanctifying grace is not an added life, placed alongside the life we already have. Rather, the personal nature we already possess is transformed so that we begin to live differently—with this new kind of life of which Christ spoke to Nicodemus.

SANCTIFYING GRACE AS REGENERATION

Probing more deeply into the mystery of sanctifying grace, we recall that the Church speaks of Baptism not only as a new birth but also as a regeneration, i.e., a process of acquiring sanctifying grace. Scripture itself does not use this word, but it is contained there implicitly.

Furthermore, the Church has on numerous occasions, particularly in the Council of Trent, used the word "regeneration" as a description of what is involved in sanctifying grace (TCT 560). This is not a matter of metaphor. Regeneration is used properly to denominate the process of sanctification by grace.

From experience and from philosophical analysis we know that generation is the action in which one living being communicates to another being the same kind of life that is possessed by the first. Animals generate animals, men generate men. When man causes some other effect, e.g., a fire, we do not say that man "generates" the heat. The reason is that he does not give the same kind of being he himself possesses. But man does generate when he is the cause of a child, for in this case he communicates human being—his own proper kind of being.

It is precisely this communication of proper being that is the foundation for the relation between the members of any species of living beings. This inter-relation takes on new depth of meaning in the case of personal beings. Here the giving of human life by parent to child is the whole basis for the unity of the family. All family life and, in a sense, all the social patterns that grow out of the family, find their roots in the gift of being from one person to another.

This ontological relationship of one to another, based upon the gift of being, lays the foundation for those unique kinds of human conscious relationships which we describe as parental, filial and fraternal love. The community of life derived from the act of generation provides the foundation and the orientation for the more conscious social union of the family.

It is in this context that we must understand the tremendous reality that God the Father gives us—his own way of being through what is literally an act of generating. This gift of being is the foundation of our relation to God the Father. In itself the gift of being already constitutes a very profound relationship, because it implies community in life. But this gift also establishes that conscious relationship we call the life of faith, hope and charity. Without the first gift of being, it would be impossible for a conscious supernatural relationship to exist, just as without that first action of generation there could be no family society. However, since in regeneration God the Father does communicate to us his own way of being, we are very literally introduced by grace into a familial context embracing Father, Son and Holy Spirit.

Though the term "generation" can be used in a very proper sense to describe the divine act by which the life of grace is given to us, we must be careful to distinguish it from the action of human generation on the purely natural level. In human generation, by which we receive life from our parents, the act of generation itself is accomplished in an instant. Though the child remains deeply dependent on its parents, still the life-giving action was completed in the generative moment itself. Once generation has occurred, the newly generated being is, as it were, self-sustaining. Its own life forces now begin to assimilate whatever is necessary for the development of that life. The function of parents is now a non-generative and post-generative matter. Their contribution is restricted now to preserving, developing and encouraging the life they have given.

Where supernatural life is concerned, however, this cannot be the case; for there is nothing within the being that can continue what God has granted. God himself must be continually generating, continually giving the gift of new life. The reason is simple: both the sustenance and the development of grace lie beyond the competence of nature alone.

God's generative action in grace differs in a second way from purely human generation. The parental gift of life is what brings the individual into existence. The divine gift of the life of grace, on the other hand, comes to a person already established in being. Therefore, it cannot involve the giving of the first, or substantial, level of existence; this is already present. Though the reality we call sanctifying grace does indeed involve a very radical change in man, it is a change which, philosophically speaking, we would classify as *accidental* rather than substantial. Nevertheless, though sanctifying grace does not bestow on man either his being or his personality, it still functions in a profoundly important way to transform both being and personality. Since the divine gift of life in the supernatural order differs in these two ways from natural generation, we apply to it the term "*re*generation."

GRACE AND PARTICIPATION

One of the most profound descriptions of supernatural life, or sanctifying grace, is that given in the second letter of Peter. Here the early Christians are told that they are "partakers in the divine nature" (2 Pet 1:4). The same idea is contained in germ in the Old Testament and explicitly elsewhere in the New. St. Paul's constantly used formulas "with Christ" and "in Christ" emphasize our profound sharing in that supernatural life Christ himself has as man, though they involve both the humanity and divinity of Christ.

The Greek fathers of the Church, particularly Athanasius, Cyril and the Cappadocians, emphasize the fact that grace is a participation in divinity. Athanasius says: "God became man so that men might become gods" (Ep. de Synodis: PG 26, 784. 5. 1). Cyril of Alexandria, who follows him, concentrates on man's assimilation to God, on his participation in divinity (In Joan. Comment: PG 73, 157. 1. 1. 1-13). When we come to the Cappadocian fathers, we find the same notion stressed. In defending the divinity of the Holy Spirit against the heresy of Macedonianism, they argue from the fact of man's divinization by grace. The third Person of the blessed Trinity must be in the strictest sense divine because he is the cause of grace—i.e., since grace is divine life, he who causes this life must himself be divine. The direction of their argument shows us the profound sense in which these early fathers of the Church understood how grace involves a sharing by man in God's divine nature.

The concept of our participation in the divine nature, our sharing in God's own way of being, is open to much misunderstanding. It is clear that we do not become part of God, for God has no parts. It is equally clear that we do not lose our identity in some kind of pantheistic merging into God. Discounting these two hypotheses as possible explanations, what precisely do we mean by the phrase "participation in divinity"?

At the root of this difficult and crucial truth of our faith lies a profound philosophical problem that has plagued speculative thinkers over the centuries.

Even before Plato, the problem of participation troubled the emergent philosophical thought of mankind. In Plato's Dialogues it occurs as a critical and agonizing question which Plato, with all his philosophical genius, never satisfactorily solved. This unsolved problem, persistent throughout much of the history of occidental philosophy, has posed special difficulties for those who want to explain the community of beings in being and yet maintain their distinctness from one another.

Fundamentally, the difficulty lies in correctly understanding the nature of efficient causality. In efficient causality, the agent communicates something of himself to what he effects; but, in this process, he is not essentially changed as agent. In analyzing any situation involving efficient causality, we must beware of drifting into emanationism— i.e., the notion that something flows from the agent into the effect. Rather, we should attend to the fact that the agent assimilates to himself what he effects, so that the change takes place in what is acted upon. Thus the agent, insofar as he is agent, neither gains nor loses anything intrinsically. In all such cases of efficient causality, the effect will participate in the nature of the cause—at least in that one area in which the change takes place.

Now, the specific type of participation of interest to us in our discussion of grace is spiritual participation. Here, where a person causes an effect in the spiritual being of another person, we have participation of a unique kind. The first person has shared with his friend the conceptions, convictions and hopes he himself possesses, so that the second person now has the same ideas. Nevertheless, the ideas of the first person remain his own, even though they have also become a proper possession of the second person. Characteristic of this kind of sharing is its unlimited quality. In cases of material causality, one finds that limits are always marked off (which is why we can measure reactions in physics or chemistry), while in spiritual causal participation there are no such bounds. It makes no difference whether I communicate my idea to one person, or to ten persons, or to ten thousand persons. Increasing the number of sharers does not mean that each of them receives less of my idea. This kind of spiritual participation is, in its own order, a more profound basis for community than any communication of material or bodily perfection.

Another feature of spiritual participation is this: while a very profound unity can be established on the basis of sharing ideas, such unity (which is unity of consciousness) always implies also a definite polarity. Personal consciousness always involves a distinction between a knower and a known. Consciousness necessitates an element of otherness in the object or person known; therefore spiritual participation simultaneously achieves self-distinctiveness and union with the person who is known.

In the light of these remarks about the philosophical meaning of "participation," what does it mean to say that we share God's way of being, that we are participating in divinity? Our existence will always be creaturely existence. Men will never cease to be men. Furthermore, the mystery of grace can in no way be explained as some kind of pantheistic assimilation to God. What kind of sharing, then, can there actually be? The sharing that occurs in relation to grace must be seen in terms of efficient causality, correctly understood.

God communicates to us a possession that is his. In giving it, he in no sense loses anything. God assimilates us to himself, but this by way of effecting or causing something in us, not by way of emanation. However, we must admit that in the causing of sanctifying grace there is greater intimacy than in other instances of divine causality. In chapter three, we saw that the effecting of grace in us is inseparable from the transforming presence of the three divine Persons.

In trying to understand a little more deeply the kind of participation involved in sanctifying grace, it is good to remember that by this perfection we share in God's own way of personal being. The inner life of the divinity is tri-personal. One identical life of consciousness and love is shared by three distinct persons. Sanctifying grace introduces us into this circle of personally shared consciousness. We participate in divine life precisely as such life is personal and trinitarian. By virtue of the life of grace, we are able in our consciousness and our love to direct ourselves distinctively to each of the three Persons. The fact that we are able to do this is grounded in the fact that we are pointed by grace toward that very personal activity which is possessed by the three divine Persons.

We do actually share in God's personal way of being. We are what God is, but we are not that way infinitely or necessarily or substantially. We are related to each of the Persons in God. However, in our case this relation does not constitute our personality, as it does for the divine Persons. Obviously, then, when we speak of participation in divine nature, there is no question of our sharing in the absolute perfections that distinguish Creator from creature. One cannot be partially infinite, partially eternal, partially simple. But in the area of personal perfection, there is such a possibility of sharing in divine life. We are sons of the Father, though not infinitely, not substantially, not necessarily. The divine life that is given to us comes as something modifying accidentally our substantial being, which already exists. Grace can come and go, but the human person remains intact in his substantial being. But in God this divine life, possessed infinitely and eternally, is the very nature that is shared necessarily and immutably by the three Persons.

SONSHIP, INHERITANCE, MERIT

SANCTIFYING GRACE AND DIVINE SONSHIP

In speaking of grace as regeneration, we mentioned that it brings us into a family circle. It is similar to ordinary human generation inasmuch as it is also a basis for those relationships which we call fatherhood, sonship and brotherhood. In the order of grace, since there is a genuine reception on our part of the divine way of life, and since this life is continuously given to us by God the Father, there results a relation which is genuinely sonship. St. Paul's letter to the Galatians tells us quite explicitly that we are able to turn to God the Father and say "Abba! Father!" because the Holy Spirit is working in us in grace (Gal 4:6). Our sonship really deserves to be called sonship because it is grounded in grace as a continuing regeneration.

We know that the creative activity which produces sanctifying grace is an activity shared by all three divine Persons. For that reason, if we are to speak accurately, we must remember that all three Persons constantly cause this reality in us. But we must also remember that the grace we possess, since it involves genuine sonship, does have some special relation to the sonship of the second Person of the blessed Trinity. Like him (rather *in* him) we are related to God the Father in a way not directed to either the Son himself or the Holy Spirit.

Christ himself taught us to pray to God the Father as "our Father." This special filial quality of our sanctifying grace, and the particular resemblance it gives us to Christ in his divine Sonship, is based on the fact that our grace is a participation in Christ's sanctifying grace, which he possesses as a modification of his humanity and as head of the mystical body. His sanctifying grace acts as the instrumental cause of our supernatural sanctification. All our grace is grace that comes from Christ, and it bears the mark of Christ who, in his personality, is the second Person of the Trinity, the Son. We are very profoundly sons of the Father in and through Christ the Son.

Despite this profound relationship of our sanctifying grace to the sonship possessed by the second Person of the blessed Trinity, there are also most important differences between our sonship and Christ's. His sonship is what constitutes his divine Person, whereas the sonship we possess by grace is something we acquire after God has already established us in our existence and substantial being. Again, the sonship Christ possesses comes to him in a complete and total, infinite and eternal possession of the divine nature given him by the Father. In our case, possession of the divine nature is partial, finite and accidental.

To indicate these fundamental differences between our sonship and that divine sonship which Christ has through his eternal generation, we say that our grace gives us "adopted sonship." However, in the use of this term we must be careful not to lose sight of the fact that our sonship is not based on a legal fiction as is "adopted sonship" in its ordinary usage. This expression, as applied to sanctifying grace, in no way denies the real, physical nature of the sonship we have from God the Father. It merely emphasizes the fact that our sonship is in a profound way different from the sonship of Christ.

GRACE AND DIVINE INHERITANCE

St. Paul tells us in the letter to the Galatians that because we are sons of God, truly sons, we are heirs also, sharing the inheritance that belongs properly to

Christ (cf. 4:7). The connection between inheritance and sonship is an immediate one. Chosen by the Father to be his sons by sharing Christ's own sonship, we are also given the right of sons to possess the inheritance—God the Father himself. What belongs to Christ as Son is the Father; what Christ shares with us, his picked and chosen brethren, is his Father. In the gospels we cannot miss the eagerness of Christ to communicate to those who are his own the knowledge and love of his Father, so that those who are his own might come to know and love the Father and thereby possess him.

The possession of the Father, given us in the Christian mystery, goes even deeper. It comes in the very communication of life to us by the Father, and it is on this basis that we can turn to the Father and claim him as our own. The inheritance that we possess as the result of sanctifying grace is a genuine right of strict justice and is grounded in the gift of sonship. The goal or purpose involved in this reorientation of our natures by grace is the possession of God the Father in personal union. Unless we by our own free choice reject this orientation, it will remain as something which must bring us to ultimate fulfillment, since God will be true to the orientation he has placed in us.

GRACE AND MERIT

When we speak this way of inheritance, we are speaking of what is the ground of our ability to merit and to possess God finally as our destiny. We would fall into the heresy of Pelagius (who in the fifth century taught that man could reach his destiny by his own natural power) were we to think that our own actions, no matter how good, could of themselves deserve the supreme good, God himself. No one of our actions, nor any aggregate of them, could ever deserve the slightest degree of sanctifying grace, much less the fulfillment that comes in union with God. However, once we have been given supernatural life, once we have been given a vital orientation toward activity on the divine level, we are then placed in a new context in which we can and do deserve God himself. This supernatural life that God gives us is a life that directs us back to him, through the power and grace of Christ working in us. And in proportion as this life is deepened and amplified (through development of faith, hope and charity) this vital directedness becomes deeper and more definite.

Fundamentally, to merit means to develop our capacity for supernatural living. The greater the capacity, the greater will be the fulfillment due the capacity so that it may be satisfied. It is in this context that the Church, particularly at the Council of Trent (TCT 606), speaks of our ability to merit, teaching that we can merit: 1) increase in the grace that we possess, 2) fulfillment of this life of grace in beatific vision and 3) the extent to which we will share in beatific vision. If we look at these three aspects of merit carefully, we shall see that what is involved is this: if we cooperate with God in our organically developing supernatural life, that life will grow in its capacity for ever-greater vitality and thereby serve as a measure of our capacity for personal living in the next life.

CONSECRATION AND UNION

GRACE AS CONSECRATION

In Baptism, a real consecration is effected by the sacramental character. By this character, we are set aside for participation in Christ's redemptive work. A second consecration comes about through sanctifying grace. Grace, therefore, is a special kind of dedication.

"Dedication" means that something is designated or set aside for a particular purpose; it is directed to some specific kind of activity. Thus, we dedicate a building, indicating that it is to play some special role in people's lives. Furthermore, when we speak of a dedicated person, we mean one unswervingly intent on the attainment of some goal. A dedicated physician is devoted heart and soul to his medical practice; a dedicated scientist is wholly absorbed in his scientific research.

"Consecration" is a particular kind of dedication. It is the setting aside of someone or something for a sacred purpose, for sacred action. The very etymology of the word consecration indicates this. It comes from two Latin words: *cum* and *sacer*. Its root idea, therefore, would be "with the sacred." In an act of consecration, a person or thing is taken out of the secular realm and set apart for sacred purposes.

There is much we can learn about the revealed meaning of consecration by studying the Old Testament. We know that Moses himself was selected from among the people of Israel, set aside for the task of leading Israel out of Egypt, through the Sinai desert and into the promised land. Moses was a person dedicated to the service of Yahweh, consecrated by the fact that God singled him out and gave him a special role. Scripture describes the consecration of Moses as something that was determined by more than externals. We are told that Moses possessed the spirit in a special fashion (Num 11:25). The spirit working in him enabled him to carry out the task for which God had selected him.

David, too, was given the spirit in a special action of anointing that quite clearly symbolized the bestowal of Yahweh's spirit. This gave David the power he needed to carry out his kingly role (1 Kings 6:13). Again, at the time of the consecration of the Jerusalem temple under Solomon, Mount Sion—and more particularly the temple that was built there—was specially set aside for the worship of God. According to the book of Kings, a bright cloud descended upon the Holy of Holies, the most central portion of the temple, indicating that God himself was taking special possession of this place (1 Kings 8:10-11).

In the consecration of the priests set aside for the functions of the temple ceremonial, we see the importance attached to the anointing with blood. If we recall that the ritual use of blood at Mount Sinai indicated a sharing of life with God in covenant (Ex 24), we can see that consecration with blood would, for an Israelite, point to some introduction into God's own sphere of life. We could multiply such instances. However, from those already mentioned we can conclude that in Old Testament thought consecration is an action in which God takes possession of a place as his own, or of people by giving them life.

With Christ, the notion of consecration is fulfilled in a unique way. Christ's humanity is possessed by his divine Person in the mystery of incarnation, and his priesthood comes to him as man by that unparalleled anointing he has as God-man. Not only is there a designation of his human nature for the service of his Father, there is also the intrinsic ontological assumption of his humanity to the Person of the Son. Scripture points to this consecration of Christ's humanity when it describes the mystery of Jesus' conception by saying that the Holy Spirit overshadows the blessed Virgin (Lk 1:35). As an external manifestation of this solemn consecration of Christ for the messianic work of redemption, the Spirit shows himself in visible form (as a dove) at the baptism and again (under the sign of the cloud) at the transfiguration (Mt 3:16; 17:5).

This unique consecration, possessed by him as an individual human, Christ then extends to his Church, the mystical body. He does this by the gift of the Spirit, whom he sends into the infant Church on Pentecost, so that the Spirit may be the soul of the Church, the principle of its life and unity. Because of this indwelling Spirit, those who make up the Church, or Christ's Body, form the new temple fashioned from living stones (1 Cor 3:16-17; 6:19), set aside and anointed by the Spirit who is himself their anointing (2 Cor 1:21; Eph 1:13-14).

Working within each individual Christian, the Spirit both possesses and transforms him through sanctifying grace. This makes the Christian the Father's special possession, his son. It is in this sense that sanctifying grace is an intrinsic consecration, a reality that sets man apart from profane existence and introduces one into the most sacred of all situations—the inner, personal familial life of the three divine Persons. The reality that makes the three divine Persons especially present to the Christian is sanctifying grace itself. By it he is sanctified in his being and his activity. This is the essence of Christian sanctity. Basically, it does not derive from what the individual Christian does, but from what God does to him. All genuine Christian holiness is a development and expression of this new life principle, sanctifying grace.

GRACE AND UNION WITH GOD

As we have seen, sanctifying grace is a supernatural life principle, a sharing in God's own way of life. As such it is meant to find its perfect fulfillment in that conscious personal union with the three divine Persons which the blessed have in beatific vision. However, even in our present life, sanctifying grace is already a union with the blessed Trinity.

Since we have this divine life through an act of regeneration, God must be intimately present to us as long as we possess grace. The divine action must be continually taking place within us in order to sustain the existence of a reality which we with our unaided natural powers can neither produce nor preserve. This special presence, which we call the "divine indwelling," involves a personal union between the divine Persons and ourselves, more intimate than any other kind of personal union we know.

Sanctifying grace itself does not formally constitute conscious union with God. Conscious union takes place in the acts of faith and hope and charity; but sanctifying grace is the deeper power that makes it possible for us to have these conscious acts of personal union. Grace turns us toward God in the very roots of our being. By grace we are directed to knowing and loving the divine Persons as they know and love one another. Thus, personal union is incompletely achieved in this life by faith and love, and is fully achieved in the next by beatific vision.

Because the life of beatitude will be the full flowering of our life of grace, it may help our understanding of grace to study briefly the Church's teaching regarding beatific vision. Drawing from the statements of the later medieval Church, particularly from the famous *Constitutio Benedictina* of Benedict XII (TCT 886), we see that the union we are to have with the divine Persons in the next life will be one of astonishing intimacy.

In this life, we know nothing except through some medium. No matter how deep our knowledge of another person becomes, we must always pass through that other person's manifestation of himself in order to understand the personality that lies beneath it. Even in our knowledge of ourselves there is never complete directness. We discover ourselves only by observing ourselves in our actions, above all in our states of awareness and in our reactions to people. In all our understanding of persons, no matter how deep or intimate, there is always the medium of our own ideas. We relate to any given person according to the idea we have of him.

In our personal awareness of and love for God in beatific vision, nothing will intervene. There will not be even the medium of an idea between ourselves as knowing and the three divine Persons as known. What exactly this will be like, we can only imagine. Yet, if we reflect upon our most intimate moments of personal living in this present life, we can obtain some inkling of the kind of union we will possess with the divine Persons in our life of beatitude.

However, our life of beatitude will not differ essentially from our present life of grace. In order to have the intimate conscious union with God we are promised in beatific vision, we will have to possess a supernatural nature, so transformed that it can serve as the ultimate intrinsic source of so exalted a union. This supernatural transformation of our deeper principles of activity is exactly what we mean by sanctifying grace. As we examine the life of beatitude, we see that it must involve three elements; the reorientation in completely supernatural fashion of (a) our knowing and (b) our loving, and (c) a transformation of the deeper principle of activity which is our nature. Of these three elements we now possess two: sanctifying grace (transformation of nature) and charity (reorientation of love). Only the first will be changed, for knowing by faith must give way to knowing by vision. We can see, then, that our present life of grace is already a state of most profound union with the divine Persons.

JUSTIFICATION AND TRANSFORMATION

GRACE AS JUSTIFICATION

When we speak of sanctifying grace as "justification," we are using what is probably the most common name for this reality, apart from the name "sanctifying grace" itself. This term is rooted in the writings of St. Paul, who often speaks of man as "justified" by Christ. It is also important because medieval, early Renaissance, and Catholic-Protestant discussion of man's sanctification turns about the question of how man is justified. What constitutes his justification? The Reformation and Post-Reformation controversies about grace centered around this question. Because much modern theology still deals with these controversies and with Trent's formulation of doctrine on the subject (cf. TCT 556-607), books about grace treat justification quite generously.

To some extent the problem of justification posed at the time of the Reformation was stated too strongly, as though there were an irreconcilable opposition between two propositions: we are justified by our good actions; we are justified by the merits of Christ. Probably it would be better not to phrase the difficulty this way. What is really at stake is whether God's justifying action is merely an external legal affair or an action that effects our internal reordering, and whether or not our human freedom is a necessary correlative to God's justifying act.

The Catholic position is that God does indeed justify us in the external public order by forgiving our sins, but that his forgiveness goes beyond this and actually restores to us the divine life that is sanctifying grace. This divine life, since it involves the personal relationships that flow from love and consciousness, is something that cannot be imposed on a person. Therefore it can only be effected in us if we open ourselves by our own free choice to God's loving and justifying action.

In both the Old and New Testament we find the same basic approach to the notion of justification. There is no doubt that God, spoken of as a just God with regard to men, is the one who must make man just.

In Old Testament times, God had already pointed out man's inability of himself to turn himself to the divine, to order himself to his destiny, to make himself just. God alone, by his divine action, can turn sinful man back to the right path and lead him in peace and harmony to the true promised land. Yet God promises to do precisely this. In the famous passage in Jeremiah 31:31-33, God says through the prophet:

This is the covenant which I will make with the house of Israel after those days, says the Lord: I will put my law within them, and I will write it upon their hearts; and I will be their God, and they shall be my people.

Certainly, there is promise here of more than just external forensic pardoning of the sinful man or sinful people.

Yet it is also clear—tragically clear on many occasions—that man's free acceptance of God's justifying action is a necessary element in the picture. In the earlier strata of Old Testament thought, in the time before the people's spiritual understanding had deepened to any great extent, they thought that the justification bestowed on Israel was unconditioned. Yet, by the time of the prophets and the Deuteronomic movement, we find it explicitly stated that God's selection and sanctification of Israel (and of the individual Israelite) is dependent on man's turning to God in free choice. If Israel will but turn to God, then the divine action promised through the prophets will take place, and Israel will become once more the Just of God. Fundamentally, justification will occur in freely accepted redemption—which only an omnipotent God can accomplish in man.

Against this background, we can see that when the New Testament says that man is justified by faith (Rom 10:4-10), it means that only God, working in the mystery of the incarnation and through the merits of Christ, can be the cause of man's redemption or reordering. Yet, in the pages of the New Testament it is abundantly clear that Christ does not force his healing upon anyone. Before he can work his wonders in man, Christ must find faith. If faith is there, then Christ's power enters into a man in order to overcome the evil that abides in him (Mk 9:22-23). This internal reordering, to which both Old and New Testaments refer, is "sanctifying grace."

It is, then, a new and more intimate ordering to God that sanctifying grace gives us. We are directed to union with the three divine Persons in knowledge and in love. This ordering is, because of the fallen state of man, a re-ordering; it is a *redemptive ordering*. Adam had this supernatural order through grace and lost it through original sin. Original sin, and our own personal sin, cause in us, too, a fundamental disorder. We need redeeming. Christ's saving action effects our redemption precisely by causing in us that internal reordering which is sanctifying grace. Because grace orders us to God, because it "rectifies" our being, we call it "justification."

The Council of Trent in its treatise on justification (TCT 556-607) makes it clear that sanctifying grace is that intrinsic, reordering reality:

. . . the only formal cause [of justification] is "the justice of God, not the justice by which he is himself just, but the justice by which he makes us just," namely, the justice which we have as a gift from him and by which we are renewed in the spirit of our mind (TCT 563).

The Catholic position does not deny that there is a legal aspect to the justification of man. God does consider man just because of the merits of Christ. But the

Church insists that the divine forgiveness goes beyond this, and that the merits of Christ (which are really the power of his "grace of the head" expressing itself in his death and resurrection) work for the intrinsic reformation of man.

Through Christ's grace man is reordered to God. The reality which is the reordering is sanctifying grace. Thus, sanctifying grace is within us; it is a constant dynamic principle, remaking us according to the sublime pattern of the new Adam, Christ.

GRACE AS TRANSFORMATION OF PERSONALITY

We have seen that grace, viewed under the aspect of justification, involves a reordering within man, an intrinsic transformation of the individual. This change in man, fulfilling the promise of Jeremiah 31:33, is referred to by St. Paul's writings as the "new man . . . created in Christ Jesus" (Eph 2:15, 10; cf. 3:10). The recipient of grace is not merely restored to Adam's original condition. Because he has been changed by the sanctifying grace coming from Christ's death and resurrection, man is in a superior situation. That is why the liturgy of Holy Week can refer to Adam's sin as a "felix culpa," a fortunate transgression.

The change effected by sanctifying grace does not put man in the position of having a completely human nature. A "state of pure nature" is something no human being has ever possessed. Adam himself was in a state of nature already transformed by grace. Later, because of his sin, he passed into a state in which nature was deprived of its original supernatural orientation (TCT 372). In the Christian dispensation, we have a nature reordered by the grace that comes to us through Christ. We who have this status as "the new man in Christ" exist in a transformed fashion, touching our personal way of being and action.

What does it mean to say that grace is a transformation of our personal nature? Perhaps we might preface our answer to this question by addressing ourselves to a more basic one. What does it mean to be a person? When we discover what is distinctive in our human way of being, we see that we are creatures who open up, in a privileged way, to things around us. Animals, it is true, know the things around them, and they are aware in some sense that they know them. But it is also true that they know only material things, things which can be seen, heard, smelled, tasted and touched.

We humans, because we are spirits or persons, are not thus limited. Because of our distinctive powers of knowledge and affectivity we are able to extend our sphere of knowing and loving far beyond what we can see and hear and touch. Given enough time and proper scientific instruments, we can penetrate thousands of years into the past and millions of miles into space. This means we have an incredible capacity for enriching our way of being—a conscious and loving way of being. We can constantly bring into our lives all the things we come to know, most importantly the persons. The only limit to the extent of possible growth is that imposed by the human life span. Again, our ambitions and hopes are not limited to what pertains solely to ourselves. Rather, through what we call personal friendship, we can identify the good, the hopes and the ambitions of others as our own. We can, quite literally, seek their good as if it were our own good. As a matter of fact, because of our love for them it does become our own good.

In this way, through knowing and loving, we can extend the periphery of our own existence. As persons, we share our lives with others, and we share in their lives. Furthermore, because we are persons with freedom, we are not deterministically ordered to the future. Rather, within a certain range of capabilities and circumstances, we are able to shape the future according to our own desires and hopes. Concerning the things deepest in us—whether we will be loving or hateful, whether we will seek knowledge or not, whether we will be honest or deceitful—we exercise the determining causality as to what we will be.

In this process of opening up to reality in knowledge, love and freedom, and in extending the sphere of our own existence and activity, we have in a sense an unlimited potential. Only the shortness of our lives and the weakness of our powers of observation limit the scope of our learning and our friendship. While our powers of knowledge and love are confined properly and directly to the created world of things and persons in our immediate experience, we are able even by our natural powers to know of the existence of a God beyond this world. However, it is still correct to say that our openness as persons, as an openness to direct knowledge of others, is restricted to the limits of the created universe. Naturally speaking, our powers of thinking and loving do not have God as their direct object. They can contact him only indirectly—insofar as he can be seen to be demanded by the being, the truth, the finality of creation.

Human activity on its highest level is spiritual; it is an activity of personal awareness and love. To support this spiritual way of action there must be an underlying ontological principle, directed to personal being and personal activity. This we call human nature. It is this principle, at the heart of our being, that directs us outward to the world. It directs us particularly to persons and ultimately, though indirectly, to God himself. Since this human nature specifies our existence, we *are* or *exist* openly. And because our activity is the expression of the kind of being we are, we *act* openly.

Sanctifying grace comes to this open way of being, to this root of personal spiritual activity, and transforms it. Grace exists to be a further opening up, a reorientation, a redirecting, a transforming intensification. To use the common theological term, grace is an elevation of the nature of man. It would be incorrect to think of sanctifying grace as something that is simply added to, or laid on top of, human nature. Grace comes as a radical transformation, developing the potential of man's nature, bringing his capabilities to fuller realization. God's personal way of being is superior to man's; it absorbs man's into itself without destroying any of its own intrinsic values. "Grace perfects nature; it does not destroy it." This supernatural life, therefore, touches us at the very core of our being, at the very root of all our human activity, expanding our basic personal openness so that a whole new range of being and activity is now ours.

Because of this amplified power of personal activity, we are able to relate ourselves in direct familiarity to the three divine Persons as distinct persons. We are able to include them within the sphere of our own conscious living. Because of this new relationship to the divine, we can relate ourselves in a more profound way to created persons and to the entire created universe. This we do by exercising the new life-powers of faith, hope and charity, which spring from the transformation of our nature in grace.

BIBLIOGRAPHY FOR CHAPTER 4

WORKS ON SANCTIFYING GRACE

B. Fraigneau-Julien, "Grace and the Divine Indwelling," *Theology Digest* 4(1956), pp. 79-83. Interesting discussion of Scheeben's teaching on grace and divine indwelling, followed by extensive bibliography on the divine indwelling.

P. Fransen, "Towards a Psychology of Divine Grace," *Theology Digest* 6(1958), pp. 79-83. Interesting study of grace and freedom, drawing from contemporary work in phenomenology and psychology.

R. Gleason, *Grace,* New York, Sheed and Ward, 1962. Standard presentation of the major aspects of Catholic teaching on grace.

H. Küng, *Justification,* New York, Nelson, 1964. A famous doctoral dissertation in which the author argues that the Calvinist Karl Barth and the Catholic Council of Trent are in substantial agreement about the nature of God's justifying grace.

L. Lavelle, *Evil and Suffering,* New York, Macmillan, 1963. The second portion of the book (pp. 93-152) is a stimulating essay on the relation of *presence* to grace, by one of today's leading personalist thinkers. As background for these pages, one might profitably read Lavelle's essay, "In the Presence of Being," pp. 43-64, *Modern Catholic Thinkers* (R. Caponigri, ed.), London, Burns Oates, 1960. It might also be helpful to read, in the same volume, the article by E. Mounier "The Self amongst Others," pp. 200-221.

J. Mouroux, *The Christian Experience,* New York, Sheed and Ward, 1954. An important presentation of the Catholic teaching on the life of grace, rooted in scripture and theology but presented in the context of human experience. A profoundly Christian work.

H. Rondet, "The Divinization of the Christian," *Theology Digest* 7(1959), pp. 113-122. Brief review of the historical position taken by theologians in explaining grace as divinization, followed by the author's own theological conclusions. This article is immediately followed (pp. 123-126) by a related study: F. Bourassa, "Son of God or Son of the Father?" which discusses grace as a personal relationship.

5

CHRISTIAN DECISIVENESS

•

THE SITUATION OF TEMPTATION

•

TRANSFORMATION OF OUR POWERS

CHRISTIAN FREEDOM

The transformation of the Christian personality that takes place through sanctify-ing grace is meant to find its fulfillment in a new exercise of human freedom. "For freedom Christ has set us free" (Gal 5:1; cf. Jn 8:32-36). It is, therefore, especially in the exercise of freedom that we are to manifest that sonship we possess through our identification with Christ. Christian spirituality is, in a pro-found sense, a shaping of our lives according to the pattern of Christ's. This demands that each of us consciously choose what he wants his life to be and his personality to become. Each of the sacraments is, in its own way, a sign of the basic Christian choice of life, an acceptance of Christ on his own terms, an accept-ance of a role in the community of the Church, a commitment to the use of personal freedom in genuine Christian maturity.

A NEW DIMENSION

Sanctifying grace, because it is a reorientation of our nature, directs us to this new decisiveness in life. The transformation of our powers of understanding and love, accomplished in faith, hope and charity, brings the finality of grace into our personal living. Faith enables us to live our lives with the vision that God, Father, Son and Spirit, is working in our history to redeem mankind in and through the mystery of the risen Christ. Moreover, faith enables us to take Christ on his own terms, with the wisdom he imparts to our human prudence, and to realize that the answer to our existence in this world is to be found through identification with Christ's own death and resurrection. It is faith, too, that gives us the ability to see the deeper meaning of any human situation and the somewhat hidden workings of God in and through the risen Christ. In becoming incarnate, Christ transformed the total context of human living. It is faith that enables us to make the Christian effort to transform the world, according to his pattern and by the power of his Spirit working in us.

In addition to the new vision that comes with faith, we are also given hope. Hope provides the courage to overcome life's difficulties and to pursue with patience the goals presented by faith. The transformation of human history which faith proposes to us is a task beyond our merely human powers. Moreover, the Christianization of the world will be accomplished in the face of continued resistance from the powers of evil. Hence, struggle and some discouragement are an inevitable part of the Christian endeavor. Purely human courage would not be sufficient for us to carry on practically and with patient aggressiveness the task of the Christian community, the task to which we commit ourselves in Baptism. Only hope, by transforming our ability to face life, makes it possible for us sincerely and constantly to make those decisions demanded by our Christian vocation.

Again, we could not love deeply enough either God or our fellow man, nor could we give ourselves to life with the wholeheartedness demanded of a Christian, except for the fact that the life of grace transforms our very powers of affective response. Supernatural love or charity directs us to a depth of loving and an openness in personal relationship expressed in a personal dedication of ourselves to the task of remaking the world. Christianity is the mystery of the transformation of human history through the power of love. This involves more than human love. Divine love works through us, transforming our human love, and accompanies our attempts to make the lives of our fellow men more meaningful.

Thus transformed, the Christian goes out into the world and encounters a life that demands decision. He often finds himself in situations of basic moral decision, which we call temptations. If we are to understand this human experience of temptation, we must approach it not with mere human understanding, but with an educated faith. Since faith finds its direction and formation in the revelation God has given us in Christ, a Christian should evaluate his own experience of temptation in the light of the temptation of Jesus himself. We know that the gospel account of the temptation of Christ has been preserved for the sake of our instruction about this continuing human situation. Therefore, we should utilize this gospel lesson in deliberating decisions of daily life.

TEMPTATION OF CHRIST

A Recurring Challenge

In studying the temptation of Christ, we note first that it is not described as an isolated event. We have already seen (in chapter one) that it is inseparably linked with Christ's baptism by John, and that these two scenes really form one mystery. But Christ's temptation is not linked to his baptism alone; it is linked to everything that follows—including his death and resurrection. In a sense, the temptation provides the norm for interpreting the other, later occasions of decision encountered by Christ in his public life. Analysis of what Christ did here will help us understand certain of his later actions.

Examination of Satan's temptation of Christ indicates that the tempter was suggesting that Christ exercise his messianic role in a manner other than that intended for him by the Father. The Old Testament had predicted that the messianic figure was to be a "suffering Servant" (cf. Is 52-53), and the gospel text of the baptism shows us that Christ at this moment was publicly asserting his identity as this Servant. Now, in the desert, the tempter encourages him to find some other way of saving mankind.

Reading further in the gospels, we see that Christ encountered this suggestion as a recurring temptation. His family tried to have him work wonders at the great feasts and so win notoriety and power (Jn 7:1-10). His own apostles told him that he should not go down to Jerusalem to face suffering and death. The scribes and pharisees tried to convince him to join forces with them and accept their solution for the salvation of Israel. Finally, in Gethsemane, his human nature recoiled from the threat of suffering and death. In all these situations we see that the key to understanding Christ's temptations and his answer to them is his free decision to faithfully fulfill the messianic task of redemption as it had been committed to him by the Father.

Maturity of Christ

When we reflect on this, we can see that free decisiveness is at the very core of Christ's response to life, and that he had to renew this response continually in the face of ever new challenges. His Father had given him a task to accomplish. His recurrent temptation was to turn away from this particular task and try to find some substitute more pleasing to his humanity. The temptation was to follow human wisdom rather than the wisdom of the Father. It is precisely here that Christ's human holiness is manifest. He straightforwardly accepts the concrete challenge offered him; he honestly faces his task, and makes the decision to follow his Father's will. When the gospel describes Christ's *human* sanctity, we see that this sanctity clearly involves his completely mature confrontation of life in honesty and in love.

In the gospel descriptions of his baptism, Jesus is paralleled both to Adam and Israel. The first man and the chosen people had made false choices. Christ is now pictured as reversing those choices. For that reason, Christ's response to Satan's temptation is already part of his redeeming work. On Calvary Jesus overcomes evil by freely accepting the Father's will. He did not defeat evil simply by dying, but by accepting his death in obedience to the Father. In obediently and freely choosing to undergo death, Christ rejected, freely and totally, the temptation to try some other way of saving men. It is on the cross that Christ definitively says No to the tempter, and Christ's choice there sets a pattern for human decision directly opposed to the false choice made by Adam. In doing this, Christ is redeeming mankind. Yet what Christ does on the cross is only part, though a most important part, of this mystery of rejecting evil. All his earlier victories over temptation form part of this same mystery.

The temptations of Jesus described for us in the synoptic gospels demand reflection upon the precise issues involved. What happened to Christ is meant to teach us about our own Christian situation. Satan's suggestion that Christ seek salvation by false paths points up the fact that men frequently choose the wrong means to salvation.

The first proposal of Satan, to change stones into bread, touches on the preservation of life. This temptation grows out of the human tendency to become excessively concerned about material security. Men all too commonly equate life with bodily life, with what is vegetative and sensitive. There is little awareness that, on its most important level, life is related to thinking and loving. It is not easy for a human being to risk or to lose his bodily health or life in order to preserve the true personal levels of his being. This requires uncommon courage. Even when our life is not so sharply threatened, or our health endangered, there is still a very subtle tendency to allow ourselves to become almost totally absorbed in providing for what is less important in our life.

Christ spoke about this in the sermon on the mount when he said: "But seek first his kingdom and his righteousness, and all these things shall be yours as well" (Mt 6:33). In the temptation in the desert Christ's answer to Satan conveyed this same point: "Man shall not live by bread alone, but by every word that proceeds from the mouth of God" (Mt 4:4). The word of God is a life-giving force. It is the creative power which governs each detail of our life on earth. This word touches the most profound personal depths of our human living in order to nourish them. The first temptation that confronted Christ urged him to abandon true Christian perspective. It suggested that he place the pursuit of material things before personal values, that he subordinate people to things.

The second temptation involved trying to dictate to God a better way of doing things. The Old Testament had predicted that God would guard his Messiah in a special way. Satan told Christ that he should test God to see if God really keeps his promises. However, this is not just an arbitrary testing of God. The issue is rather our human tendency to prefer our own way of accomplishing good. Then, when the path we have chosen in preference to God's has led us into danger or problems, we turn to God telling him that we are his sons and that he should take care of us. We prefer our own human judgments to the divine wisdom expressed in revelation, and then we foolishly expect God to act miraculously in order to compensate for our mistakes. As we shall see, this is true of any person who needlessly places himself in an occasion of sin.

The final temptation is more obvious, though still very fundamental. Satan offers all the wealth and power of the world to Christ. This is of course suggested under the guise of saving men and bringing them to happiness, as though the answer to life's problems comes with the possession of wealth and power.

TEMPTATION OF THE CHRISTIAN

A Christian Commitment

With this brief analysis of the temptations of Christ as a guide, we can study our human experience of temptation in order to see, from a Christian point of view, the fundamental issues we must face.

In our day by day experience of temptation, we generally think of it as something that involves accepting or rejecting some particular temporal good incompatible with our destiny. Such false goods do enter into the situation as an important element. However, an analysis of temptation shows that something more basic is present. The real issue is whether we will honestly pass judgment according to the Christian values we professed in our Baptism, on the created good concerned. The issue is our commitment to a Christian vision of life. Do we genuinely accept that wisdom of Christ which St. Paul in his first letter to the Corinthians admits is a "stumbling block to Jews, and folly to Gentiles"?

Temptation is really a test of our Baptism, just as the temptation of Christ was a test of the commitment he had made publicly at his baptism. In Baptism we accept wholeheartedly the meaning and the power of Christ's death and resurrection. We profess the fact that these mysteries give value to human life, and we reject the value connected with the opposing view. "I do renounce Satan and all his works and all his pomps." Every life-situation we experience is judged by one of these two value systems. Whenever he is tempted, a Christian must evaluate the demands of the moment by applying the values that he accepts in Christian faith. In his Baptism he pledged himself to this; to reject these values would constitute infidelity to his Christian vocation, unfaithfulness to his membership in the body of Christ.

If we view temptation this way, we notice that it cannot be isolated in one moment of choice. It frequently embraces an extended period of time during which one wrestles with the problem of evaluating a certain course of action. In fact, the need to apply Christian values is a continuing challenge to which we are more or less deeply responding at any given moment. In this way we are steadily preparing for those specific instances when a clear crisis or decision emerges.

Temptation may also be analyzed in relation to the genuinity of our Christian love. In any situation in which we are being tempted to a false course of action, there is a good that appeals to us in one way or another, a good that promises some happiness. If these apparent goods are able to draw us away from God, if we permit some material thing or temporal pleasure or pursuit of personal power to take precedence over our genuine concern for a fellow man, then genuine Christian love is not the ruling force in our life.

This does not mean that we Christians, in situations of temptation, must deny the attraction of created goods. Rather, it is a question of balancing our attraction to this or that good with a still greater attraction toward God in love. It is not Christian to stand in haughty superiority above created things and claim that they do not appeal to us. Christian triumph over temptation is a triumph of love, love of Christ and of all mankind.

This has important practical implications. When we are faced with a particularly difficult decision, when we are strongly moved by emotions of fear or desire, personal love for Christ must be brought into play. Obviously this love cannot be developed at a moment's notice. We must draw upon a growing gift of self to Christ, upon a deep personal commitment to living the whole of our lives along with Christ, upon a developed loyalty that will cling to those values for which Christ laid down his life. Such love for Christ brings a Christian great freedom from unbalanced attraction to things or persons.

Maturity of the Christian

Every temptation is a temptation to deny love; every sin is a concession to this tendency to barricade oneself and turn inward; it is a denial of genuine love for God, one's fellowman and oneself. Scholastic theologians speak of love as the "form" of all the other virtues; conversely, in every sinful act we find a lack of love. Every temptation, then, is a choice to give or to deny love.

One of the most important aspects of temptation is that it tests personal maturity, personal ability to govern life in free decisiveness. An adult is a person whose human activity grows from his self-awareness and his own responsible choices. An adult works with patient endurance toward the achievement of goals that befit him as a person. Though he may be in difficult circumstances, he determines the kind of life he truly wishes to live. Though he is sensitive to the reactions of other persons and aware of the opinion they have of him, though he may be deeply emotional, still he does not allow himself to be unduly affected by human approval or by emotional attraction toward one or other course of action. He allows neither of these two influences to destroy the very values most meaningful to him as a Christian.

It is in situations of basic choice, of temptation, that one most manifests the presence or absence of maturity. When we look at the Christ of the New Testament, one of the things that is most striking about him is the way in which he is always completely in command at the great moments of choice. Whether confronted by Satan in the desert, or assailed by the scribes and pharisees as he preaches in the temple, or facing Pilate on Good Friday, there is never a time when Jesus is not the master of himself as well as of the situation. At the moment of greatest decision, during his agony in the garden, Christ reasserts the choice that has governed each action of his life: "Not my will, but thine, be done" (Lk 22:42).

A mature Christian is one who has reflected upon the values that he wishes to guide his life. He is conscious of the goals toward which he works, and has chosen to live according to these goals and values. When temptation occurs, he is not stampeded into a course of action by fear or desire or anger. No man can predict all the judgments he will have to make, but a mature person possesses those elements of understanding and motivation that will be effective in times of critical judgment. It is clear that he must constantly develop these elements through reflection, reading and prayer. But when the moment of decision comes, the individual, notwithstanding his dependence upon the community and all the support given him by his friends, must stand alone and make his choice in somewhat frightening isolation. It is the mark of a person that no one except himself can ultimately decide for him what is to be his destiny.

Perhaps the most basic element in any temptation is this: for any human being and more particularly for a Christian, a situation of moral choice requires an honest and realistic acceptance of one's own life. Each individual has certain practical demands established for him, at least in a general way, by his personal potential or deficiencies, by his obligation to family or civic society or professional life, by his educational background, by the relations he has with various people and by the grace God has given him. In each case the combination of these elements is unique. They point to a role within the mystery of the Church that is not given to any other person. The Christian, like Christ in the desert, faces the obligation to accept honestly his function in life.

The moment of temptation demands something all too rarely found, a courageous and honest appraisal of self in the face of a concrete situation. Some people try to overreach their gifts and powers by striving for unattainable objectives. Others are more gifted but fearful about exploiting their gifts, because they lack the hope that is needed for achievement or are unwilling to encounter the difficulties that will ensue; they try to ignore their capabilities and settle for a lifetime of mediocrity. One must love deeply and possess mature honesty in order to evaluate objectively both oneself and the circumstances in which one is situated. Finished and perfect Christian adulthood is not easily achieved.

THE HELP OF GRACE

THE NOTION OF SELF-SUFFICIENCY

INADEQUACY OF HUMAN EFFORT

This brief analysis of the Christian's need to confront moral decision with mature honesty and love indicates that life is not an easy affair. Faith tells us that man by his unaided efforts is not able to handle the situation adequately; he needs that transforming help we call grace. The Catholic view of man is not pessimistic; on the contrary, it holds that man can attain a destiny of glory. But he is able to do so only in close dependence upon divine assistance and never by his efforts alone.

This need for the special help of grace, making it possible for man to do what leads him to his goal in life, has been insisted upon since the days of St. Paul. Even prior to that, in the Old Testament, revelation taught that man is unable to do what befits his dignity unless he is helped by the graciousness of God (Jer 31:31-34; Hos 13:4-10). The people of Israel more than once trusted in their own ways, their own devices, their own human power, and abandoned the paths of the Lord. In each instance disaster resulted. Only by repeated failure did the people gradually learn their deep need for God.

In the New Testament, many passages teach the same lesson. Two in particular are rather striking. In the fifteenth chapter of St. John's gospel, we find the Church described under the figure of the vine and branches. Christ, after telling his apostles that they are to be the branches, drawing their life, strength and fruitfulness from him who is the main stock of the vine, tells them very clearly, "Apart from me you can do nothing" (Jn 15:5). The context of this passage refers to what we now call the supernatural order, the order of grace. Christ is indicating that no work that is to be truly fruitful in the supernatural order can be accomplished by purely human powers. Again, in the letter to the Romans, St. Paul, after sketching the insufficiency of man in the period before the Law, then describes the continuing inadequacy of human determination and motivation even with the guidance of the Mosaic Law (Rom 7). Against this background, he points to the grave problems facing man. Left to his own devices, even with the guidance of revelation, man finds that he cannot accomplish the things that he would, and finds himself doing what he does not wish to do (Rom 7:19). Only one thing can solve this basic inadequacy: the grace of Christ (Rom 8:9-10). Following this lead of scripture, the Church has always taught that man stands in absolute need of the special help of God. Only with such help can he accomplish what is good and achieve his destiny (TCT 648).

The lesson of man's dependence on grace is very much needed. The revelation that man must receive special help from God works against our human tendency to think ourselves completely autonomous and self-sufficient. Man inclines toward naturalism, trusting in the complete adequacy of his own powers. This he does because he is unaware of the magnitude of the supernatural order and of the harm that has come to him by sin. The supernatural order, the order of grace, is participation in God's own way of being. Consequently it completely surpasses the natural drives, motivations and powers of human nature. Since supernatural life is divine, man must be given divine help in order to live at this level. Furthermore, man has been seriously harmed by sin—Adam's sin and his own personal sin. As a result, he often rejects what is best for him, closes himself off from the world of truth and goodness and beauty, the world of his fulfillment, and turns in on himself, perverting the basic law of his being as a person. This tendency has a number of historical antecedents.

PELAGIAN HERESY

In the early centuries of Christianity, we find this supposed self-sufficiency of man expressed in a heresy known as Pelagianism. Pelagius and his followers, teaching and writing in the fourth and fifth centuries, rejected the basic teaching of the Church with regard to the special order of grace that makes us Godlike. Without going into the whole complicated development of Pelagianism, we can summarize its main tenets:

While Pelagius and his followers admit that Adam may have committed a sin that can be called original sin, still no real harm came either to human nature or to human powers of free decision as a result of this sin. Adam's fault hurts the human race only insofar as it provides a harmful example that human beings tend to follow.

There is no real intrinsic need of the supernatural help from God which we call grace. God does give grace, but this is merely to make it easier for man to do what he should do. Grace is not necessary to raise man to the level of divine activity nor to work against the harmful after-effects of sin.

Since no intrinsic damage remains in man because of sin, there is no real need for redemption. Christ did redeem, say the Pelagians, but this redemption consists solely in the fact that he gave us an example counter to that of Adam, and so leads us to our destiny. Christ did not redeem by effecting anything intrinsic to human nature or personality.

The basic error in each of these three tenets of Pelagianism is that man is able, by his unaided natural powers, to reach a destiny which is truly supernatural. Pelagianism does not recognize the existence of a supernatural order. The end or goal it envisages for man is a goal completely proportioned to nature and to natural powers of action.

Pelagianism was condemned by the popes and fathers of the Church who lived and taught at that time. In a series of synods, the African hierarchy denounced the teachings of the Pelagians. The bishops insisted that man does need grace in order to perform actions that are proportioned to his supernatural destiny as well as to overcome the results of original and personal sin. Alerted by the investigations and discussions of the African hierarchy, the popes of the period, Zozimus and Innocent I, joined in the condemnation of Pelagianism (TCT 536, 369). Unfortunately, because of difficulties in language and the subtlety with which the Pelagians explained their position, a synod held at Jerusalem early in the fifth century appeared to support them. The confusion was caused by a failure to understand the real Pelagian teaching. Not long afterwards, at the Council of Ephesus in 431, the Eastern Church also condemned this heresy.

Semi-Pelagianism

The tendency to look upon man as capable of solving his own problems is something deeply rooted in human nature. Even after the condemnation of the Pelagian heresy, a subtler form of the same error appeared again, particularly in the Church of Gaul (cf. TCT 543-549). Semi-Pelagianism is often connected with Cassian, one of the great leaders of monasticism in the West. In urging their monks to resist sin, some monastic teachers seem to have excessively stressed the role of human effort (TCT 630).

Semi-Pelagians admitted that grace is needed. Furthermore, it is needed as a reality intrinsic to man. It enables his human nature to operate on the supernatural level and to overcome the pernicious results of sin. However, grace is, at least in some cases, owed to him in consequence of his naturally good actions. If a man does the best he can, if he performs good acts, then his actions *deserve* grace. Such a doctrine is, of course, heretical. Grace always comes first, and man's act comes in response to grace.

Drawing from the writings and insights of St. Augustine, the Church, at the second Council of Orange, consolidated its opposition to Semi-Pelagianism. At this local council, held in Gaul and later approved by the pope, the Church's position on grace was very clearly stated (TCT 543-549). Grace, God's special supernatural help, is needed if man is even to begin a supernaturally good act. Prior to what man does, grace is already present as the first movement toward supernatural fulfillment. Not only must grace be present to help man begin a supernaturally good act; it must remain with man as he continues his action. It is grace, flowing into man's activity, that directs it toward that fulfillment which is his eternal destiny. Therefore, we can say that grace begins, grace accompanies and grace crowns human supernatural activity. This teaching of the Church, formulated at II Orange, has become a classic guide for all theologizing in the western Church with regard to the need and effectiveness of grace. Even the more detailed teaching at the time of the Council of Trent still follows the guidelines laid down by II Orange and St. Augustine (TCT 556-607).

NECESSITY OF GRACE

THREE SITUATIONS

The teaching that began at Orange, continued throughout the Middle Ages and terminated in its classical form at the Council of Trent, can be applied to three concrete situations—each of which illustrates the necessity of grace.

The first situation is this: a man who is not yet justified is moving along the path toward Baptism and sanctifying grace. During this initial stage, he is in need of supernatural help in order to continue performing good actions over any appreciable length of time. Obviously, there are certain good actions, like a mother loving her child, which come easily to any normal person and require no special help. However, if the performance of good actions is to be continued over a long period of time, some special help is required. This help is not just natural; it is, according to the teaching of the Church, supernatural. It is grace. Clearly, the grace that is given in such a situation is not yet sanctifying grace, for it is sanctifying grace that establishes justification. Therefore, the special help that is given is what we call actual grace. It is a less permanent form of supernatural assistance given by God in order to provide a supernatural illumination for man's power of understanding and a supernatural impulse for the power of choice.

The man who is moving toward justification needs actual grace not only to persevere in living a good moral life; he also needs it in order to start out on the road that leads to justification. As he begins to respond to the information he receives about the Church, as he follows his conscience in searching for the true religion, he is actually taking steps leading to justification and, therefore, to his ultimate supernatural destiny. Since justification and ultimate glory are intrinsically superior to human nature and intrinsically beyond merely human powers of achievement, already in these early stages the man must be given some supernatural help from God. To put it another way: as a man begins to move toward justification and glory, he must have elevating grace. Since habitual elevating grace (sanctifying grace) is not yet present, it is clear that actual grace is the supernatural help given him so that he can approach the state of sanctifying grace. We find this process admirably described in the sixth session of the Council of Trent. Here the stages leading from faith, through conversion, hope and repentance, to charity and justification are clearly delineated (TCT 562). Thus we can see the Church's teaching that man, in his approach to justification, has need of the transitory supernatural help we call actual grace.

The second situation is that of a man who, having been justified, lapses from the state of justification through deliberate and grave sin. In many respects, this man is in practically the same situation as the one being led to justification. Just as the beginner cannot take the first step toward justification by himself, so the sinner cannot make the first move toward sorrow for mortal sin. Without grace, he will never be able to redirect himself to the state of grace.

What differentiates the second man from the first? In most cases, the sinner retains faith and hope, even though he has lost charity. Without charity, faith and hope are not there in full force. Nevertheless, they are present to some extent as a bridge to help man regain grace. Even with such faith and hope, man must have actual graces guiding him to repentance. He must have grace both to begin the act and to accompany it, in order that he may make an act of contrition, approach the sacrament of Penance and again be justified.

The third situation concerns a man who is in the state of sanctifying grace. His nature and powers of action are transformed by sanctifying grace and the infused supernatural virtues of faith, hope and charity. This means that he has, as a habitual possession, dynamic powers of acting in harmony with his supernatural state and destiny. These powers are caused in him by continuing gifts of God and, since it is the three divine Persons who are actively working this special transformation, we say that they dwell with him. Such dwelling, obviously, is not a static reality, but a dynamic presence inseparable from the very causing of grace. This man's intellect is being constantly illumined, and the drive of his will toward good constantly transformed. Even when he is not personally acting (as during sleep), his basic powers of action are being supernaturalized, so that when a situation demanding activity does present itself, no new divine gift is required at that moment.

The transformation that comes with grace and the virtues elevates man and his powers. Simultaneously, it repairs the deviation resulting from original and personal sin. Such grace is both elevating and healing. Without the continuing special act of God, an act by which he communicates a share in his own way of being to man, man would be incapable of growing in the life of grace or of performing meritorious actions. Even when a man has been justified by God, he cannot go on to develop this life by himself. The three divine Persons must constantly abide with him, communicating to him the sustenance and development of supernatural life.

ATTEMPTS TO LIMIT GRACE

It is clear, then, from the teaching of the Church that every human being has an absolute need for sanctifying grace. Adults have a like need for actual grace if they find themselves without sanctifying grace. Correlative to this doctrine on the necessity of grace is the Church's teaching about the universality of the gift of grace. Although we do not know exactly how this gift is given to non-Christians who comprise a large portion of the human race, still faith teaches that all men are given sufficient grace to reach their eternal destiny. No man will be damned, unless he deliberately so chooses. This teaching of the Church has not always been accepted. In fact, it has occasioned considerable dispute.

At the time of the Protestant Reformation, John Calvin and his followers rejected the universality of God's redemptive grace. Their effort to limit the gift of grace was based on the Calvinist idea of predestination, namely, that God has once and for all selected a certain part of the human race for salvation and another part for damnation. Only those predestined to be saved received grace sufficient for salvation. Because predestined by God, neither group was truly free to determine its own destiny.

Calvinism was rejected by the Council of Trent (TCT 591). However, in the centuries that followed upon the Reformation and Trent, certain currents of thought within the Catholic Church continued in the same direction. One of the most prominent and disastrous of these was Jansenism. Claiming to find its roots in the writings of St. Augustine, the Jansenists maintained that man was under the absolute domination of one or other impulse. He is directed either by the good spirit or by the evil spirit. Either spirit is irresistible. In its own way, though it was expressed in milder form than Calvinism, Jansenism effectively denied the universality of grace for all men. Once again the Church reacted against this unjustified limitation of redemption to a certain group of men. She condemned the main theses contained in Jansen's book *Augustinus* (TCT 627-631), and, somewhat later, the expanded form of his teaching as found in disciples like Quesnel (TCT 632-644). However, the impact of Jansenism persisted long after its official condemnation, and it has to some extent influenced European and American Catholicism up to the present time.

GRACE AND FREEDOM

LIBERATION FROM EVIL

One of the most debated and most important areas of the Church's teaching on grace is the teaching on the relation between grace (whether sanctifying or actual) and freedom. A few preliminary remarks may help clear away some common misunderstandings. First of all, it is not correct to assume that man by his nature is in a state of perfect equilibrium with regard to choices of good and evil. His nature, left to itself, is not completely neutral. If there were, and there is not, such a thing as perfectly integral and unharmed nature, it might be accurate to say that the function of grace is to tip the scales in favor of the good choice. So conceived, grace would appear as a limitation on man's freedom, for it would introduce an impulse in one direction that would make it more difficult, if not impossible, to choose the alternative.

When we look at what revelation tells us about the relation between grace and freedom, about the present state of man's powers of free choice, we find a quite different picture. Both St. Paul (Rom 7) and St. Augustine point to the fact that man is enslaved. Because of his own sins and the sin coming from Adam, man is not truly free. He requires liberation from evil. It is because man is given the grace of Christ that he has the freedom required to do those things he most deeply wishes to do, those things most compatible with his nature as a free and dignified individual. To put it another way, we may very truly say that the more a man loves, the freer he is. A man is not most free when he equally desires opposites. A man can have so great a love of one thing or one person, that he would not want to choose anything that would involve the loss of that person. It would be a perversion of the meaning of person to say that such a man would be less free because he is doing precisely what he wishes to do.

Another point should be kept in mind when we discuss grace and freedom. Grace and the supernatural virtues work in the very depths of man's nature and powers of activity. We should not think that grace is given in a very specified and definite form for just one action, or for that one situation of temptation. The transformation wrought by grace and the virtues extends to the roots of man's active powers, transforming them at that profound level at which they are, in a sense, oriented to all possible personal acts. By transforming this wider potential of man, grace is automatically introducing into his life all the supernaturalization, all the elevation, all the healing required to provide for any of the individual situations in which he might find himself. And so grace does not enter human life as a reality that directs man to this or that specific action.

SIMULTANEOUS ACTION

Over the past three hundred years or so, there have been frequent and sometimes bitter discussions between those who tend to see grace as a determining reality leaving apparently little freedom for human choice, and those who, by stressing human choice, seem in the eyes of their opponents to detract from the infallibility and universality of divine providence. To some extent these disputes have grown less important and less bitter because historical studies have questioned the basic positions on which both theories were grounded.

Actually, what is at issue in these disputes is the relationship between human effort and divine grace. Perhaps the solution does not lie in trying to reconcile two things that are thought of as opposites. Rather, we ought to see that in a sense—a very true sense—God is constantly working in man. From this divine action flows everything man does, and yet man is actually performing something proper to himself. In all that he does he is dependent; yet it is *his* choice to accept or reject the grace offered him. Everything a man does that is salutary, everything positively ordered to his supernatural destiny, flows from the grace God is giving him. Without this grace, man would be completely incapable of doing the things he should do. On the other hand, what man does is his own proper action. Therefore man truly merits, even though this merit is grounded in grace. In discussing the problem of grace and freedom, we are really dealing with one aspect of what is most difficult for us to grasp: the simultaneous action of God and man in human activity, be it natural or supernatural. This is the philosophical problem of understanding the nature of secondary causality—that creatures do act in total dependence on the first Cause.

No matter how man may wish to describe or explain in detail the process of the human free act, or more specifically the human free act in the context of grace, it remains true for the Christian that the Church's teaching recognizes both the need for special divine help (supernatural grace) and the fact of human freedom. Grace is necessary in order that man may act in a way that leads to his supernatural end. But it is the man who chooses. He does have, as grace works in him, the ability to take the good or evil course of action. Man himself, and not the divine action in him, is the only source of evil. For the evil choice does not demand that any new reality be introduced into the picture. Rather, the evil choice is due to the inadequacy of the human action. Evil in a human choice is not something essentially positive; it is the privation of something that should be there.

THE SACRAMENT OF PENANCE

RESTORATION OF ORDER

RECONCILIATION AND PEACE

Baptism implies a fundamental self-commitment. Through Baptism we are incorporated into Christ and possessed by the Holy Spirit. Divine grace transforms not only man's nature but also his actions. Nevertheless, moral evil continues to affect human life. Frequent infidelity to his Christian vocation is a sad and disconcerting experience for every Christian. Only the Mother of God possesses that fullness of grace which enables her to avoid all sin. Because of the ever present mystery of evil in the Christian's life, there is a continuing need for reconciliation with Christ and with his body, the Church—to which each of us has been more or less unfaithful. Christ provides for this reconciliation by continually forgiving sin through sacramental action. To complement the sacrament of Baptism, and its power to remit sin, the sacrament of Penance functions throughout the Christian's life.

Since its earliest days, the Catholic Church has defended the sacramental power to forgive sins as one of the most valuable possessions given it by the risen Christ. The power to forgive sins has not gone unchallenged. It is a most unusual and, seemingly, an audacious claim. Yet many incidents in the gospel narrative depict Christ forgiving sin (Mk 2:1-12; Mt 9:2) and communicating the same power to his Church (Mt 18:18; Jn 20:19-23). From these texts it is clear that the Church was fully conscious of the fact that Christ gave her authority over the mystery of evil. Time and time again in the pages of the gospel, Christ is described as forgiving the sins of men. This wish to remove malice from human lives is one of the most evident and deepest desires of Christ. Among the apparitions of the risen Christ, the first fully public appearance on the night of the resurrection was concerned with Christ's communication to his disciples of this power over sin (Jn 20:19-23).

Literature from the immediate post-apostolic period shows that the Church continued to be aware of its power to forgive sin. Already in the Didache, which may antedate some of the New Testament writings, forgiveness of sins is mentioned in connection with the Eucharist. Both Clement of Rome and Ignatius of Antioch, writing at the turn of the first century A.D., connect forgiveness of sins with the jurisdiction possessed by bishops. The earliest Christian writers state quite clearly that sin will be pardoned no matter how great the malice, provided the person genuinely wants to return to Christ and the Church.

We have evidence of a fairly strong tendency, during these early centuries, to harshness on the part of many Christians. More than a few (Tertullian is a tragic example) were critical of the bishop of Rome because of his willingness to forgive some of the graver sins. There were those in the Church who were inclined to refuse sacramental pardon until the moment of death and, in certain cases, even then. Nevertheless, in the midst of this excessive harshness the Church maintained its basic orientation of merciful forgiveness and insisted that its right to forgive sins could be traced back to the apostles themselves. In the *Apostolic Tradition* of Hippolytus (which gives an insight into the liturgy of Rome at the very beginning of the third century) the text for the consecration of a bishop mentions his authority "according to thy commands to loose every bond according to the authority that thou gavest to the apostles."

In the early practice of the sacrament of Penance there is some indication of private confession, but the data on this point is not too clear. Documents from the time of St. Augustine and Pope St. Leo I definitely distinguish between the private confession of sins made to the bishop and the public performance of the assigned penance. Moreover, there is a distinction between the penances. For sins publicly known, public penance is the rule; for sins known only in private, private penance is enjoined. As liturgical practices connected with the sacrament of Penance developed, there was increasing emphasis on penance imposed as a means of rendering partial satisfaction for an offense. It is in this context that the role of the priest became more important and more noticeable—because he had to impose penances commensurate with the fault confessed. However, despite increasing emphasis on penances, the basic meaning of the sacrament always remained one of reconciliation with the Church, a reconciliation that could only take place on condition of genuine repentance and conversion.

Throughout these early centuries, the sacrament of Penance was administered only sparingly and, for the most part, only for grave sins. Thus, early patristic thought recognizes, though details are not developed, that the sacrament of

Penance involves both a reconciliation with God and a certain healing of the penitent's faults. Reconciliation is obtained by submitting to the penance imposed by the Church. And reconciliation with the Church, which the absolution signifies, is an effective sign of peace which restores the life-giving Spirit to men.

The renewed gift of the Spirit was clearly connected with Penance. For many centuries in the Church's history the sacramental sign of forgiveness seems to have been the imposition of hands. We know, from evidence in scripture itself, that the basic significance of imposing hands is the giving of the Spirit. While a certain amount of flexibility and fluidity remain in the details of penitential practice until the time of the Council of Trent, the basic elements—confession of sins, reconciliation with the Church, absolution through the gift of the Holy Spirit—remain constants in the sacrament of Penance.

What, then, are the main elements that pertain to the sacrament, to its nature and practice? First of all, it is clear that the sacrament of Penance is a sacrament of peace. Its function is one of reconciliation; it is meant to restore the order that ought to exist between the individual Christian and the Church to which he has been somewhat unfaithful. It is meant, too, to restore the personal order that should exist between the Christian and Christ, who has been abandoned, totally or partially, by sinfulness. This reconciliation takes place in the context of Christianity, which is a new covenant dispensation. We know from scripture that what characterizes the situation of one who is united with God in covenant is peace. It is to restore this peace connected with the new covenant, the Eucharist, that the sacrament of Penance functions. It causes peace by restoring order.

Moreover, we would misunderstand this sacrament if we failed to recognize that it causes peace within the individual himself. It reorders him according to the pattern established for the first time in his Baptism. It gives him that peace which comes with the gift of the Holy Spirit, the peace which Christ himself said the world cannot give. Such peace can be achieved only through redemption.

Furthermore, the sacrament of Penance is a sacrament of peace on many levels. It is meant to create an atmosphere of peace in the Christian's life, by giving him the consolation of knowing that this means of reconciliation with God is available to him. It is meant to reestablish peace between the individual, the Church and Christ. It is also meant to reestablish within man himself that order among his powers of action which underlies psychological and personal peace.

Christ significantly chose Easter evening as the occasion on which to give his Church the Holy Spirit for the forgiveness of sin. The sacrament of Penance, like the other sacraments, is an action of the risen Christ living on in the Church. Christ continues to do what he began to do in his public life, to forgive sins. Furthermore he does it not just by pardoning the sinner and so restoring him to favor; he actually remakes the individual. If one is to be truly reconciled with God, the disorder caused by his personal sins must be rectified. Christ continues to do this by acting on men through the mystery of his resurrection. The sacrament of Penance is, for the Christian, the occasion on which he can encounter the risen Christ and present his need for redemption.

The priest's judgmental decision to forgive, expressed in the action of the sacrament, is meant to bear directly on the individual's need for redemption. When a priest absolves a penitent, he does not give a generic absolution applicable to any or all penitents. He passes judgment in the light of this particular individual's need for redemption. However, in order that the priest may purposely direct the redeeming power of the risen Christ to a specific penitent, he must know what the penitent's need is. This is why sins must be confessed. The actions of both priest and penitent pertain to the sign of the sacrament. Because this external sign is one of judgment, it requires two parties: one who judges and another who is judged.

Since the causality of the sacrament of Penance is affected by the priest's intention, which is guided by the penitent's confession, it is clear that the penitent ought to be capable of accurate self-appraisal. Only then can the truly basic disorders of the individual be subjected to the healing powers of the sacrament. The sacraments are signs which cause according to their significance. The sacrament of Penance, therefore, will be more effective in proportion as it is explicitly directed to the specific redemptive need of this individual. Seen in this context, Penance transcends the bounds of a purely legal concept of divine pardon. It actually touches the very roots of culpability. As Christ's instrument, it heals those devious tendencies which in themselves may not be explicitly culpable, but are nevertheless aberrations in the psychological make-up of the individual. These are conducive to sin and are often the result of previous sin. In this context, we can see the value of frequent confession, even repeated confessions of the same fault.

By his Baptism, a Christian is committed to working with Christ in the struggle against evil. His capacity to do so is hampered by his own sinful involvement in the very evil he should be combating. He needs, therefore, to be constantly liberated from his own enslavement to sin so that he can be an apt minister of Christ, assisting him effectively in his redeeming work. Penance exists in order to achieve this liberation and so prepare the members of the Christian community for their apostolate.

PREPARATION FOR EUCHARIST

The sacrament of Penance also takes an intrinsic orientation toward deeper participation in the Eucharistic action of sacrifice. St. John's gospel (Jn 13:2-14) describes the way in which Christ prepared for the last supper by washing the feet of his disciples. This act clearly places him in the position of fulfilling the messianic role of the Servant. The biblical text itself was part of the early Church's required catechesis in preparation for the Eucharistic action. Some scripture scholars, particularly in non-Catholic circles, prefer to interpret this scene as part of the catechesis of the sacrament of Baptism. But it can just as well, and perhaps even more correctly, be considered part of the catechesis for the sacrament of Penance. The scene as described in the gospel of St. John clearly pictures not a first washing nor a total washing, but the partial washing required for removing dirt acquired after one has already been totally washed (Jn 13:9-10).

Even if this passage did not clearly refer to the sacrament of Penance and only indicated some need for purification prior to the Eucharist, other texts from the synoptic gospels certainly place the forgiveness of sins in a sacrificial context. The power of forgiving sin which Christ exercised in the public ministry replaced the standard Judaic practice for obtaining divine forgiveness, namely, the offering of trespass- and sin-sacrifices. In replacing these sacrifices, the sacrament of Penance was clearly doing what a sacrifice would do. Not only that, but these Old Testament sacrifices for trespass and sin were seen, in the context of levitical legislation (Lev 5-7), as preparations for a deeper sharing in the most important kind of community sacrifice, Old Testament covenant sacrifice or peace offering. So also, Christ's forgiveness of sin points to the new and definitive offering of covenant peace, the Eucharistic action.

The Eucharistic orientation of confession and forgiveness of sins is found in the Didache. Even if the Didache's reference to confessing sins does not directly concern the sacrament of Penance itself, it still indicates the direction of thought in the primitive Church. Confession of sins is something that should be done before the community enters into Eucharistic sacrifice. This relation between Penance and the Eucharist continues through the patristic tradition. Thus we see that Penance is not something that exists solely to reconcile the individual to the Church and to Christ.

There is no sacrament whose externals are more clearly social in nature than those of Penance. This sacrament involves an exercise of judgment by an authorized delegate of the Church community. The purpose of his judgment is to reinstate the individual into the community, to reconcile the Christian more deeply to the Church to which he has been more or less unfaithful. Penance achieves this reconciliation in order that the community as a whole may be prepared for fuller participation in the sacrifice of the Mass. Viewed in this perspective, the sacrament of Penance, like all the other sacraments is intrinsically ordered to the full expression of Christian life in the action of the Eucharist. Its purpose is to purify and prepare the community for a fuller and more integral expression of its dedication to Christ.

In this way the sacrament of Penance continues the work begun by Baptism and Confirmation. Baptism achieved a total forgiveness of sins through insertion of the individual into the corporate mystery of the Church. Confirmation deepened this entry into Christian life. In both instances there was an essential ordering to the community's specific and proper action, the worship of God in the Eucharistic sacrifice. The individual, because of his sin, and the community as a whole, because of the frailty and sinfulness of its members, are never totally faithful to these Eucharistic orientations of Baptism and Confirmation. Consequently, there arises the need for a constant and deep restoration; this comes in Penance. The very liturgy of the Mass seems to indicate this. The prayers at the foot of the altar, while not a sacramental form of penitential accusation and forgiveness, mirror the spirit of the sacrament of Penance. The community and priest alike confess their sins, and the priest begs forgiveness upon the people and upon himself.

BIBLIOGRAPHY FOR CHAPTER 5

WORKS ON CHRISTIAN DECISION AND TEMPTATION

B. Cooke, "The Hour of Temptation," *The Way* 2 (1962), pp. 177-187. A more extended treatment of Christian temptation.

L. Lavelle, *Evil and Suffering,* New York, Macmillan, 1963. The first part of this book (pp. 1-92) is a stimulating approach to the role of Christian freedom and decision.

A. van Kamm, *Religion and Personality,* Englewood Cliffs, Prentice-Hall, 1964. There is a growing literature on the psychological aspects of Christian behavior; this book by van Kamm is one of the best and most balanced examples, by a man who is both psychologist and theologian.

WORKS ON THE SACRAMENT OF PENANCE

P. Anciaux, *The Sacrament of Penance,* New York, Sheed and Ward, 1962. Simple but accurate study of the history and nature of Penance by one of the leading authorities in the field.

P. Palmer, *Sacraments and Forgiveness* (vol. 2 of *Sources of Christian Theology*), Westminster, Newman, 1959. Very helpful collection of texts illustrating the historical and doctrinal development of the sacrament of Penance.

B. Poschmann, *Penance and the Anointing of the Sick,* New York, Herder and Herder, 1964. Excellent doctrinal history of the two sacraments, probably the most comprehensive work to date. Good bibliographical helps.

A. von Speyr, *Confession, the Encounter with Christ in Penance,* New York, Herder and Herder, 1964. Reflective theological essay on the sacrament of Penance; filled with valuable insights on Penance as an integral part of Christian living.

6

CHRISTIAN MATURITY

·

THE SACRAMENT OF CONFIRMATION

·

HISTORICAL BACKGROUND

THE MYSTERY OF PENTECOST

Christian Baptism, because it is an act of incorporation into a community, makes it impossible for genuine Christian life to be individualistic. Acceptance of Christianity necessitates concern for one another within the Church as well as concern for the redemption of all men. Such unselfish involvement in the lives of others demands a large measure of Christian maturity, an openness in love to one's fellow men, a prudent and adult decisiveness. Two sacraments seem especially ordered to satisfying this need: Confirmation with its intensification of the baptismal commitment, and Matrimony with its transformation of the human experience of love.

Christ's sending of the Spirit into the individual Christian and into the corporate reality of the Church leads us to reflect further on the mystery of Pentecost. Then, for the first time, the risen Christ sent the fullness of his Spirit to animate his body, the Church. The mystery of the gift of the Spirit is still operative in the Church and will continue to be operative until the end of time. While all the sacraments of Christian living involve action by the Spirit, the sacrament of Confirmation signifies, and therefore causes, in special fashion, the conferring of Christ's own Spirit.

EMERGENCE OF THE SACRAMENT

At the present moment a considerable amount of study and reevaluation of this sacrament is taking place among theologians, Catholic and otherwise. This investigation is in some respects still in its beginnings. However, the scholarly work of the past few decades has done much to clarify our understanding of the reality and role of Confirmation.

A special difficulty faces the scholar who attempts to clarify the early history of the sacramental rite of Confirmation. In the early Church one sacramental rite was not sharply distinguished from another, as is presently the case. Above all, the rite of initiation, which included what we separate into Baptism, Confirmation and Holy Eucharist, was a ceremony in which the Christian passed through three distinct sacraments, thinking of them as one mystery of entry into Christ's death and resurrection. After being baptized, the Christian was anointed, the bishop imposed his hands, and the sign of Christ's cross was placed on the recipient's forehead. Immediately after this, the individual participated for the first time in the Eucharistic action of sacrifice. While the early Church clearly saw that these signs (i.e., anointing and imposition of hands) signified and conferred the Holy Spirit, it did not consider them as signs to be distinguished, either in themselves or in their effect, from the baptismal and Eucharistic rites. Therefore, in the writings of the early Church fathers and theologians, it is impossible to find a description of Confirmation apart from Baptism.

It was only in later centuries that the Church became more conscious of Confirmation as a distinct sacrament, and separated this rite from that of Baptism. However, the very association of Confirmation with Baptism and the Eucharist tells us a great deal about the role it plays in the Christian mystery. No one of the sacraments can be known in isolation from the others. This is particularly true of Confirmation, whose very purpose is to intensify what was accomplished in Baptism, and to prepare the Christian for fuller participation in Christ's act of Eucharistic sacrifice. The very name, Confirmation, indicates its purpose—to strengthen the Christian vocation first conferred sacramentally in Baptism.

BASIC SYMBOLISMS

ESSENTIAL MEANING

Without making any detailed study of the historical development of the sacrament of Confirmation we can look at some early writings to find what meanings were inherent in that portion of the initiation rite which, over the centuries, became recognizable as the individual sacrament of Confirmation. The most fundamental meaning is found in the expression "conferring of the Spirit," which refers to the dedication, sanctification and strengthening of the new Christian. In different portions of the Church, different aspects of the various significant actions were regarded as more important. However, three signs seemed to be of key importance: imposition of hands, anointing with chrism and signing with the sign of the cross. A fourth sign appears quite universally as a complement to the sacrament—the conferring of the kiss of peace. By studying in some detail these four gestures, we can recapture the thinking of the early Church, and better understand the role that Confirmation played in the early centuries of Christianity.

The imposition of hands.   This gesture, in which a priest or bishop imposes his hands upon the head of a Christian, is found in many contexts besides that of Confirmation. In all its various applications, the basic symbolism seems to be *conferral of a blessing or,* more specifically, *of the Holy Spirit.* It is found in conjunction with the exorcisms preceding Baptism, with the blessing given catechumens at the time of their instruction; it is used as a sign of reconciliation in the early practice of the sacrament of Penance and as a sign conferring the Holy Spirit in the sacrament of Holy Orders. Furthermore, this gesture had still another meaning when it was used after Baptism within the rite of initiation.

In point of fact, imposition of hands can be traced back into the Old Testament. The patriarchs passed on from generation to generation the special blessing of God by laying their hands upon the head of the one to whom the primogeniture belonged. The same gesture is used by a prophet or a judge to indicate the transfer of the spirit. Generally, this is done to a person who himself will exercise a special role. The spirit of God is given to him to fulfill this role (1 Kings 18:12, 46; Ezek 3:14).

Exactly how we are to understand each of the various scenes in which Christ lays his hands on people is difficult to say. In many cases, Christ's act of touching a person or laying his hand on him is connected with the fact that the Spirit of God is working to heal that person, either physically or spiritually. Realizing that the gospels are, in large part, sacramental catechesis, it is not accidental that Christ is so often described as using this particular gesture.

Throughout the patristic writings and in the early sacramental formulas for the various rites of initiation, it is clear that the action of imposing hands is seen as a gesture that effects something. It results in an intensified possession of the Holy Spirit by the person on whom hands are laid. Some of the invocations indicate as much. It is also important to notice that the action of imposing hands is consistently spoken of as something proper to the bishop. The initial anointings in the ritual might be performed by others; a priest (other than the bishop) could perform the actual baptizing, but imposition of hands and anointing with chrism were the proper office of the officiating bishop.

The chrismation.   In studying early accounts of the rite of initiation, we must carefully distinguish the various anointings described there. In some churches, two anointings took place after the Baptism—in addition to the anointing which immediately preceded it. In other places, only one anointing, the chrismation, followed the Baptism. In any event, in all the sacramental rites of initiation, we find an anointing with chrism (not with oil) which is consequent upon the Baptism itself, and which must be performed by the bishop.

This anointing with chrism is compared in many of the texts to the anointings of priests and prophets of the Old Testament. It gives the Christian his name. Christian means "anointed." To be anointed means to be dedicated to the service of God, to be set apart as sacred, to be united with Christ in the messianic office of the Anointed One.

Scripture itself points to the meaning of the word, and the texts in patristic documents are quite explicit on the point. It is not clear whether or not in the early Church the anointing was performed simultaneously with the signing of the forehead. In some cases these two actions seem to have been distinct; in others they are combined. In any event, the basic significance of the anointing is the giving of the Spirit. The external sign of chrismation points to that inner dedication—or inner anointing—which is accomplished by the Spirit himself. This is sometimes put so strongly that the Spirit is himself described as the anointing.

In addition to this basic significance, the early Church fathers also teach that the anointing with sweet-smelling chrism means that one is made specially pleasing to God. The fragrance of the chrism in the external ceremony functions as a sign of the inner fragrance given the soul by the mystery of transformation in grace. Furthermore, anointing a person with oil was associated with strengthening him for combat; and it may well be that the notion of preparing a person to face the difficulties of Christian life, or conferring Christian strength and adulthood, was attached to the use of oil. Placing chrism on the head was meant to emphasize bestowal of the seven-fold gift of the Spirit, through which one would, with fuller consciousness and more loving dedication, enter into the mystery of Christ celebrated in the Eucharist.

The signing. There is a great deal of controversy about the exact significance of the sign used in the initiation rite. Was it connected with the sacramental character, or with grace, or with the Holy Spirit himself? At least this much is perfectly clear in the universal practice of the early Church: in that portion of the initiation rite which immediately followed the actual Baptism, there was a signing of the forehead of the new Christian with the sign of Christ. This signing indicated alignment with Christ in the work of redemption. It pointed to the fact that one was set aside, dedicated to Christ, marked for entry into that work which found its focus in the death and resurrection of Christ. The fathers compare the Christian to a soldier who is branded for the service of a specific king. They also compare the signing to that which formalizes the making of a contract. It seems quite clear that some early explanations of this sign point toward a theological recognition of the sacramental character. In this rite it is precisely the signing with the cross that indicates the Christian aspect of this particular ceremony. It points to the mystery of Christ's death and resurrection.

THE PRESENT PRACTICE OF THE CHURCH

According to the present method of conferring the sacrament of Confirmation, the three significant actions just described are combined into one. In the early Church, there was a similar tendency to combine these actions, particularly the anointing and the signing. Today, if one carefully observes the sacramental gesture of the bishop, one will see that it is simultaneously an imposition of the hand and an anointing with the sign of the cross. Although it is now a single, somewhat amplified sacramental action, Confirmation still retains all the significance of the three distinctive signs. The external rite still points to the conferring of the Spirit as the great blessing given to the newly baptized Christian. The Spirit, whom he possesses and who possesses him, anoints him from within, setting him aside as consecrated to the service of God, strengthened for activity within the Christian mystery and marked in more intense fashion as belonging to the service of Christ.

The kiss of peace. Our present ceremony retains in a modified way another significant action, which is not of the essence of the sacrament. The bishop, when he has confirmed a Christian, strikes him lightly on the cheek. This gesture is not meant to be—as popular fancy would sometimes have it—a warning that the one confirmed will have to bear hardships for the sake of Christ. Rather, it is a vestige of the bishop's kiss of peace, given new Christians in the early Church's initiation rites. In the early centuries, the kiss of peace was very likely part of the Eucharistic ceremony which followed immediately upon the ritual of Confirmation. Later, when Confirmation became a separate, distinctly recognized ceremony, the kiss of peace was added to the imposition of hands, the anointing and signing as a complementary gesture indicating the relationship of paternal love existing between the bishop and the Christian who was part of his flock. Today, the gesture of the bishop, though more difficult to recognize in its externals, is still meant to retain this fundamental significance. By conferring the Spirit in a more intense degree, the bishop bestows upon the Christian that peace which Christ himself described as the atmosphere accompanying the action of the Spirit.

EFFECTS OF CONFIRMATION

SIGNIFICANCE TODAY

With this background we can, in summary form, answer the question: As administered today, what does the sacrament of Confirmation mean?

A deepening of the Christian vocation. All the evidence from the past points to the fact that the Church has always viewed the sacrament of Confirmation in relation to the sacrament of Baptism. What Baptism begins, Confirmation continues and deepens. In this context we can see that the sacrament of Confirmation points to the reception of a deeper participation in that call to Christian life which began with Baptism. Normally the person who receives Confirmation has been living as a Christian for some time since his Baptism. He now reiterates his initial choice of the Christian way of life. The externals of the sacrament also signify a solemn introduction to deeper and more mature participation in the life of the Christian community. The very presence of the bishop as minister lends to Confirmation an official atmosphere for the most part not found in Baptism.

Since the action of Confirmation is a sacramental one, the internal deepening of the Christian's participation in the Church is effectively caused through this sacramental action. What happens to the individual is specifically the same as what was accomplished in Baptism—the causing of the sacramental character and sanctifying grace. Both realities are deepened in a new way.

Sacramental character of Confirmation. Very early in the history of the Church it was recognized that the sacrament of Confirmation, like the sacrament of Baptism, caused a sacramental character in the Christian. In this respect, we can speak of a second character, one in addition to Baptism (TCT 673). Yet, the effect caused in Confirmation is certainly very closely related to that caused in Baptism. Really it would be more accurate to think of it as an intensification of the baptismal character.

The sacramental character of Baptism is a share in Christ's priesthood, a power of entering with him into the redemptive action of the Church. What is effected in Confirmation is a strengthening of this ability to cooperate with Christ in his priestly mission. Confirmation therefore deepens and expands the character given at Baptism. It does not produce a second, separate reality. Because of this character, the confirmed Christian possesses greater capacity for participation in the Christian mystery. Such increased participation will permeate his Christian life, the life through which he shares in the Church's prophetic office. This character pertains most particularly to the exercise of priesthood in the sacrament of Matrimony, to participation in the priestly sacrifice of the Mass, and finally to increased sharing in the life of glory hereafter.

Along with the amplification of the sacramental character, Confirmation also affects the gifts of sanctifying grace imparted to the Christian by his Baptism. A new kind of supernatural life is not added. But the same life has now a new and special characteristic because of Confirmation. Not only is the life of sanctifying grace deepened because of this sacrament, but this life is now meant to be lived in a more mature, more profound fashion. In a sense, the sacrament of Confirmation puts the finishing touches on that introduction into the mysteries of Christian life and sacrifice which began in the sacrament of Baptism.

Possession of the Holy Spirit. All the sacramentals of Confirmation point to a special coming of the Holy Spirit. Baptism already involves the gift of the Spirit, who causes in us that life which he shares with the Father and the Son.

In Baptism the Holy Spirit, by taking possession of the newly baptized, displaces the evil spirit who rules those still in original sin. In the sacrament of Confirmation, however, there is a new and fuller dwelling of the Holy Spirit within the individual. Consequently, that individual can lay greater claim to the Holy Spirit as his own possession.

What does it mean to say that one has more of the Holy Spirit after Confirmation than before? This question is part of a larger one about the indwelling of the blessed Trinity in a Christian through sanctifying grace. We may say that the extent of the divine indwelling is proportioned to the extent to which the individual has been transformed. A spirit is present by what he effects. Since the Holy Spirit possesses and transforms the individual more deeply and more completely through Confirmation, he can be said to dwell more fully in that individual, to give himself in greater measure.

Sacrament of Christian Apostolate.   In the last few years it has become somewhat common to speak of Confirmation as the "Sacrament of the Christian Apostolate." To what extent is this description justified by the traditional teaching of the Church and by theological clarification of this sacrament? In virtue of his Baptism the Christian already shares in the priesthood of Christ. Therefore he possesses by Baptism a vocation to the apostolate. Nevertheless, Confirmation does entail a more reflective and adult acceptance of Christian life. It involves an intensified participation in the mystery of Christ's priesthood. Baptism is a vocation to share in the messianic office of Christ. Confirmation is a calling to an even deeper participation in this mission.

In relation, then, to the sacramental character connected with Confirmation, one can justifiably speak of a fuller and deeper vocation to Christian life and to the Christian apostolate. This deeper call to be a Christian finds its completion in the action of sacrifice we call the Mass. But it also finds its application in all the various aspects of Catholic living in which one exercises the prophetic, priestly and kingly roles which Christ gives to his Church.

MATRIMONY

LOVE IN THE TRINITY

LIFE-GIVING LOVE

God has revealed not only his desire to give life but also the fact that he actually does give it. Revelation emphasizes the importance of life and the creation of life by a transcendent God. Old Testament revelation was fulfilled in this respect by those particularly significant actions of Christ which we call the miracles. These were directed either to giving or to bettering human existence.

The final stage of this revelation, manifested in the Christian sacraments, both teaches and gives life.

Revelation connects another theme with the theme of life, namely, life comes from love. In some respects this is the deepest and most persistent theme in all God's communication to man. We shall study it in connection with the sacrament of Matrimony.

Nature shows us that the power to give life comes only with mature possession of life. In the case of human beings, biological maturation should not be considered sufficient. The personal maturity that comes with deep and genuine human love is also very necessary. In this way, love of man and woman in marriage is meant to reflect God's own life-giving love.

THE TRINITARIAN EXEMPLAR

Christian understanding of human love must spring from faith-understanding of Trinitarian life. In the depths of the mystery of God, the Father gives himself totally to his divine Son. So great is the Father's love, so total his self-giving, so complete his identification with his Son that there is absolutely nothing of his own being and perfection which he does not communicate in consciousness to the second Person, his Word. It is precisely because his self-communication is so absolute and unrestricted that this second Person, who is the term of this life-giving process, is just as infinitely God as is the Father himself.

In a second instance of divine life-giving, the love of Father and Son so binds them in total identity and is so rich that it gives expression to a third Person who also possesses the infinite being which is theirs. Nothing but a divine Person could express the depth and completeness of their love for one another. This third Person, the Spirit, possesses without qualification the divine nature possessed by Father and Son. He is God coequally with them. The richness of the giving and depth of union involved in this divine life of love are beyond anything we can possibly experience in the realm of created love. What human love strives for is achieved in God. A human lover tries to give himself, strives for union and even identity with the person he loves. It is part of the frustration of our creaturely status that we can neither give ourselves completely, nor achieve with another that identity which we seek. Only in the Trinity is this goal attained. Yet to the extent that we humans learn how to love truly, our love shares in and reflects the mystery of the divine loving.

Flowing from the mystery of the Trinity, not by necessity but because of the free love of these three divine Persons, life is extended to creation and specifically to man. This extension of life to personal creatures, to created spirits, is an expression of love freely given. Such love is not weak or soft; it is powerful enough to create an entire universe. Upon reflection, we realize that at the roots of all the dynamism in creation lies this limitless force of divine loving. All the energy and power of nuclear development, all the tremendous and awesome forces of the universe are but a created expression of this greater power from which they all spring. Not only is love the source of all creation, divine love is the reason why all that God has made is good; for evil cannot spring from love. Only in the denial of love does evil find its origins.

MARRIAGE IN SCRIPTURE

YAHWEH AND ISRAEL

Man could never have grasped the depths of divine love had it not been for the supernatural revelation of this love which the three divine Persons give us. Even prior to the New Testament revelation of the Trinity, the Old Testament people were given a deep insight into divine love. From the beginning, God manifests himself as a being who loves. He shows his interest in and his care for the special people whom he picks as his own (Ex 19:1-6). He provides for their physical well-being (Ps 77:13-16; 24-27). He gives them a law to guide them and to shape their social living (Ex 20-23). He protects them from their enemies (Ex 23:20-35), and leads them from evil. They are, as he tells them, his chosen ones. Prophets, trying to describe the love which God has for his people, speak of Israel as Yahweh's flock (Mic 7:14). Israel is a vine which he has planted and tended with great care, a vine which, tragically, had proved to be unfruitful (Is 5:1-4). In spite of this, we find the deepest and most significant revelation of the love of God for his people in the magnificent passage of Hosea (chapter two) which contains the imagery of husband and wife. This prophetic image, introduced into the religious life of Israel in the eighth century B.C., becomes the classic image of the relationship of Israel to Yahweh.

In the second chapter of Hosea, as in later prophetic literature, Israel's crime in abandoning Yahweh is described as adultery. Israel is pictured as an unfaithful wife who has gone off with false lovers, the idols of the country, and abandoned her spouse, Yahweh. Yahweh, in return, has given Israel a bill of divorce; he rejects her children because they are the children of prostitution. Yet, the second half of the chapter goes on to predict that Yahweh will recall Israel, his faithless bride. Just as in the days of her youth he had led her out of Egypt to woo her, so he will again call her into the desert and make her his own. In that day, the day of conversion, Israel will no longer call upon the Baal; their name shall no longer cross her lips. She shall no longer commit the abomination of calling even Yahweh himself by the name "Baal." Yahweh will once again give Israel a situation comparable to Paradise. Those who had not been his people shall be called his people, and Israel shall turn to Yahweh and call him "my God" (Hos 2:23).

This beautiful passage depicts the covenant relationship between the people and their God in terms of the most profound human relationship, that of husband and wife. It is important to note that a double deepening of religious understanding results from Hosea's imagery, which continues in prophetic usage. There is, quite obviously, a deepened understanding of the familiar and personal aspect of God's relationship to his people and of their relationship to him. There is, at the same time, an important transformation in Israel's understanding of human marriage. In the ancient world this is an extremely important religious message. Once this imagery has been used to describe Yahweh himself, then the understanding of marital love takes on an unsurpassable dignity, sublimity and personal depth. In this prophetic understanding of human love and marriage, there is a deepening of the significance already pointed to in Genesis (2:24), which speaks of marriage between husband and wife as a thing blessed by God, a unique love which takes precedence over all other natural bonds.

CHRIST AND THE CHURCH

One of the most profound claims of Christ to be the God of the Old Testament was his identification of himself as the bridegroom. In one of his early encounters with them, the scribes and pharisees accused Christ of being too lenient with his disciples. They pointed to the fact that they and their own disciples fasted regularly, as did the disciples of John the Baptist. But the disciples of Christ did not fast. Jesus, in answering this charge of the Jewish leaders, said something which, against the background of the Old Testament, was a clear claim to who he was. He asked: "Can the wedding guests fast while the bridegroom is with them?" By this question, he clearly pointed to himself as that bridegroom and to his apostles as the bridegroom's friends (Mk 2:18-22).

Again, in the course of his public life, Christ pointed to his intention to give to marriage the full dignity that it was meant to have as a unique love between man and wife. He did this when he declared that he no longer intended to countenance the provision of law which permitted Jewish husbands to divorce their wives, as had been the case in preceding centuries (Mt 19:1-9). Marriage was to be restored to what Yahweh had originally intended it to be—an indissoluble union, characterized by a profound personal element. Nevertheless, the fullness of Christ's revelation regarding the sacrament of Matrimony comes only with the last supper and Calvary. This Eucharistic meal fulfills those parables (Mt 22:1-14) in which the kingdom is described as a marriage feast. In his death on the cross he gave himself for the life of the Church.

Reflection upon these latter mysteries of Christ's life led the Church in its early decades to discover its own identity as the spouse of Christ. With this discovery came the final stage of revelation about human marriage. The classic text here is the statement in the fifth chapter of the letter to the Ephesians. This is one of the richest passages in the New Testament about the nature of Christianity, the Eucharist, Baptism and grace, as well as Matrimony.

Be subject to one another out of reverence for Christ. Wives, be subject to your husbands, as to the Lord. For the husband is the head of the wife as Christ is the head of the church, his body, and is himself its Savior. As the church is subject to Christ, so let wives also be subject in everything to their husbands. Husbands, love your wives, as Christ loved the church and gave himself up for her, that he might sanctify her, having cleansed her by the washing of water with the word, that he might present the church to himself in splendor, without spot or wrinkle or any such thing, that she might be holy and without blemish. Even so husbands should love their wives as their own bodies. He who loves his wife loves himself. For no man ever hates his own flesh, but nourishes and cherishes it, as Christ does the church, because we are members of his body. "For this reason a man shall leave his father and mother and be joined to his wife, and the two shall become one." This is a great mystery, and I take it to mean Christ and the church; however, let each one of you love his wife as himself, and let the wife see that she respects her husband (Eph 5:21-33).

The passage begins with a statement about authority within the family. St. Paul makes it clear that it is the husband who is in the first position. But the kind of authority he enjoys is quickly clarified. And this immediately brings us to a deeper level of meaning: wives are to be subject to their husbands as to the Lord. We are reminded of that passage in which Christ explained to his disciples the way in which authority was to be exercised in his kingdom, the Church. "The rulers of the gentiles," he said, "lord it over them . . . It shall not be so among you; but whoever would be great among you must be your servant . . . even as the Son of Man came [and he clearly came with supreme authority] not to be served but to serve, and to give his life as a ransom for many" (Mt 20:25-28). This passage, in which Christ identifies himself as the Servant, sets the pattern for all exercise of authority within the Church, and particularly in that most intimate society which is the Christian family.

The husband's position as head of the family is described in terms of Christ as head and savior of his body, the Church. The passage indicates the ideal that is to characterize Christian marriage. The husband is to love his wife as Christ loves the Church. Now Christ loved his Church to the extent of giving his life for her, so that in the sacrament of Baptism he might sanctify and cleanse her, preparing her for the day of glory when he would espouse her to himself without wrinkle or blemish. In like manner, husbands should love their wives and be willing to give up their lives, if necessary, in order to communicate to them that life of consecration to God which is sanctifying grace. The measure of a man's love for his wife should be his love for himself, for it is in loving his wife that he loves himself. At this point St. Paul refers again to Genesis 2:24. And in so doing he gives it its final and undreamed-of interpretation. The ultimate reason why man and woman are bound together indissolubly in the marriage union is because that union takes place within the context of the mystery of Christ and the mystical body. This must be pondered deeply and prayerfully, for St. Paul reminds us that it "is a great mystery." Matrimony has the dimensions of a truly Christian mystery because of its intrinsic relationship to the mystery of Christ and his Church.

EXERCISE OF PRIESTHOOD

In Matrimony, two Christians exercise that power of causing grace which they possess in virtue of the sacramental character of Baptism and Confirmation. The sacrament of Matrimony is not just a matter of husband and wife encouraging one another to sanctity. They do more than dispose one another for God's grace by their acts of mutual love and kindness, or by their exchange of insights and motivation.

In the sacrament of Matrimony, beginning on the day of their nuptials and continuing throughout their entire lives, the husband causes the wife's grace, and the wife causes her husband's. This causation of grace, a truly priestly inter-action when we examine it, is effected in terms of the sacramentalism they exercise. The husband is the sacrament, the symbol of Christ, and the wife is the sacrament, the symbol of the Church. Thus the relationship between husband and wife is not just a more or less convenient parallel to the relationship of Christ and his Church. Matrimony is not just a human institution whose pro-fundity and depth of meaning can throw some light on the mystery of the Church as related to Christ. There is an intrinsic causal link because of the respective significance of the two. The significant (sacramental) causality of husband and wife shares in the significance of Christ and his Church.

There is a *counter-symbolism*, too, in what St. Paul says. In the Christian life of husband and wife the husband is meant to be a sacrament, a symbol, a wit-ness, a revelation of Christ and his love for the Church. The wife, similarly, symbolizes and opens up the mystery of the Church's love for Christ. Apart from the Eucharist which itself fulfills the significance of Matrimony, the deepest revelation a Christian wife will receive about Christ's love for her is her expe-rience of her husband's love. On the other hand, in experiencing her own response to her husband's love, in experiencing growth in her personality because of it, the wife becomes aware of the way in which all members of the Church are meant to grow by receiving Christ's love.

The husband, in his experience of what it means to love his wife, gains an insight into the fact that Christ wishes to give himself to, wishes to find identi-fication with, the human beings he loves. Christ wishes as far as possible to be identical with us. He wants to give himself—even surrender his life if necessary —for us. A Christian husband should be helped to understand in greater depth how Christ thought and felt when he said that he was eager to encounter death (Lk 12:50). Then, too, he experiences the fact that his wife— who receives and responds to his love, assumes a position somewhat subordinate to him and accepts his destiny and his name as her own—is in no way demeaned. Rather, she acquires greater self-identification than she had before; she achieves fulfillment and happiness, she becomes more deeply a person. For him, all this emphasizes the fact that the members of the Church should go through the same experience. They will successfully do so only if they accept the dependence that is necessarily involved in opening themselves to God's infinite love.

Husband and wife, then, living in the lasting communion of love, are a revelation first of all to one another, secondarily to the whole Church. They reveal the mystery of God's love, specifically the love between Christ and his Church grounded in the mystery of the incarnation. The fact that this love brings forth children (to the Church) reveals the intrinsic link between love and life. That love should want to give life is something that a married couple deeply understand. They receive an insight into the mystery that even the three divine Persons wish, freely and deeply, to communicate their life to man in the mystery of sanctifying grace.

The symbolic role which husband and wife play with respect to their children is also of great importance. The father is meant to be the image and symbol of God the Father. He stands as a revelation of and witness to God the Father's love for his children. This function of the human father is one of the most important educational influences in the life of his children. If he genuinely fulfills the image of fatherhood, his children have the necessary human analogue, to help and not hinder them when they try to understand the person who is God the Father. On the other hand, the mother should symbolize the maternal role of the Church, the role to which we refer when we speak of "holy Mother Church."

Then, too, the love between father and mother, as shared by the entire family, is meant to be one of the deepest experiences the children will ever have. If children grow up in the atmosphere of their parents' love, it becomes a part of their own understanding and evaluation of personal relationships. If they grow up to trust the reality of love, if they see that it is an important and warming and fulfilling human experience, they will profit from it throughout their lives. This family experience will be a bridge to understanding the supernatural mystery of divine love. On the other hand, if the children are deprived of parental love in their own home, it will be extremely difficult for them ever to come to an understanding of the revelation that God is love.

Thus marriage between two members of the Church is a sacrament. It is also a sacramental society, that is to say, it is rooted in the causative significance of Christ and his Church, a significance in which the two individuals share. Christian marriage is unique because husband and wife participate in this significance, because their love is meant to deepen the relationship between Christ and his Church, because they witness to all the meaning of the Christ-Church relationship. It is indissoluble because its sacral significance necessitates indissolubility. Christ cannot abandon his Church; the bond between them is one that must last throughout all the ages of human existence. Christian marriage is also different from all other marital relationships because it is inconceivable that the Church could worship any other god or give herself to any other Lord than the Christ who is her head. Christian husbands and wives will attain the greatest depths of love by consciously expressing in their own lives together the love of Christ and his Church. Genuine marital love, even among non-Christian couples, is a human experience of deep meaningfulness, but that meaning is profoundly transformed within the mystery of Christ.

A EUCHARISTIC BOND

Before leaving the topic of Matrimony, we might mention something that will become more apparent as we study the Eucharist in later chapters. For a married couple, the experience of their consecrated love for one another is the most important preparation for intelligent participation in the sacrament of the Eucharist. Their special function in the congregation is to act as a sign that leads to understanding the significance of the Eucharist itself. However, it is in their participation in the Eucharistic action that they become most aware of the dignity of their love for one another. When they receive the body of Christ, a bond is established between them. This bond is the final achievement of the identity they seek with one another. In accepting identification with Christ in Holy Communion, they accept Christian identification with one another. The sacrament of Matrimony bears this profound inner link with the Eucharist because the significance of the Eucharist is the same as the significance of Matrimony. The same sacramentalism binds them together: the relationship of love between Christ and his Church.

BIBLIOGRAPHY FOR CHAPTER 6

Works on the Sacrament of Confirmation

M. Bohen, *The Mystery of Confirmation,* New York, Herder and Herder, 1963. Balanced study of the historical development and theology of the sacrament, with added pastoral and catechetical suggestions. Good bibliographical aids.

P. Camelot, "Towards a Theology of Confirmation," *Theology Digest* 7(1959), pp. 67-71. Short but valuable discussion; describes and evaluates contemporary attempts to delineate the specific effect of Confirmation.

B. Luykx, "Confirmation in Relation to the Eucharist," *Readings in Sacramental Theology* (C. Sullivan, ed.), Englewood Cliffs, Prentice-Hall, 1964, pp. 187-209. Interesting study by one of the leading exponents of Confirmation as a "sacrament of initiation."

Works on the Sacrament of Matrimony

J. Caffarel, *Marriage is Holy,* Chicago, Fides, 1957; and *Love and Grace in Marriage,* Notre Dame, Fides, 1960. Combining theological insight and pastoral experience, Caffarel is one of the few contemporary authors dealing with the *sacramental* aspects of marriage.

J. Guitton, *Essay on Human Love,* London, Sheed and Ward, 1953. Stimulating essay by one of the leading lay theologians in the contemporary Church.

J. Kerns, *The Theology of Marriage,* New York, Sheed and Ward, 1964. Despite the title, it is essentially a historical approach to the topic; as such it is a valuable clarification of many Catholic positions on the sacrament of Matrimony.

G. Thibon, *What God Hath Joined Together,* Chicago, Regnery, 1952. Like the essay of Guitton (above), it is a bit dated, but it is still a worthwhile attempt to probe into the deeper meanings of marital love as transformed by the mystery of Christ.

7

CHRISTIAN PRIESTHOOD

•

PRIESTHOOD AND REDEMPTION

•

THE CONCEPT OF MEDIATION

SIGNIFICANCE OF THE INCARNATION

Though all the preceding millennia of human existence had been a preparation for the coming of Christ, and the centuries of Old Testament history had pointed to his advent in a very direct way, the work of human salvation takes on a radically new reality with the actual occurrence of the incarnation. This most mysterious entry of God into the very course of human history makes the salvation of mankind a work "from within." God no longer stands apart, as it were, from man's existence on this earth; he no longer looks down upon man in mercy, sending him prophets and teachers to guide him to his destiny. With the incarnation, God identifies himself with men; the second Person of the Trinity actually becomes a member of the human race, so that he can share our human experience and human destiny—or rather, so that we may share his human experience and human destiny.

The incarnation is not a static reality; it is an infinitely dynamic happening directed to the transforming redemption of all mankind. God the Father's own Son, his Word, takes to himself a human way of being and living (without ever ceasing to be and live divinely) precisely in order to redirect the life of men. Christ, as incarnated Word, is ordained (i.e., directed) to the work of redemption, to the unification of men with God, to the overcoming of evil. To express this a different way: by the very fact of the incarnation Christ is a priest, a mediator between men and the Father.

One must be careful not to think of Christ's priesthood as no more than a title attributed to him in recognition of his supreme human dignity. His priesthood is not accidental to his God-manhood, nor to his work as redeemer; it is of the very essence. Moreover, his priesthood is utterly unique; it fulfills and supplants all other priesthoods. No other mediation can compare with that of him who is both God and man.

Ancient Conceptions

Many ancient priesthoods grew out of the institution of kingship (or something similar, like the role of the pharaoh in Egypt), and quite understandably so. The king was thought to be a special person; he had not just his own individual identity but to some extent a "corporate personality." In his person and actions he caught up in himself the existence, meaning and destiny of the people whose king he was. If he was especially related to his people, he was also thought of as especially related to the gods they worshiped. He was considered a relative of the gods or at least the favorite of the gods. Quite commonly, ancient peoples referred to their king as "the son of the god."

Because he was closely associated with the gods, the king was the logical person to perform the religious rituals which linked the people and their gods. Frequently the king did exercise such priestly functions. More often, however, he delegated them to a group of professional priests. Such professional priesthoods rapidly became independent, and at times even exercised a controlling influence over the kingship.

Among the Israelites the pattern seems to have been different. From Israel's early days, the tribe of Levi apparently exercised a distinctive role in the worship of Yahweh. This role was not connected with or derived from kingly power. Instead, according to what seems to have been a very ancient concept in Israel, the entire people was considered sacred and dedicated to Yahweh. To their ancient Semitic way of thinking, this dedication of the entire people would have been most logically expressed by having the oldest son of each family set aside for the special service of God. However, as a substitute for this arrangement, one of the twelve clans (the tribe of Levi) was designated as a priestly group and functioned in this way.

Gradually, some families within this tribe became more prominent than others, and there developed—particularly after the Babylonian exile—a distinction between the high-priestly family, the priestly families and the Levites. All exercise of priestly function was limited to the priestly families. For this reason the element of lineage was most important. Priesthood was based entirely on heredity, though bitter dispute broke out in the centuries immediately before Christ regarding the legitimacy of some priestly families.

CHRIST THE UNIQUE PRIEST

The New Testament writings refer to Christ as "high priest according to the order of Melchizedek" (Heb 5:10). This indicates that Christ is not priest by reason of any of the Old Testament "orders" or family claims; his possession of priesthood has nothing to do with ordinary human lineage. Just as the patriarchal traditions enshrined in the book of Genesis say nothing about family lineage in narrating the priesthood exercised by Melchizedek, so too Christ does not depend on this source of priestly power. He is priest because he is the Son of God.

Ancient kings were also considered priestly because of their role as corporate personalities. In the case of Christ, this notion receives unparalleled realization because he recapitulates the historical existence and destiny of men and transforms them. St. Paul speaks of Jesus as a new Adam, as one who begins a new mankind; he speaks also of the "new man in Christ Jesus." Several of the New Testament writers describe Jesus as "the first-born," as the one who somehow contains in himself the whole life-force of the transformed human race, and who can, therefore, represent the whole human race in a most proper and intrinsic manner.

If an ancient king could justifiably function as a priest because he was considered "the son of the god," it is clear how unique is Christ's claim to be a priest; for he is the incarnated Son of the Father. He enjoys complete familiarity with and acceptance by the Father. This guarantees the Father's acceptance of the priestly offerings that Christ will make on behalf of his fellow men. Christ's kingly and priestly dignity is based not on the fact that he is the favorite of the gods, but on the fact that he is himself God in the fullest sense.

One final aspect of the uniqueness of Christ's priesthood should be considered: its universality. In all other situations, priesthood was exercised for one particular group of people—one clan, one nation, one group of religious devotees. Only in Christ's case is priesthood a reality that embraces the whole human race. For this reason, his priesthood, once established in the redemptive action of last supper-cross-resurrection, replaces all others. There is now only one intrinsically effective priesthood—Christ's. It provides for all men.

CHRIST'S PRIESTLY FUNCTION

Priesthood is, most fundamentally, mediation; and it is obvious that Christ is unparalleled mediator between man and God, mediator as no one else could possibly be. A mediator is one who brings two parties together (in this case, man and God), and the union of divine and human natures in Christ is an utterly unprecedented instance of mediation. The very source and principle for the union effected in this mediation is the divine Person of the Son. Basically, the Son of God mediates in the mystery of his becoming man by being the Person he is (the Word) and by being the Person he is for men (the Word incarnate).

Priestly mediation is a two-directional reality: a priest somehow brings the divine to men, and men to God. So it is that in Christ's mediation there are two movements: he brings divine life and redemption to men and he carries the worship of men to his Father.

In the redeeming aspect of his priestly role, Christ brings into human life the transforming reality of sanctifying grace. Identifying men with himself (which he does most radically in becoming man), he who is the Son shares this sonship and the divine life connected with it. He is sent by the Father into the world of men so that men may be regenerated in the mystery of grace-life. He, the incarnate Word, is sent as the fulfillment of Israel's prophets to speak in revelation to men, so that mankind's thinking may be transformed by truth. He is sent as a king who will rule men's lives by love and service, and so transform the patterns of human society.

On the other hand, Christ brings to his Father the worshipful acknowledgment of mankind. In his human knowledge, Christ recognizes in unique fashion what it means to be the Son of this Father. Consequently, his human act of accepting the reality of his Father is an incomparable act of worship. But Christ does much more than express his own individual recognition of his Father. In his whole life of human consciousness and love, and most especially in the redeeming action of Holy Week, Jesus acknowledges his Father on behalf of all men, as the head of this new mankind. No other act of worship now has validity except insofar as it is connected with or related to this act of Christ. Once incarnated, Christ is the only high priest for all mankind.

Reflection upon the seventeenth chapter of St. John's gospel indicates that Christ thought of his priestly role and work in terms of unity. Already embarked upon the solemn and final phase of his priestly work, he prayed to his Father that men might be united among themselves and to God. This expresses in different form what he had done in his public life by gathering men together, as a shepherd does his flock, and then guiding them to his Father.

Moses had united the somewhat disparate Israelitic tribes into the people of God by leading them to make a covenant with Yahweh. The great mediators of Old Testament times had preserved or restored that unity by insisting on the observance of the covenant. Christ not only is the mediator of the new covenant that unites men to God and men among themselves; he *is* the new covenant. The words of institution of the Eucharist—particularly those spoken over the wine— make it clear that Jesus is the new covenant, and precisely as giving himself as the source of life to men.

Since the result of observing the covenant is peace, Christ's priestly work is one of establishing peace. Peace is the condition of tranquility that accompanies correct order; order within the individual, order among men in human society, order between men and God. Christ had been expected as "the prince of peace"; but the various messianic writers of the Old Testament, who had used this term to describe the awaited human savior, had not anticipated the priestly fashion in which Jesus actually established peace in the new covenant.

CHRISTIANS AS PRIESTS

During his public life, Christ often told his disciples that he would give them his own mission, his own priestly task. Once the full redemptive act begins at the last supper, Christ starts to confer this priestly commission on his apostles. He completes it by sending the Holy Spirit on Pentecost. We can see that the apostles were clearly aware of their priestly identity and power because of the fact that they began to celebrate the Eucharist immediately after Pentecost.

However, it would be wrong to think that Christ established Christian priesthood in a way in which it might have been established in some ancient religion or even in Israel. Christian priesthood is not essentially an institutional structure of the Christian religion; it is not a function that some men must perform so that the members of this religion may have the opportunity to participate in religious ceremonies. There is only one priesthood in Christianity, Christ's; strictly there is only one priest, Christ himself. It is only because he lives in and works through those who are members of his Church that Christians are able to exercise priestly functions. All Christian priesthood is a sharing in Christ's unique priestly office and function.

Though all the members of the Church are united to Christ in his priestly mission, there are degrees of participation in his priestly power and activity. The whole people is a mediator for the rest of mankind; but there are some who act as mediators between Christ and the Christian community itself. These are given a greater share in Christ's priesthood, a more specialized role in the priestly tasks of apostolate and worship, in order that they may act as servants of the Christian people and aid them in performing their own proper priestly role. This higher degree of priesthood is conferred in the sacrament of Orders.

SACRAMENT OF HOLY ORDERS

A SPECIAL COMMUNAL OFFICE

HISTORICAL DEVELOPMENT

There are traces of the origins of the sacrament of Orders in the New Testament, particularly in the Acts of the Apostles and in St. Paul's letters to Timothy and Titus. It is clear that the apostles delegated to others some of their duties as leaders of the community and witnesses to the gospel. It is also quite clear that they arranged for others to succeed them in the various Christian communities they founded. However, it seems evident enough that an imposition of hands was connected with this commission to share in the apostolic task. Writing to Timothy, St. Paul says: "Do not neglect the gift you have, which was given you by prophetic utterance when the elders laid their hands upon you" (1 Tim. 4:14).

We cannot reconstruct all the details of the process by which the various levels of the priestly office emerged in the first few decades of Christianity, but it is clear that before the end of the first century A.D. there was already an established pattern of bishop, priests and deacons in every major Christian community. This we know from the letters of St. Ignatius of Antioch, himself one of the most prominent bishops at the turn of the century. On his way to Rome, shortly after 100 A.D., he wrote letters to several of the Christian communities that had sent emissaries to console him on his journey to imprisonment and martyrdom. In these letters he refers constantly to the role of the bishop, and exhorts priests, deacons and people to work in close union with the bishop.

By the beginning of the third century, and probably for quite some time before that, all the various minor and major orders existed. We have in the *Apostolic Tradition* of Hippolytus (a work that records the Roman liturgy at the beginning of the third century) a description of the ordination ceremony for each of the orders, including that of bishop. Though it is not a sacrament in the full sense in which the episcopate, priesthood and diaconate are, the subdiaconate is considered a major order because of the subdeacon's close involvement in the Eucharistic liturgy. On the other hand, lector, porter, exorcist and acolyte, since they do not function immediately at the altar nor share so directly in the priestly action, are considered minor orders.

OFFICE OF THE PRIEST

It has become common to think of priesthood as a state in life. More properly, it is a function within the Christian community. One is ordained by the sacrament of Orders to execute a specialized function in the Church. The fullness of this role *belongs* to the bishop who, in each diocese, is the high priest (always, of course, derivatively from Christ and in union with him) and who communicates to his clergy the powers and tasks that are his. In the explanation that follows, we shall discuss the priestly function in general, without constantly referring to the distinction between bishops and priests.

The sacraments of Baptism and Confirmation enable the members of the Christian community to cooperate in a specific way with Christ, in his continuing work of redemption and worship of the Father. The sacrament of Orders directs some Christians to an even more specialized role in the same task. Baptism and Confirmation give this directedness by causing in the Christian the sacramental character, which is a share in the priestly power of Christ, an effective authorization to participate in the Church's life of worship and sanctification. The sacrament of Orders provides a third level of sacramental character, intensifying and amplifying the share in priesthood conferred by the other two sacraments. Orders, therefore, involves an authoritative delegation to perform certain tasks required by the Christian community.

Many of the priest's actions in the Church's life are sacramental acts of giving the Spirit. This is closely allied with his own fuller possession of the Spirit through the sacrament of Orders. While the entire Church possesses the Spirit as its animating supernatural principle, the bishops and priests are able by virtue of their office to communicate the Spirit more directly and more fully. All the men of Old Testament times who exercised special mediatorial roles were thought of as spirit-bearers in the midst of the people. So, too, in Christian times the ordained priest is specially associated with the Spirit's action in the Church.

This directedness of the priest to a specialized Christian role through the sacramental character and the power of the Spirit is indicated by the external sign of Holy Orders. From the earliest days of the Church this rite seems to have involved an imposition of hands (the usual sign for the conferring of the Spirit) and an invocation for the descent of the Holy Spirit. Over the centuries a number of other symbolic actions were associated with the ceremony of priestly ordination: conferring priestly vestments, handing over the chalice and host, anointing the hands. In recent times, however, the Church has stated that the essential act of the sacrament is the imposition of the bishop's hands on the head of the ordained together with the accompanying words which invoke and indicate the gift of the Spirit (TCT 852).

ROLE OF THE PRIEST

Although there are many ways of describing and classifying the priesthood, we shall limit our discussion to the following three points:

Ministry of the word. It is clear that the Christian people do need some explanation of the word of scripture and sacrament. The priest gives them this in his teaching. However, the purpose of his instruction is to lead them to an understanding of God's own word, and the priest's chief task in this area is to announce to them (particularly in the Eucharistic assembly) the inspired word of sacred scripture. All the theological formation given the priest in his seminary years is meant to prepare him for this task. His whole intellectual life and life of prayer should be developed in the context of this task which he will undertake for the sake of the community on the day of his ordination.

The Church is a community of faith; the priest is ordained for the development of that faith community. Like all societies, the Church finds its life rooted in the exercise of an authority commensurate with the proper objective of its societal existence, in this case the profession of Christian faith. The priest is delegated his particular role in the Church, and he is given authority by Christ through the working of the Spirit—all for the sake of the Christian people. His priesthood is meant to be a service of the word of God and of the people.

Offering of sacrifice. Ordained as he is for the sake of that community which is the Church, the body of Christ, the recipient of Orders plays a fuller role in the Mass, the greatest action of that community. His position with respect to the Mass has primacy even over the role he is to play in the sanctification of the community, for the community itself exists in order to worship the Father. The ordained priest is meant to have a special part in the community's act of worship. He is to stand at the altar in a distinctive mediatorial position, for he represents at the same time both Christ and the people. In union with Christ he is to present to the Father the intent of the community; he is to bring from the Father that gift of life by which the very existence of the community is continued.

The priest at the altar functions as a father at a meal, for the sacrifice of the Mass is a sacred covenant meal that binds the community together and expresses and sustains its life. His is a special role in announcing and explaining the word of God. He takes the offering of the people, raises it as a sign of its sacralization, and then lays it on the altar as something now set aside as God's possession. He speaks publicly to God of the people's desire to be consecrated to God and separated from what is profane.

But his most important function is to transform the offering, to be the minister of the divine action which changes the profane elements of bread and wine into the sacred reality of the body and blood of Christ. Again, the priest acts as the minister of Christ and the Father when he feeds the community with the body of Christ. Through the sacramental action he gives the very life of grace for which the priesthood of Christ exists.

Thus, his ordination to sacrifice, to the sacred act of worship, is the primary element in his priestly Orders. His whole life is meant to center around this sacred action. The ceremonies of his ordination point to the fact. In the imposition of hands, the Holy Spirit is communicated to him in fullness. The hand of the bishop is laid on his head, since the action of sacrifice the priest performs is essentially a conscious human action. In the course of the ordination ceremony, the priest's hands, the instruments of his sacramental action, are anointed with sacred oil. He is clothed in the sacred vestments which will distinguish him from the rest of the community where he stands at the altar of sacrifice. Into his hands, now consecrated and set apart for the act of worship, are placed the sacred vessels of sacrifice, the chalice with paten and host. The significance of these acts is very clear: to the priest is given the sacred trust and fearful obligation of standing between the people of God and the God whom they worship.

The transformation of men. From the key action (the consecration of the bread and wine) that he performs in the sacrifice of the Mass, we can see that the ordained priest is meant to be a minister of transformation. What he does in the Mass, he does sacramentally. To some extent the role the priest plays in the offering of the oblation is a special expression of the priestly power possessed by the entire community. But what is most proper to him, what is not shared by the community, is his function as divine minister in transforming the bread and wine. This act, since it is a sacramental one, causes what it signifies. Hence, the priest, in transforming the bread into Christ, is God's minister in transforming the people into that new way of living which is the life of sanctifying grace.

The priest's role, then, is one of transforming human existence. This finds its focal expression in the very act of the Eucharistic sacrifice, but it extends to the rest of his priestly activity. As teacher, he announces and explains the word of revelation so that it can transform human consciousness. From this word, man should have a new vision of life. Human insight into what man is, what the world means and what man needs to reach his destiny should all be transformed by faith-understanding of God's workings in men.

Human society is to be transformed by the love of Christ. The priest's words and actions should teach this love to the community and assist it in forming a genuine community based on Christian love. Love is a unifying reality, and one of the foremost responsibilities of the priest is to be a principle of unity, a peacemaker, in the Christian community itself and among all men. Christ indicated this in his own priestly prayer at the last supper (Jn 17), when he asked his Father for the gift of unity among his followers.

Above all, in bringing to the community the gift of grace, the priest fulfills what is signified by his specific contribution at Mass. We call this action of the priest the "consecration." It makes something sacred which before was substantially profane. So, also, the role of the priest in society is to help transform that society with all its profane goodness into a reality consecrated to the Father.

FATHERHOOD OF THE PRIEST

One final fact about the priesthood, to which the ceremonies of his ordination and his actions in the Mass point, is that priesthood is an exercise of supernatural paternity. We can say this because in the Mass the priest gives the faithful the living body of Christ under the appearance of bread. His action is similar to that of a father who continues his initial gift of life to his children by providing them with their daily bread. In feeding them from day to day, the father of a family signifies his intention to sustain the life he originally communicated to them. In the sacrifice of the Mass, the priest continues to give those who are his children by Baptism the bread which is the body of Christ; he signifies and effects in them the enduring gift of supernatural life.

In this action, the priest does not give his own life; rather, he is the mediator of that divine life which comes to them now from the Father "from whom all fatherhood is named" (Eph 3:15). To speak of the priest's actions as fatherly is not simply to speak metaphorically. The priest is truly performing a paternal act; he is really giving to those who are members of his flock that life which comes from God the Father.

The paternity exercised by a priest in his sacramental functions of communicating grace is itself a "life-giving" that should spring from love. In the situation of giving natural life within the sacrament of Matrimony, a human father exercises his fatherhood because of his self-giving love for his wife. So, too, a priest's love for the Church should be the basis for the exercise of supernatural fatherhood. He should love the Church (i.e., the Christian community) as a husband loves his wife. As the sacrament of Christ he should have Christ's own desire to give life to the Church. In a sense the priest has the Church for his spouse, for he possesses a special kind of identity with Christ.

For this reason, there is special appropriateness in the celibate priesthood of the Latin Church. The priest has accepted his spouse, the Church, as the object of his unique love, the one to whom he wishes to give children. As a sign of this complete dedication, as a sign of his total self-giving to the Church, the priest forgoes the gift of self to another in marriage and the joy of fulfillment in natural fatherhood.

Thus, Matrimony and Holy Orders stand together as complementary sacraments, signifying to all the world the paternity of God the Father which is the source of all life, natural and supernatural. Both sacraments point to the profoundly mysterious relationship of love between Christ and his Church. Both sacraments find their fulfillment in the sacrifice of the Mass, which points to such great love on the part of the Father that he sends his own Son to communicate supernatural life to men. Both sacraments point to the basic obligations of all human beings to give life, to increase life, to help life find its fulfillment in and through the gift of love. "This is my commandment, that you love one another as I have loved you" (Jn 15:12).

BIBLIOGRAPHY FOR CHAPTER 7

WORKS ON THE GENERAL ASPECTS OF PRIESTHOOD

Y. Congar, *Lay People in the Church*, Westminster, Newman, 1957. Still one of the basic books on the topic.

H. F. Davis, "The Priesthood of the Faithful," *Theology Digest* 1(1953), pp. 49-52. Largely a presentation of the pioneering studies of P. Dabin, this is a clear summation of the main ideas— though it has been somewhat outdated by the developments accompanying Vatican II. Followed by a short bibliography.

E. Sauras, "Is there a Priesthood of the Laity?" *Theology Digest* 4(1956), pp. 110-114. Studies the priesthood of the faithful precisely in relation to the Eucharistic sacrifice; needs only slight modification as result of decrees of Vatican II.

C. Heris, *The Mystery of Christ*, Westminster, Newman, 1950. While not formally concerned with the topic of priesthood, this book on Christology— because of its emphasis on the priestly role of Christ himself—provides valuable background for any study of Christian priesthood.

WORKS ON THE SACRAMENT OF ORDERS

J. Bligh, *Ordination to the Priesthood*, New York, Sheed and Ward, 1956. In the course of describing the historical development of the rite of priestly ordination, this book contributes many interesting insights into the nature of the sacrament.

J. Lecuyer, *What Is a Priest?* New York, Hawthorn, 1959. Short study of Orders by one of the leading scholars in the field.

The Sacrament of Holy Orders, Collegeville, Liturgical Press, 1962. A collection of essays by a number of the finest theologians and historians in France. One of the very few worthwhile books on this sacrament.

8

•

THE EUCHARIST AS SACRIFICE

•

SACRIFICE IN SCRIPTURE

•

SACRIFICE IN THE OLD TESTAMENT

PRELIMINARY REMARKS

From the earliest days of Christianity, the Eucharistic action has been the center of the Church's life. It has been the supreme prayer and act of worship, the most important occasion of Christian instruction, the source of unity and love in the community. All the other sacraments point toward the Eucharist and find their own fulfillment in it. The Eucharist is truly the center and the epitome of Christianity.

Our treatment of the Eucharist (and we will use this word "Eucharist" to refer to the action of the Mass) will be divided into four chapters: the Eucharist as *sacrifice*, as *worship*, as *word*, and as *redemption*. These four approaches to understanding the Eucharist cannot be rigidly separated one from another. There will necessarily be a considerable amount of overlap. But each approach will provide a different point of view from which to study this extremely complex yet amazingly unified action. This present chapter will be divided into three major sections: 1) the Old Testament practice of sacrifice; 2) Christ's action of sacrifice at the last supper and on Calvary; 3) Christ's continuing act of sacrifice in the Christian Eucharist.

ANCIENT NOTIONS OF SACRIFICE

According to the Mosaic traditions that underlie the books of the Pentateuch, the Old Testament people came into existence as a unified group at Mount Sinai because of the action of Yahweh in forming a covenant with them. This covenant was formalized in a sacrificial act in which the blood of a victim was shared between Yahweh and his people (Ex 24). Thus, sacrifice is central to the approach of man to God in the Old Testament centuries that prepared the way for Christ.

However, we must not think of sacrifice as something unique to the Israelites. Actually, in all the ancient religions we know of, there was some manner of ritual act resembling the sacrificial acts of Israel. We cannot determine with absolute accuracy the various purposes of the different mystery rites. Some basic purposes can be recognized in almost all ancient religions, including that of Israel.

Perhaps the most fundamental objective of ancient ritual was to establish some contact with whatever powers controlled the forces of nature. Man tended to think of these ultimate powers as personal, and so he attempted to render such "divinities" present by the force of his religious ceremonial. This ceremonial used some sacred object (like a statue) to portray the god, or saw him as present in some sacred element (like ritual fire). In some cases the ritual reenacted myths about the people's gods, and so "made present" those acts of the gods which they wished to guarantee.

With the god or gods present to him in ritual, man could now become united to divinity. This he did by offering gifts that would win favor and establish peace, or in some cases appease an angry god and avert his harmful activity. In other situations the ritual consisted of a sacred meal in which the divinity somehow shared food with the devotees. Having eaten together, the god and the people were united in a contractual bond.

Another meaningful feature of ancient rituals had to do with *sacralization*. The offering brought to the sacrificial act, and the people symbolized by the offering, were joined in the realm of the sacred, set apart as dedicated to the divinity. This making sacred could come about by lifting up the offering, or by placing it in a sacred spot (for example, upon an altar), or by the change effected through some force like sacred fire. Sacrificial dedication or sanctification seems to have been thought of as involving an entry into the realm of the sacred.

Again, all religious ritual implied an acknowledgment of an already existent religious relationship, or an attempt to establish relationship with a god. Sacrifice could serve to express the recognition of human dependence upon divine forces at work in nature. Or it could express a particular people's allegiance to their special protecting god. Or it might manifest the desire for reconciliation with some offended deity, thought to be showing his displeasure through some plague or disaster. The attitude of genuine personal thanksgiving seems to be missing.

Are not the rituals that seem to be thank offerings really payments to the god of what was promised in earlier rituals of petition and bargaining?

ISRAELITIC NOTIONS OF SACRIFICE

On the surface, the ritual actions of the people of Israel appear similar to those of neighboring peoples. Actually many of the external ritual forms found among the Israelites were borrowed from Mesopotamia, Egypt or Canaan. However, there is a radical difference between Israel's religious ceremonials and those of other ancient peoples. This difference is clear in the externals of the characteristically Jewish festivals, but most importantly in their inner spirit and meaning.

Beginning with the experience of the Exodus, the Israelitic expressions of faith are distinctive because their divinity, Yahweh, was unique among ancient gods. Because Yahweh was spiritual, not attached to any particular place, not immanent in the processes of nature, the whole notion of establishing contact and making him present drastically differed from similar concepts in other religions. Because Yahweh could not be represented (graven images were prohibited), Israel did not have a ceremonial re-presentation like that, for example, of the New Year's festival in Babylon.

What was represented in Israel's festivals was that *historical* act which lay at the beginnings of the people's existence and which was seen by faith to be the result of Yahweh's special intervention in history. In the course of the Exodus from Egypt, Yahweh had made the covenant with his people at Sinai, a covenant that established Israel as a nation consecrated to this divinity. So it happened that sacrificial ritual during the Old Testament centuries never lost the central implication of covenant. The peace offerings celebrated on all the great feasts were essentially ceremonial reiterations of the Mosaic covenant; they were sacred meals shared by Yahweh and his people to express the union binding them together. Passover, Tabernacles and the Harvest Festival all commemorated in their liturgical rites various aspects of the Exodus experience of Israel.

Along with these peace offerings, in which the sacrificial meal was shared by God and the people in attendance, the Old Testament people also practiced the holocaust. As far as we can reconstruct the mentality of the ancient Israelites, it seems that the holocausts signified recognition of the sovereignty of this God who had brought their fathers out of Egyptian bondage into the land promised them. One can misinterpret the holocausts, seeing in the victim's destruction the essence of the act of worship. However, it seems that the Israelites did not think of the fire as something that destroyed the victim; rather, it was an action that *transformed* man's gift into the invisible element of fragrance that was thought pleasing to Yahweh. Moreover, it was Yahweh himself who transformed the offering, using fire as his instrument. The Israelites did not see fire itself as something divine, but like most ancient people they did look upon it as a force especially associated with the divine, as Yahweh's own instrument, used by him to draw their sacrificial offering to himself. The fact that the fire sent up pleasing smoke to Yahweh was a sign of Yahweh's acceptance of the offering. When man consecrated his offering by laying it on an altar, Yahweh concurred by transferring it into a way of being more like his own.

When he came to the action of sacrifice, the Israelite thought of himself as bringing a gift to Yahweh. As a matter of fact, the Hebrew word "gift" comes closest to being the generic name for those Old Testament actions which we call sacrifices. Not that Yahweh needed the gifts that the people brought to the shrines. Especially in the later Old Testament centuries Israel realized that all creation belonged to Yahweh, that he had need of nothing, and certainly not of the animal offerings made to him in the temple courts. However, the bringing of a gift had several meanings. It represented a self-offering, a desire to establish peaceful relations with God—or to reestablish them if reconciliation was necessary. Not only was the bringing of the gift filled with meaning, but Yahweh's acceptance of it, through the fragrant burning action of the fire, signified his divine good will toward Israel.

An interesting mentality, and one that Israel shared with other ancient peoples, is reflected in the offering of the first fruits of the harvest and flocks. Apparently, according to nature, the earliest heads of wheat or the first bunches of grapes were thought to contain the whole life force of the crop. If this first, full, divinely given life was offered in sacrifice, the whole crop or vintage was rendered sacred, and a sacred people could then have sacred nourishment. Furthermore, the success of the rest of the crop was guaranteed because the entire harvest had been rejoined to its life-source in the offering of the first fruits. This notion of the offering of first-fruits to their divinity was so strong among some ancient peoples that they mistakenly sacrificed even their first-born children. There are signs in the Old Testament that the people were not completely immune to this false idea. They had to be reassured by their religious teachers that Yahweh did not will human sacrifice. Instead, they were to offer to Yahweh the substitute gift of two lambs or two turtledoves.

In the later centuries of Old Testament history, especially in the strictly Judaic period that followed upon the Babylonian exile, the notion of *expiation* became quite prominent in the sacrificial ritual. The great annual feast of Yom Kippur (Day of Atonement) emphasized the people's reconciliation with Yahweh and the making of amends for the transgressions of the people. In addition, a whole array of sin- and trespass-offerings came into being. These served as liturgical reconciliations with God for individuals or the community. It seems that the historical tardiness of these expiatory sacrifices was at least partially due to the fact that a true sense of personal guilt and sin came into prominence only with the prophetic movement. Until men have seen their relationship to God as a *personal* reality, there cannot be that realization of sin which makes real religious expiation necessary or understandable.

Throughout the sacrificial ceremonial of Israel there runs the influence of Israel's God. Yahweh, who brought the people out of Egypt with power and a mighty right arm, is the divinity to whom each act of Old Testament ritual is directed. Yahweh's transcendence and spirituality impart their meaning to these actions and elevate them to a level not shared by other ancient religions.

HISTORICAL COMMEMORATION

Most characteristic and unique in the religious rites of the Old Testament people is the *commemorative* character of their sacrificial acts. Their sacrifices involved, as an essential part of their meaning, references to the great events of Israel's history. But the ritual commemoration was more than mere remembrance of past happenings. It also provided, for those who participated in the ritual, an opportunity to share in the significance of the original happenings, to enter into their spirit and so pledge themselves as a continuing covenant people.

A most fascinating aspect of this commemorative nature of Old Testament liturgy is that it is a developing reality. While the commemorative significance of sacrifice remains essentially unchanged (it is always a recalling of the Exodus), a deepening of understanding takes place over the centuries. Consequently, we find increasingly more detail and explicitation in the ritual itself. Cultural and historical influences have their impact, too, with the result that we find considerable accretion developing around the earlier and simpler ceremonial forms. What is notable in this complex process of liturgical growth is the influence of Israel's concept of Yahweh and her recollection of his intervention in human history. By intervening, he radically transformed the new elements that came into the picture and made them part and parcel of the Old Testament world. In this process, the natural religious insights of ancient man, expressed and retained in his religious ritual, were brought into relationship with the truths of revelation and so transformed.

CHRIST'S SACRIFICE

EXTERNALS OF THE LAST SUPPER

Any study of the Christian notion of sacrifice must necessarily center much of its attention upon the scene of the last supper. Here Jesus gathered together his apostles to perform that action which is the origin of the Church's Eucharistic celebration. Great care must therefore be given to analyzing this *supper* scene if we are to understand the Church's teaching about sacrifice. Because genuine sacrifice consists of an interior attitude expressed in some external sign, we shall have to examine both the externals of the last supper and the inner attitude of Jesus during it.

Christ's actions during his life on earth have always been the object of Christian contemplation and study. These actions form a pattern for our own human living and decision. In the case of the last supper, there is an additional reason for examining in great detail the external aspects of the scene. This was a supremely sacramental action, the beginning of the greatest of the Christian sacraments, the Eucharist. Since a sacrament is distinguished from other human actions by the fact that it produces its effect by meaning or signifying something, it is important that we study the meaning of the last supper. The nature of Christian liturgical life, the nature of the Church and the nature of salvation itself are dependent upon the significance Christ and his apostles attached to the external ceremonies and words of the supper event.

When Christ gathered with his apostles in the upper room on the night before he was to die, he did so in the context of a Passover dinner. Though there is some scholarly dispute about whether or not the dinner was eaten on the day of the official Passover celebration, it is quite clear that the whole spirit and atmosphere of the meal was that of the Passover feast. This dinner would have had for Jesus and his disciples the same significance it had for any devout Jew of the time.

We know that for centuries prior to Christ the Passover dinner was already a yearly festival in Israel's liturgical calendar. Perhaps more than any other feast celebrated by the Old Testament people, it focused upon the commemoration of the great events of Old Testament history, particularly those events which marked Israel's origins as a people. Even today the ceremonies of the Passover dinner, as celebrated by Jewish communities, make it clear that the commemoration of the Exodus is central to the meaning of this meal.

The meal, taken in a family context in which the father officiated in a priestly role, was patterned after the meal described in the book of Exodus. On the night before they left Egypt the Israelites gathered together in haste and, standing with staffs in hand, ate the lamb whose blood they had smeared above their doors as a mark of salvation. Each year, as the Jewish family celebrated the Passover dinner, the youngest child was required to ask of his father the significance of the action they were performing—the meaning of the lamb, of the unleavened bread, of the bitter herbs. As the father recalled aloud the events which showed God's providential care for Israel, each member of the family had the opportunity to link himself psychologically with the heritage of his people.

Not only did the Passover dinner recall the flight from Egypt, it recalled the entire Exodus history. Consequently, it included the enactment of the covenant at Sinai under Moses' leadership. At Mount Sinai, Moses gathered the people about him and, according to the tradition contained in Exodus 24, built an altar. He took the blood of the animal to be used for the sacrifice, poured half of it upon the altar, and sprinkled the other half upon the people. This he did as a sign that God was linking his people to himself in a blood bond, in the familiarity of a clan relationship. So, the annual Passover celebration recalled to the people their own covenant relationship and commitment to the God of their fathers. It provided an opportunity for them to enter by their own decision into the history of their people and to make it meaningful in their own lives.

Another theme that originates with the Exodus and continues throughout the history of the Old Testament is that of God dwelling with his people. Though they were conscious that their God could not be constrained either by time or space, the Israelites still felt that God exercised a special providence over them. This special dwelling was symbolized during the desert wanderings by the tent, or tabernacle, pitched over the ark of the covenant, and later by the Jerusalem temple. The Passover dinner, both in its spirit and in its ceremony, retained this notion of the providential presence of Yahweh with his people. The ceremony was filled with expressions of thanks for Yahweh's continued care for his chosen people.

During the desert years, a sign of this special care was the giving of the manna. The eating of the bread at the Passover meal was related to the manna. Not that the Passover bread (the unleavened matzos) was seen as anything but ordinary unleavened bread; but this ordinary bread was considered to be as much a gift from Yahweh as was the extraordinary food given during the years in the desert.

At the last supper, as they were gathered together with Jesus, the apostles were conscious of all these Jewish meanings of the Passover celebration. Christ's own awareness went far beyond theirs. He saw all the historical significances of the dinner. He also knew that this was the beginning of the new Exodus, and that his presence with the apostles was the fulfillment of the idea of God's dwelling, for he was God, living among men.

Looking at the externals of the action that took place in the upper room, we become conscious of the fact that this is not a simple enactment of the Passover dinner ceremony. What began as a celebration of the Old Testament Passover was transformed into a meal that is at once the fulfillment and replacement of this Old Testament feast. The action of the last supper, as recorded for us in the gospels, constitutes the formation of the new covenant which replaces the Sinaitic covenant commemorated each year in the Passover ritual.

One can see from the gospel text that Christ's action of changing bread and wine into himself is clearly linked in his thinking with Moses' sacrificial action at Sinai. There Moses, after taking the blood of the victim and sprinkling it on the people, said: "Behold the blood of the covenant which the Lord has made with you in accordance with all these words" (Ex. 24:8). The blood of the new covenant is not merely sprinkled externally upon the people; in a more sublime way Jesus distributes the blood of the new covenant by giving his disciples the cup to drink. The parallel between Christ's words at the supper and those spoken by Moses at Sinai indicates that the last supper is the establishing of the new covenant in an act of sacrifice.

Christ's action was not simply a more intensified stage of the same covenant begun by Moses. It was, rather, the new covenant predicted by Jeremiah and Ezekiel, which was "not like the covenant which I made with their fathers when I took them by the hand to bring them out of the land of Egypt" (Jer 31:32). This was a new covenant in which the Law would be written on the hearts of men instead of on tablets of stone. This was the new covenant which, in the minds of the prophets from Jeremiah onward, was to be effected when Yahweh came on the "day of the Lord" to bring salvation to his people.

Though the gospel text is very succinct, there can be little doubt that Christ was conscious of this passage of Jeremiah when instituting the Eucharist. This was truly a new covenant, established in Christ's own blood and based on that new Law which Christ himself is. Moreover, this new covenant fulfills the prophecy of Malachi that a new and spiritual sacrifice, a truly free inner offering of self, would mark the relationship of man to God on the day of the Lord.

Reflection on the relation of the supper both to Sinai and to the prophecy of Jeremiah leads us to conclude that Christ and the early Christians saw it as a sacrifice. Just as the old covenant had been enacted in sacrifice, this act of the last supper, which was the fulfillment and realization of Sinai, also had to be sacrificial. Besides, the words of Jesus when he speaks of his blood—"This is my blood of the covenant, which is poured out for many" (Mk 14:24; cf. Mt. 26:28)—point to the ritual use of blood in the sacrifices of the Jerusalem temple. In the Septuagint, the Greek word used for "poured out" is the technical word for the pouring of the sacrificial blood upon the altar of the temple. Again, Christ's words when he changes the bread into himself indicate a sacrificial oblation: "This is my body which is *given for you*" (Lk 22:19).

From beginning to end the last supper is a sacrificial action. It is not only, as is sometimes said in oversimplification, the act of Jesus changing bread and wine into himself; it is also the transformation of the entire feast of Passover with all that it means. The Old Testament liturgy and system of sacrifice is radically transformed by being absorbed into the mystery of the new covenant. As we examine the action of Christ at the last supper, we can see that it fulfills all the various types of Old Testament sacrifice. It fulfills the holocaust because Christ's offering of himself to his Father is a total oblation; it fulfills the peace-offering because the last supper is a sacred meal shared by God and the new chosen people; it fulfills the offering of the first fruits because Christ is here being set aside in solemn consecration to his Father and is, as St. Paul tells us, the first-born of creation, the first-born from the dead.

One aspect of the Passover that is absorbed into Christian liturgy at the last supper is its festive spirit. It is one of the characteristics of Old Testament liturgy that the great gatherings of Israel in the temple courts were, for the most part, looked upon as occasions of rejoicing and thanksgiving. These were the times when God's people were gathered in his presence to eat together, to drink together, to sing together, to praise the Lord. Probably, no Old Testament feast preserved as much of this spirit of joy and comradeship as did the Passover, which was celebrated within the family circle. This spirit of joyousness was clearly indicated by the context of the last supper, despite the sadness of Jesus over Judas' betrayal. It is explicitly underlined in the last discourse, in chapters 13-17 of John's gospel, all of which are Eucharistic catechesis: "These things I have spoken to you, that my joy may be in you, and that your joy may be full" (Jn 15:11). It passes into the Christian Eucharist as a principle for interpreting the spirit that should guide the Christian community in the celebration of Mass.

The externals of the last supper contained, in implicit and highly compressed form, much that was profoundly significant. They can be better understood if we view them in relation to the actions and words of Christ which precede the supper. When we analyze the earlier scenes of Christ's public career, we begin to realize that all his actions and teaching form a background for understanding the supreme action which begins in the upper room. Christ relating himself to the Jerusalem temple, Christ pointing to himself as the Messiah expected by Israel, Christ's teaching by parables that he would establish his kingdom as a nuptial meal, scenes like the multiplication of the loaves followed by the beautiful Eucharistic discourse at Capharnaum—all these point to that culmination of Christ's prophetic witness which took place at the last supper. This also confirms the sacrificial character of the last supper as well as the reality of the transformation of bread and wine into Christ. If Christ, in the assertions he made during the previous three years and in the extraordinary actions of healing that he performed, was pointing progressively to something which would be his supreme act on behalf of mankind, it certainly would have been anticlimactic had the last supper not been a genuine sacrifice, had Christ not truly given himself under the form of bread and wine.

The event which perhaps points most clearly to the last supper, and helps us to appreciate its full meaning, is the multiplication of the loaves. When the gospel account of this event was written, the early Christian community had already been celebrating the Eucharist for two or three decades. Hence it is not surprising to find the text filled with more or less technical expressions from the Eucharistic liturgy. This very fact points to the insight of the early Christians into the relationship between the episode of the loaves and the supper event.

The narrative begins by saying that the crowd had followed Christ into a desert place. The very use of the word "desert" recalls the Old Testament Exodus, when Yahweh led his people into the desert. Christ is faced with people who, for the moment at least, are deprived of the ordinary means of sustenance, as were the Israelites in their sojourn in the desert. Like Yahweh of old, Christ now in extraordinary fashion provides bread for the multitude. Clearly the Gospel writers intended to show Christ exercising the role of the Old Testament God, giving bread as a sign of the giving of life. The next day, when Christ (as we know from St. John's gospel) addressed the crowds in Capharnaum, he tried to show them the deeper significance of the miracle he had worked. He spoke of a future gift of himself as source of life, a gift which would one day be provided for them under the external sign of bread. The fulfillment of this promise took place in the upper room when Christ initiated the Eucharistic action which still continues in the Church.

By way of summary, our examination of the externals of the last supper reveals the following.

1. The scene was quite clearly a Passover dinner in which Christ, gathered together with his disciples, acted as the father of the family.

2. It was a transformation of the Passover into something new; it was the establishment of a new covenant.

3. This action at the last supper was simultaneously the fulfillment and the replacement of the old covenant made by Moses at Mt. Sinai, since it was the new covenant described in the prophecy of Jeremiah and Ezekiel.

4. The earlier scenes of Christ's life, particularly miracles like that of the multiplication of the loaves, were part of the pedagogical preparation for understanding this crowning action of the supper.

5. Externals point to the fact that the supper, as the fulfillment of Moses' action at Sinai, is an act of sacrifice.

CHRIST'S INNER ATTITUDE

When Christ was involved in the action in the upper room, what specified his human consciousness, what was he aware of, what were the intentions which governed his activity? Fortunately, many indications are provided by his external actions. Even clearer are the words recorded in the gospel narratives of this scene, and in St. Paul's first letter to the Corinthians.

Quite logically, we argue from the externals, both gestures and words, to an understanding of Christ's consciousness at this moment. These externals are visible expressions of his invisible inner life. We saw that these externals point to the fact that Christ intended to establish a covenant. He was giving himself as an oblation for men. He was fulfilling the Old Testament Passover at the very moment when he was radically repealing it. He was establishing the new covenant in his blood, a covenant which was to be continued through the commemorative action of his followers. However, we wish to probe more deeply into the mentality of Christ at this moment, because his human attitude during the action of the supper must be the model for all Christian participation in the Eucharistic action and, therefore, for all Christian spirituality. There was, of course, only one state of consciousness in Christ. We can better understand its complexity by reflecting upon the way in which it was an attitude of obedience, worship, sacrifice and thanksgiving.

An attitude of obedience. Scripture itself tells us that Christ's act in freely undergoing death was one of obedience by which he merited redemption for us and glorification for himself. Superficial understanding of this obedience sees it as conformity to an arbitrary law laid down for him by his Father. Something more radical is involved, namely, acceptance of the creaturely status bound up with his humanity. This involves admission of dependence upon a creator God, as well as acceptance of those other factors of human life which bring man not just growth and development but also suffering, pain and eventually death. Christ, in being obedient to his Father, was unreservedly accepting the lot which was his as a man. He did this in the concrete historical situation in which he found himself.

Christ's act of obedience involved an integral confrontation of reality. At no moment in his life was there the least compromise in Christ's acceptance of his human situation. As he approached the moment of greatest difficulty, his passion and death, Christ solemnly consecrated to the Father this fullest expression of his earthly existence. The action of the supper expresses this inner obedience of Christ. Particularly significant are his changing bread into his body and his statement that he is putting himself aside as an oblation to his Father for the sake of men.

An attitude of worship. In a later chapter, we shall see in greater detail how the supper is an act of worship. Fundamentally, of course, Christ's act of submission to the Father in obedience is worship. In worship man acknowledges the sovereignty of God. In the Christian context, worship cannot be merely a matter of recognizing God as creator. It must include recognition of God as Father. New Testament literature reveals how profoundly Christ's human consciousness was dominated by the mystery of the fatherhood of his Father. As Christ approached the supreme action of his redemptive work, all his consciousness and all his affectivity were directed toward his Father. The seventeenth chapter of St. John's gospel describes Christ's state of consciousness at the last supper. Christ dedicated himself to the Father in reliance upon the Father's love, and completely accepted the role which he as the Son made man must play so that the Father might have other sons.

Christ's attitude, then, during the supper in the Cenacle was one of profound acknowledgment of his Father as the Person to whose loving care he committed himself. There could have been no more profound human trust in the fatherhood of God than Christ's willingness to encounter the mystery of death which, as man, he had never before experienced. He did this with full trust that his Father, who loved him, would raise him up in resurrection.

An attitude of sacrifice. Sacrifice as an attitude is very closely allied with worship. However, genuine sacrifice is more than interior acknowledgment of God. It must also include public manifestation of irrevocable dedication to this God. The internal attitude involved in sacrifice is what makes the externals of the act personally meaningful, truly significant. If in sacrifice we bring a gift and place it apart as belonging to God, then our internal attitude should logically and honestly be one of setting ourselves apart, a dedication of ourselves to the service of the God whom we worship. Christ was quite obviously sacrificing at the last supper because the externals of the supper were the externals of a sacrifice. By changing bread and wine into himself, he clearly set them apart from their normal profane use. His words, which accompanied this transformation, signify that this is his giving of himself to the Father. He was dedicating himself publicly and irrevocably to the task which his Father had committed to him, the task of encountering death and so destroying the mystery of evil.

Christ, in offering himself, had that internal attitude which is the heart of sacrificial action. This conclusion is confirmed by St. John's gospel, which gives us such rich insight into Christ's consciousness at this privileged moment. Christ repeatedly voices his gratitude for the task which his Father had given him to do. He gives thanks for the reality of the Father himself. He thanks the Father for the fact that he, the Christ, is now approaching death and resurrection, is coming to the moment of his human fulfillment, the moment of his glorification. Hence, Christ's gratitude is made manifest by his actions as well as by his words. The early Christian community saw this in describing the act of Christ in this way. In recording what happened, the gospel text says that Christ, took the bread, and "when he had given thanks he broke it and gave it to them" (Lk 22:19). Christ obviously intends to situate this act in the context of thanksgiving. We can see, then, that the attitude of Christ at the supper is precisely that of sacrifice. Christ was submitting himself in gratitude to his Father, to render supreme worship to him by the sacrificial gift (oblation) of himself in death and resurrection.

As we look at the concrete reality of Christ's choice at the last supper, we find that it was essentially a matter of his opening himself to a new way of life. He chose to relinquish the limited existence which we human beings enjoy in our present context of space and time, and open himself to a greatly amplified and spiritualized human existence. Since his experimental knowledge was just as human and limited as our own, Christ had no immediate experience of his coming death, nor of the new kind of life which was to be his. His willingness to commit himself to this passage through death into new life represented a profound expression of trust in his Father's providential care for him.

For the past several centuries, stress has been placed on the fact that Christ's decision at the last supper was a decision to accept death. But we must never forget that the total object of Christ's choice was death and resurrection. He did not offer himself to death in isolation from the mystery of passage into new life. To accept death is not simply to accept cessation of bodily existence. Acceptance of death was for Christ the supreme moment of his conflict with evil. Throughout his public life, from the very moment of its inception with the temptation in the desert, the suggestion had been made to Christ that he should, in order to preserve his physical life, betray the task which his Father had given him. This was Christ's basic temptation: to deny his role as the new Adam, his identity as the man who occupied the key position in human history. Had Christ given way to this suggestion, evil would have triumphed over him because he would have denied the basic orientation of his historical existence. Since this was the context of his temptation, we can see that the choice he made signified man's triumph over evil. Christ's rejection of the temptation to avoid death was not merely a meritorious action inducing God to remove evil. By overcoming temptation, he was actually victor over sin, and by going through death into risen life he made himself victor over death.

It is important to remember that Christ, by accepting death, was very literally choosing resurrection. His death and resurrection could not be isolated one from the other. Together they form one mystery of Christ's passover to his Father. In order to come into this new way of unrestricted human existing, Christ had necessarily to give up the limited context in which man finds himself. For him this was the meaning of death. However, we must not forget that Christ had an integral human experience. Therefore, he did not escape the trepidation, the uneasiness that came because of the suffering and anguish he faced and because of the inevitable natural fear of death.

Christ's acceptance of death was essentially acceptance of victimhood. If we examine the notion of victimhood when applied to a human, it means acknowledgment of the fact that one is a being to whom something is done. At the very roots of Christ's victimhood lies the creatureliness of his human nature. Accepting the fact that death would be inflicted upon him, Christ made himself a willing target for the forces of nature and the hatred of men.

But his victimhood has an even deeper reality. It involved being set aside for the Father, set apart from the profane. While it is true that Christ from the first moment of his incarnation accepted the fatherhood of his Father and the role which was his own, the last supper marks the solemn public commitment of himself to the fulfillment of this role. In saying, "This is my body which is given for you" (Lk 22:19), Christ was dedicating himself through a public cultic act to the work of overcoming evil and restoring mankind.

The death of Christ on the cross fulfills the victimhood which he accepted at the last supper. His act in the upper room said sacramentally that he was setting himself aside from the profane world; the act of dying on the cross said exactly the same thing. There is no more effective way of setting a man apart from this temporal world than by death. Nothing could so irrevocably remove Christ from the ordinary ways of human living as his passage through death into risen life.

Another important element of Christ's interior attitude toward his death and resurrection is his acceptance of both *for the sake of men.* Christ said, "And for their sake I consecrate myself" (Jn 17:19). The action of the last supper is not just a matter of Christ *giving up* his life. More importantly it is a question of Christ *giving* his life to men, of giving himself as a living person so that men might share his life. Developing this idea, we see that the mystery of resurrection is not something that happens to Christ in isolation from the rest of men. Christ takes on new life, Christ passes into resurrection to bring men to that same risen life which he himself possesses. Christ's action of giving himself to his Father is simultaneously the action of giving himself to men as a source of their new life. There is no opposition, as a matter of fact there is no distinction, between these two acts of giving. It was precisely in order to give himself to men that the Father sent him into the world in the mystery of the incarnation. Christ's inner attitude is clearly one of sacrifice, not just because he accepts death but also because he willingly passes over into the new risen life which other men are destined to share.

In summary, the last supper is essentially a sacrificial action, a preeminently spiritual and personal sacrifice, the total self-giving of Christ in his humanity to the mystery of man's salvation in conformity with the Father's will. This sacrifice recapitulates and fulfills the sacrificial liturgy of the Old Testament and of all the natural religions of mankind. It is a sacrificial action because of the inner attitude of Christ who gratefully and obediently acknowledges the fatherhood of his Father. It is a sacrifice also in its externals, linked in their significance to the entire sacrificial ritual of the Old Testament. At the last supper, then, Christ in the midst of his brethren brought to an end the validity and effectiveness of the Old Testament sacrifices. He repealed them in his new covenant sacrifice, which fulfilled the prophecy of Malachi and provided the point of departure for Christian worship of the Father. This worship continues in our own day and to the end of time in the action we call the Eucharist, the sacrifice of the Mass.

EVERLASTING SACRIFICE

THE CHRISTIAN EUCHARIST

CHRIST'S RESURRECTION

Catholic belief in the Mass as Christ's continuing act of sacrifice is grounded in the mystery of his resurrection. Because he is in this new state, to which he passed in the mysteries of redemption, he is able to abide with his Church and continue his redeeming sacrificial action in her midst. For that reason it would be good to preface our study of the Mass as Christ's sacrifice with a brief investigation of the Church's doctrine on the mystery of the resurrection itself.

The New Testament says very little about this new way in which Christ lives as man. We know, however, that Christ's resurrection brought with it an increase in his human freedom. In his risen state Christ lives in a new dimension of human bodily existence, in which he is no longer limited by the narrowness of our space and time. Strictly speaking, the risen Christ cannot be said to be in any place in our world. It is more accurate to speak of him as being present *to* a place, since no spatial situation can either contain or limit him. Again, he is not limited by our time, but lives in a new context of sequential existence whose nature we will understand only when we ourselves participate in it in the next life. Freed as he is from such limitations, he is also freed from the inability to contact more than just a small group of human beings. He needs none of the techniques we have devised to extend the range of our communication with other human persons. Instead, his resurrected humanity makes it possible for him to be present to human beings wherever they may be in the entire range of creation.

This freedom from limitation in no way denies true bodily existence. We must not get the impression that Christ in his present risen state has only a semblance of a body. Rather, in a way in which we cannot fully appreciate, he is more thoroughly human, more integrally man in both body and soul than he was in the period which preceded his death and resurrection. The mystery of death and resurrection is not a denial of bodily existence. It is the passage to fulfillment of human life, the life of a spirit incarnated in a body. The Catholic Church has always firmly insisted that the risen Christ is truly and completely man. His human nature is perfectly integral.

PRESENCE OF THE RISEN CHRIST

This means that Christ is able to be present to his Church and to baptized Christians throughout the entire world. This presence, though invisible, is a presence of immediacy. Christ does not stand at a distance from his Church, as we learn from his reminder to his disciples, just prior to the ascension: "Remember, I am with you always until the end of the world" (Mt 28:20).

Christ's presence to the Church both as God and as man is a fulfillment of the mystery of God dwelling with men. Foreshadowed in the Old Testament, this mystery finds its ultimate expression in the incarnation—in which a divine Person becomes part of the process of human history. Once this association is initiated in the incarnation, it continues unceasingly. At the present, this mystery is in what we might call its intermediate stage, i.e., between the initial stage and the final beatitude in which Christ and all the redeemed members of his body will share together the same kind of bodily life which he now has.

Starting with the letters of St. Paul, the Church has used the image of the body to describe Christ's relationship to the members of his Church. Christ is the head, the members of the Church form his body, which lives by him and under his direction. The Church serves Christ much as the human body does the human spirit: it manifests the invisible Christ externally, locates him in a given context of space and time, and is the instrument by which he acts on the lives of men. The term "mystical body" as applied to this mystery, indicates that the word "body" is not to be understood in exactly the same sense as an ordinary body in which the parts have no separate identity, proper only to themselves. On the other hand, "body" is not to be taken simply in a metaphorical sense, as in any ordinary societal grouping of men. The meaning of "body" in the mystical body lies somewhere between. In the Church, individuals retain their identity, and yet there is a truly vital principle that unites them in one life.

This presence of Christ to the members of his Church is not a static presence. Rather, it is a *dynamic* presence, grounded in his activity in their midst. He is actively present to them, and present to them precisely so that he can be actively present to the rest of mankind. In this manner he carries on the work of redemption he began in his public life and achieved essentially in his death and resurrection. There are not two redeeming actions of Christ, one consisting of death and resurrection and the other taking place now in the Church. There is but the one redeeming act of Christ, starting at the last supper and continuing unbroken up to the present moment and unto the end of time. From the fact that Christ exists now risen and dynamically present to the Church, we can come to some understanding of Christ's present human consciousness. When we inquire into his present state of awareness and into the basic decision which flows from his human act of love, we find that this inner attitude is the very one that must lie at the center of all genuine sacrifice.

First of all, Christ in his present state can acknowledge, even more fully than during his historical existence, his creaturely status as man and his relationship as man to his heavenly Father. He can still continue to accept his historical vocation—to witness to truth and wisdom even at the expense of persecution and death. Or to put it in other terms, Christ in his present state of consciousness is still fundamentally marked by that spirit of self-oblation which characterized his life on earth. It is the same conscious oblation to which he gave solemn expression at the last supper and which continued through death into resurrection.

CHRIST AS VICTIM

Oblation touches on Christ's role as a victim, because his sacrificial attitude as man involved the acceptance of victimhood. There is a common misapprehension that victimhood is essentially something passive, that it is merely a state of having something done to one. But victimhood goes much deeper than this. A person who is truly a victim recognizes that what is done to him is directed to the creature in him. Man's very being is given to him, and his activity is dependent upon the divine activity cooperating with him. He lives in a world filled with forces to which he is subject. He can control them to a limited extent, but they will, in large measure, always master him. In such a situation, man can rebel and attempt to establish a false independence, although it is the part of honesty and maturity to accept the givenness of human experience and to work with it rather than against it.

We find this illustrated in the public life of Christ, beginning with his baptism, continuing through the following three years and terminating in his death and resurrection. There was never the slightest trace of any reluctance on Christ's part to face his own actual life-situation. In being baptized, he gave public witness to his acceptance of the role of Servant Messiah. Each day of Christ's public life represents a reiteration and intensification of this baptismal promise. The final statement of his acceptance of victimhood begins at the last supper when he solemnly and liturgically sets himself aside for fulfillment of the role of suffering Servant. Thus he acknowledges perfectly his creatureliness as man, his willing acceptance of relationship to his Father, and his confidence in that Father's providential care for him in his human condition. Christ's acceptance of victimhood is essentially an acceptance of the fact that he is completely and thoroughly a man.

Though Christ had accepted his human situation throughout the whole of his life, still the last supper marks the beginning of a new stage in the redemption. In the public setting of a Passover feast, reminiscent of the covenant origins of the people of Israel, Christ solemnly and sacrificially expresses his acceptance of the task his Father had given him to do. Christ's actions at the last supper are meaningless if they do not proceed from this inner sacrificial attitude. The personal and human efficacy of Christ's action came not simply through the externals of this scene, but from Christ's inner consciousness and love and decisiveness. What made this a profoundly human act was the depth of his insight, the generosity of his love, the wisdom which guided him at this moment, and the thorough and complete decisiveness with which he committed himself to the task which he was then undertaking. *This inner decisiveness, flowing from love, was the "bridge" that Christ established between mankind and the Father*. The point of contact between man and God can come only in the consciousness and love of the human person. In the case of Christ, the human who recognizes the Father's providential guidance of human life is himself a divine person become man.

The last supper does not stand by itself, discrete and separate from what follows. Rather, it marks the first stage of that single event which continues in the death and resurrection of Christ. What unites these successive actions into one event is Christ's one inner attitude, his free offering of himself to his Father for men. This one inner attitude is translated into external expression symbolically at the supper and nonsymbolically in the actual suffering and death. There is only one action of Christ, that of self-oblation. The conscious attitude of Christ, which he maintains throughout the supper, passion and at the moment of death, is the oblatory act which marks his passage out of this life into risen life. Consequently, the three stages—last supper, cross and resurrection—form one integral redeeming action of Christ. Together they constitute a single movement, from limited bodily existence into that fuller risen life in which he will be able to share himself with the whole of the human race. The inner and truly effective force in this entire action is Christ's loving gift of himself to the Father and to men.

If it is true that one inner attitude of Christ, that of offering himself sacrificially for the redemption of man, continues unbroken from the supper, through the cross and into the resurrection, then we must conclude that Christ has the same attitude today. In his understanding of himself and in his attitude toward his Father, Christ has not changed in any way since the first moment of the resurrection. *The risen Christ today is the mystery of the resurrection.* As he presently lives and works in the Church, Christ still offers sacrifice for us. He still accepts willingly the fact that he had to die in order to give himself to men. He still accepts the Father's mandate that he give himself to men. The very choice of bread as part of the Eucharistic symbolism indicates Christ's inner desire to share with man the very same life which is his. In short, Christ now still lives in his risen state, actively present to his Church, continuing that sacrificial attitude which is the core of his redemptive activity. In his Church, Christ continues to offer sacrifice to the Father.

EXPRESSED THROUGH THE CHURCH

Sacrifice, however, is more than an internal acknowledgment of God. It is a sensible, symbolic action whose purpose is to give external manifestation of this attitude of the human mind and heart. Even though he still possessed the attitude of sacrifice, Christ would not really be offering sacrifice in this world were he doing nothing more than abiding in invisible fashion in his Church. For there to be continuing sacrifice in a true and full sense, Christ's inner attitude must find sensible expression in the context of human living. Such expression comes through his Church which, as his body, expresses him externally. Through this body he communicates to each succeeding age of humanity his continuing sacrificial acceptance of the role his Father gave him.

However, the sacraments give clearer expression to Christ's inner attitude. Particularly in the Eucharistic action of the Mass, Christ externalizes his own sacrificial attitude through the community's actions and words. He expresses his continuing acceptance of the fact that he had to undergo death; he manifests his desire to fulfill his Father's wish that he give himself as the source of life for men. This is proclaimed by the actions of the Mass performed by the Christian community. It is not accidental that the symbols used at Mass are fundamentally the same symbols as those used at the last supper. At the supper, the meal with its transformation of bread and wine signified Christ's intent to accept the death which still lay before him. In the Mass today, Christ through his Church uses these same symbols to say that he still accepts with full willingness his passage through death into risen life. At the heart of the action of the Mass, therefore, Christ stands with his human consciousness and love and decision still focused on accepting his human role as the suffering Messiah. If the Mass has efficacy as a redeeming sacrifice, it is not essentially because of the external ritual, but because of the underlying attitude of Christ which the ritual expresses. Christ's human love and knowledge is the redeeming force at the heart of human history. Through it men are transformed and made capable of achieving their destiny.

Christ's role in the redemption of man is a *vicarious role*: in suffering, dying and rising, Christ acts on behalf of the human race and not simply as an individual man. He does this representatively, because the Father has placed him in the unique position of being both head of the mystical body and head of mankind in this new life which is grace.

However, it would be a mistake to understand Christ's role as detached vicariousness, as if he acted on our behalf only because delegated to do so by his Father. Christ also acts on our behalf because of his profound identification with us. In the mystery of the incarnation he truly becomes one of the human race, and he is endowed with a special grace-life so that he can perfect mankind. Christ functions as no one else possibly could. We might call him a "corporate personality." He catches up into himself the role, the destiny and the being which mankind has in the supernatural order. He comes as the Son with whom all other men are to be identified and so attain sonship. He comes as the firstborn from the dead, so that all other men may share this new kind of life. Christ can represent the human race because he is our Lord and the source of the life we have through him from God the Father.

It is this unique kind of vicarious role, based upon the profound identification that he has with us, that explains how Christ in the Eucharist can sacrifice in and through us, and for the sake of all of us. Christ as the head of his mystical body actually can act in our behalf, giving us a share in what he himself does. Christ is the one priest who alone offers worthy sacrifice to the Father. Yet, because his members are identified with him in a bond of love, he shares with them his own unique priesthood. They become the ministers of his priestly action in the continuing life of the Church.

Mass as Anamnesis

Since Christ continues to act in his Church, offering sacrifice through those who are its members, "commemoration" or *anamnesis* gains a new meaning in the Christian context. Even in the Old Testament, salvation events were recalled in the liturgical ceremony of the various feasts, particularly the Passover. As these feasts were celebrated year after year, the great happenings of the Old Testament were brought to the attention of the people. This made it possible for each generation to make the significance of those events meaningful for themselves. Through the liturgy they could commit themselves to Yahweh. All these events were part of Christ's human experience as he participated in the great liturgical actions of his people during the years when he lived as a Jew on this earth. In the last supper he recapitulated these actions. He gave them an entirely new depth of meaning by establishing the Eucharist as the fulfillment of the Old Testament's significance.

If this recapitulation applied to the liturgical ceremonies of the Old Testament people, it applied even more immediately to the actions Jesus performed in his public life. The things that happen to any human being pass into his memory and condition his response to any later experience he undergoes. Nothing that happens to us in the course of our life is totally past, because it leaves a certain residue in our personality, in our powers of personal response to life. The same was true of Christ. The things he did, particularly those especially significant acts which we call his miracles and scripture calls his "signs," form part of the integrated human experience Christ possessed as he began the solemn redemptive action at the last supper. The man Jesus, who experienced the last supper, passion, death and resurrection, was a man in whose memory resided all those previous experiences. Moreover, the earlier actions of his public life were part of a carefully designed pedagogical sequence. By them he prepared his disciples, and those who would succeed them in the Church, for a deeper understanding of the mystery of the redemption. The supper expresses in a totally integrated way what the acts of Christ's public life said partially. It was the recollection of all the events of the Old Testament and of all the events of Christ's public life. The Mass does the same thing, because the risen Christ who acts in the Mass is the Christ who acted two thousand years ago.

Even more pertinently, the Eucharist is the anamnesis of that event which began at the last supper and continued through the death and resurrection. Here we encounter something entirely new. This is not "recollection" in the sense that a present action now recalls to our minds some previous act, past and completed, and makes this past action present to us only by way of representation and memorial. The Eucharist is the anamnesis of the redeeming action of Christ in the mysterious sense that it is *that action continuing.* The event of the supper and death and resurrection of Christ has not yet ended. Christ is present to his Church to continue this very same act. This is the act he expresses externally through the words and gestures of his Church in the ceremonies of the Mass.

The Eucharist is recollection, commemoration, in a way that is absolutely unique. It is commemoration by way of identification. The Eucharist is the continuing redeeming action of Christ. There are not two redemptive acts: one which occurred two thousand years ago in the Cenacle and on Calvary, and another that takes place now in the Christian Eucharist. The one redeeming act, totally present in what Christ himself did at the very beginning, continues to find expression through the lives and activity of today's Christians as they share in the act of Eucharistic sacrifice.

THE MASS AS THE CHURCH'S SACRIFICE

We would fail to appreciate the total reality of the sacrifice of the Mass were we to think that the Church functions as the extension of Christ in such a way as to make present only Christ's sacrificial act. *The fact is that the Eucharist is the conjoined sacrifice of both Christ and his Church*. While the Church does function as Christ's body in offering sacrifice for him, she still has her own sacrificial action of offering. The Christian community really offers the sacrifice of itself and of Christ; the liturgy of the canon of the Mass makes this clear. The Church can offer Christ and his sacrifice to the Father because Christ belongs to the Church as her head. Because of the identity in love between the Church and Christ who is her bridegroom, she can truly offer Christ to the Father. At the same time, the Church offers herself; the community of faith offers itself in its totality to the Father, through Christ and in union with him as he offers the Church, his bride, to the Father.

In describing this conjoined sacrifice, we must be careful not to think of the situation as though two sacrificial actions were going on concomitantly in the Mass—Christ offering sacrifice and the Church offering sacrifice. There is only one sacrifice, Christ's sacrifice, but the Church is granted a *share* in this one redemptive sacrificial action. It is a genuine share in Christ's sacrifice; it is not some kind of pretense. The Church has a genuinely priestly function, even though it is entirely derived from Christ's priesthood. Therefore, if we want to speak accurately, we must say that the Mass did not exist until Pentecost, when the Church began to exist. Strictly speaking, the last supper was not the first Mass. The supper is what is continued by way of commemoration in the Mass. In the Mass, Christ in his Church continues his original sacrifice and the Church, sharing now in this sacrifice, offers herself and Christ to the Father.

Obviously, we must not say that the Church supplies something that was lacking in the sacrificial act of Christ. This error can be avoided if we realize that what the Church does in the Eucharist she does completely and totally by the power of Christ. The very ability of the Christian community to offer itself effectively is based upon its sharing in the one effective priesthood of Christ. If the Church is able to perform the mediatorial act of redemptive sacrifice, it is because Christ imparts to her the very priesthood he himself exercises. There is only one Christian sacrifice, that of Christ; in the mystery of the Eucharist Christ enables his followers to share in this unique action.

In the Church's act of sacrifice, as in Christ's own continuing act, the intent of the Church is the heart of the action. External gestures and words of liturgical ceremony find their effectiveness and meaning only as a translation and expression of the Church's intent to offer itself in union with Christ to the Father. In expressing this intent, the Church shares Christ's own mediatorial role. Moreover, the Church's intent derives its intrinsic reality, its very existence, from Christ's own redemptive intent. Christ's internal attitude of sacrifice is the core of the redemptive act. Christ's sacrifice possesses salvific power because it issues from that special grace of headship which Christ has as God-man. The Church in its members is given a share in this grace-life by Christ. The members of the Christian community, because they are united to Christ, can place that supernatural intent that is at the heart of the Church's action in the Mass. Whatever Christians do in the Mass, whether from the point of view of priesthood or of grace, they do in complete dependence upon Christ from whom they derive all their authority and all their intrinsic power.

In offering the sacrifice of the Eucharist, the Church continues both to place the covenant action for Christ and to enter more deeply into this covenant herself. Like the Israelites, though in much deeper fashion, the Christians of each successive generation who celebrate Christ's Passover are given the opportunity to enter into the covenant commitment of the new people of God. This means that the Mass is our continuing acceptance of faith in the death and resurrection of Christ, for this is his Passover. In celebrating the Eucharist the Church asserts continuously and with deepening understanding its acceptance of this redeeming death and resurrection. It does this by the very action that makes Christ present, symbolically expressing his own acceptance of death and resurrection.

Again, the action of the Mass is the Church's commitment to the fatherhood of God the Father. In and through Christ, who is the Son, the Church professes her belief that God the Father is truly a Father. She pledges herself to acknowledge no other divinity. This fulfills the role of the Old Testament covenant people, for the obligation assumed by the Israelites as partner in the covenant was the duty of acknowledging only Yahweh as true God. The Church by accepting sonship in and through Christ is acknowledging the Father as true God. He alone is the ultimate explanation of reality.

Finally, the Mass is a continuing covenant action because the Church, by sharing Eucharistically the body of Christ, is performing what is essentially a covenant act. Christ in the very act of giving himself as food to men is the new covenant. In accepting the body and blood of Christ in an act of communing with him, the Christian people enter in most unique fashion into the new covenant.

The Church's communion with Christ touches upon an aspect of sacrifice that recurs consistently throughout the history of ritual. All ancient peoples, Israel included, thought of sacrifice as a means of establishing contact with their divinity, of achieving union with the god who could guarantee their life. In the Eucharist, the Church enters into profound union with Christ and through him with the Father. We can distinguish at least three important aspects of this manifold union.

Union with Christ in his unique priesthood. This is a sharing of a mediatorial role in human history, a sharing of societal power whereby the Church can officially speak the redemptive word of the Mass. It is a kind of union that involves active cooperation: the Church and Christ form one conjoined agent in the sacrificial continuation of the redemptive act.

Union in supernatural life. This union is effected through the sacramental symbolism of the Eucharistic species, i.e., the external appearance of bread and wine. The symbolism indicates that Christ's intent in the Mass is to share with his friends the very life he himself possesses. In receiving transformed bread and wine, the Christian community deliberately accepts this offer of union with Christ. Christ ratifies the offer by bringing the community ever more fully into that life which unites them to himself and to one another.

Union in faith and charity. This takes place because the community accepts Christ as its bridegroom, as the object of its love, as its redeemer and Lord. Union in faith and charity is most important because it is at this level that one's priesthood and grace-life become a conscious experience.

In these three ways, then, the Eucharistic situation achieves union between head and members, between Christ and his followers. This union of Christians with Christ is the very source of the union within the community itself. It is because we share one priesthood, because we are united in faith, because we share a common love for Christ, because we share one common life of grace that the members of the Church are knit together into a profound familial unity. This oneness of the Christian community is symbolized and effected by the Eucharist itself. The unity of the Church grows in intensity because of what occurs in the Eucharist; at the same time the Eucharistic action is the expression of the unity of the Church's life. The Church is a community that lives the Mass and lives from the Mass.

CONCLUSION

We can summarize this chapter by stating that the action of the Mass in its externals, and even more so in the underlying reality which these externals express, is a genuine sacrifice. It is the sacrifice of Christ expressed in and through the members of his Church; it is the sacrifice of the Church herself. This sacrificial action both continues and fulfills the sacrificial ceremonies of Old Testament times; but, more important, it continues the redeeming act of Christ initiated in the last supper. Because of the continuing presence of the risen Christ in his Church, the action of the Mass is not separated from the redemptive achievement of the last supper, cross and resurrection. It is the historical continuation of this very same redeeming action. In the Mass, then, this sacrifice, redemptive of the human race, continues throughout history. Christ living in the midst of the Church offers himself to the Father as redemption for men. Moreover, Christ allows those who are members of the faith-community to share in this action by offering him and themselves as a victim for the salvation of the world.

BIBLIOGRAPHY FOR CHAPTER 8

GENERAL WORKS ON THE THEOLOGY OF THE EUCHARIST

C. Davis, *Liturgy and Doctrine,* New York, Sheed and Ward, 1960. A small volume, but one which gives a very good introduction to the theological understanding of the Mass.

The Eucharist and the New Testament, Baltimore, Helicon, 1964. Valuable collection of essays on the Eucharist by some of the Church's leading New Testament scholars.

C. Vagaggini, *Theological Dimensions of the Liturgy,* Collegeville, Liturgical Press, 1957. This is one of the pioneering books. In some aspects it is slightly out of date, but it still contains a wealth of information and insights.

WORKS ON THE EUCHARIST AS SACRIFICE

O. Casel, *The Mystery of Christian Worship,* Westminster, Newman, 1962. One of the most influential books in the reorientation of theological thought about the Mass, a classic. The English translation is from the revised German edition.

B. Cooke, "Synoptic Presentation of the Eucharist as Covenant Sacrifice," *Theological Studies* 21 (1960), pp. 1-44. More extended treatment of some of the points treated in this chapter.

J. Jungmann, "Meaning of the Mass: The Mass and the Church," pp. 280-291 in Caponigri, *Modern Catholic Thinkers.* Penetrating essay on the role of the Church in the sacrificial action of the Eucharist.

E. Masure, *The Christian Sacrifice,* New York, Kenedy, 1946. The author is one of the leading theologians in the discussions about the nature of the Eucharist as sacrifice; and this is probably his most basic work. His views are somewhat outdated by more recent study, especially in the biblical background of sacrifice.

A. Vonier, *A Key to the Doctrine of the Eucharist,* Westminster, Newman, 1946. Still one of the most stimulating books on the meaning of the Eucharist as sacrifice of Christ and of the Church.

9

THE EUCHARIST AS WORD

•

WORD IN HISTORY AND SYMBOL

•

WORD AND LITURGY

CONTEMPORARY SIGNIFICANCE

Probably no aspect of the Eucharist is as ecumenically important as the Eucharist as "word." In the centuries since the Protestant Reformation it has been quite common to oppose Catholicism and Protestantism as, respectively, sacramental Christianity and evangelical Christianity (i.e., with the accent on the "word of God"). Our deepening understanding of the Mass indicates that it is impossible to establish this dichotomy between the evangelical and the sacramental. The greatest of the sacraments, the Eucharist, is eminently liturgy of the word.

The Eucharist as word can and ought to integrate our entire understanding of Christianity. It highlights the relation between scripture and sacrament. It reminds us of the continuity of God's action in history up to the present moment. It helps us understand more precisely how God operates to transform the conscious life of man. It indicates the orientations that should govern any valid approach to the Christian apostolate.

ROLE OF "WORD" IN OLD TESTAMENT HISTORY

Today we commonly refer to the process of Old Testament revelation as "sacred history" or "salvation history." We are rapidly discovering how the divine revelation given to man was inseparably linked with the series of saving actions constituting Old Testament history. Because his workings with the Israelites saved them from servitude in Egypt, from the power of their military enemies, Yahweh was seen to be a savior God. Because he formed a covenant with Israel binding the people together and setting them apart as sacred and consecrated to himself, Yahweh was manifestly an interested God. The great events marking the advances or the turning points in the life of the people all witness to the God who made Israel his special concern.

When we consider the workings of God in the Old Testament, we often overlook the function of word in this whole process. There is a most interesting Old Testament theology of the word of God. It is grounded on the role which words play in the developing faith-life of Israel. It is not enough that God lead his people out of Egypt, that he bring them to the land of Canaan, that he guide them throughout their rather turbulent history. Many other peoples besides the Israelites witnessed these happenings. But they did not see them as salvation history. The reason why the Israelites saw these events as salvific was that God sent them certain teachers, beginning with Moses, who interpreted the external occurrences for what they were: interventions of a loving God on Israel's behalf. Without this explanatory word, the great deeds of Yahweh could not have been understood as faith-events.

As the faith and understanding of the Israelites grew deeper and more sophisticated, they began to see that the explanatory words of the great charismatic leaders, especially the prophets, were more than mere explanation. The word of God as it came to the people through the special mediators God sent into their midst was a word that bore power. It was a word that effected in mysterious fashion the very thing of which it spoke. We see an instance of this in the scene of Jeremiah's vocation to the prophetic office. God says to him: "I have put my words in your mouth . . . to destroy and to overthrow, to build and to plant" (Jer 1:9-10).

First and perhaps most influential of these instances of word was the word of the Law. Spoken at the very inception of the people's existence, and gradually amplified over the centuries, the Law was one of the great influences that shaped Israel's life. Seen as the expression of Yahweh's will regarding this people whom he had chosen as his own, the Law directed their private and public behavior, the development of their social and political patterns, the formulation of their cultic ceremonial. It delineated their responsibilities, and it safeguarded the treasured rights of the individual Israelite.

In its own way, the word of liturgy was also a most influential force in the developing life and culture of the people. Recent scholarship has made us aware of the way in which liturgy influenced even the growth of the Law. It was in the great cultic celebrations, the great annual feasts at Israel's shrines, that the people gathered to commemorate the events that formed them into a people and gave them their unique identity. In these festive situations, the ceremonial reenactment of Passover and covenant was explained to the assembled people, the Law was clarified and detailed for them and the great traditions of the people were thus passed down in gradually expanding form from generation to generation. Though they were not the only places where the people preserved and developed the revelation given Israel by Yahweh, the shrine and eventually the Jerusalem temple were very important. The words of the shrine celebrations, the words of liturgy, contained in oral form the sacred traditions of Israel.

Gradually, these traditions of Law and sacred happening, as well as the traditions of prophetic oracle, were written down and slowly formed into the collection of sacred writings that we call the Old Testament. We are familiar with the idea that scripture is the word of the Law and the word of the prophets; but we do not often advert to the fact that much of this originated historically as the word of the priest in liturgy.

As this written form of the word of God came into being, it interpreted not just the historical events of Israel's life; it also interpreted the recurrent liturgical feasts that commemorated (and to some extent made present to each generation) these historical happenings. In this way, the word of scripture became an integral part of the liturgical word itself. Passages of the written word, proclaimed and explained in the liturgical celebration, formed an intrinsic part of the significance of the festive ceremony. Actually, the sacred writings functioned as the formal element in the liturgical sign, i.e., they explained the meaning of the sacred actions performed in the shrine ceremony.

At the same time, the action of liturgy prevented the traditions of Israel from being statically enshrined in a book. What the scripture spoke of, the liturgy enacted. In each shrine situation, the liturgical ceremony tended to make pertinent to a given historical period and a given group of Israelites the contemporary meaning of the written word of God. In the developing faith life of the Old Testament people, scripture and liturgy interacted continually to preserve and clarify the people's recollections of the revelation God had entrusted to them.

ROLE OF "WORD" IN NEW TESTAMENT TIMES

The interaction of word and liturgy in the life of the primitive Christian community was very similar. When the early Christians gathered for worship, especially for the Eucharistic "breaking of the bread," it was very natural for them to recall and discuss the things Jesus had said and done in their midst. In instructing converts during these assemblies, or more deeply forming the faith of the community as a whole, the apostles would give their witness to the event of Christ and its significance. This apostolic catechesis formed a more or less intrinsic part of the Eucharistic action, because the very mystery the apostles were attempting to clarify was the Eucharistic action the Christians were celebrating together.

Out of such sacramental assemblies—and we can only imperfectly reconstruct from New Testament writings the procedure of these liturgical gatherings—

there gradually emerged a body of writing that subsequently became our New Testament. As far as we can gather, and allowing of course for the action of the Holy Spirit in the process of inspiration, the reason for the writing down of the New Testament books was to preserve for posterity the apostles' witness and explanation. In this way, the apostolic explanation of sacramental action was preserved for all ages of the Church.

To quite an extent, then, the earliest Christian *sacramental practice was the cradle of New Testament literature*. Christian faith in Christ, Christian tradition, was enacted and expressed orally in sacrament before it was written down in scripture. This parallels what happened in Old Testament times; but there was a radical difference between the two situations. There had been a certain presence of Yahweh's word of power in Old Testament prophecy, liturgy and scripture; in the New Testament sacramental situation, there is present that Person who is the Word of God, Christ himself.

As the early Christians gathered together for the "breaking of the bread" (and as is true today), the risen Christ himself was in their midst. During his visible life on earth, his words and deeds had been uniquely effective in combating evil in all its forms; his word had been a word of power as he healed the sick and expelled demons. After the resurrection, as he lived on in the Christian community, his word was not less powerful; indeed, as the risen Lord, he now spoke in the fullness of his power. Hence, his words, which were spoken for him by the apostles and by the community as a whole, were effective words. Because of his continuous presence to the community, its liturgical gestures and words were now sacramental in the full sense: they bore the power of Christ's own speaking; they overcame evil; they brought Christ's own life to mankind.

Our Eucharistic celebration today is the continuation of this situation. It is still word of Christ and word of the Christian community. But before proceeding with a more detailed examination of the way in which the Mass is word, it might be worthwhile to review some considerations about the functioning of word, gesture and symbol in human life.

WORD, GESTURE, SYMBOL, SACRAMENT

Ancient man was intrigued by the reality of words. At times he tended to look on them as a magical force, especially when they were ritual words or the words of some ruler. In both cases, words were looked upon as filled with meaning and power. In our own day, faced with a revolution in communications and with the problem of trying to find words to fit our new insights into man and the world, we are once more becoming aware of the role of words. This is an age-old problem of religion, which has always faced the question of how to find words to explain and communicate the reality of divinity. It is particularly acute in the context of religions which profess belief in a God who defies definition.

Words are the expression of the person who speaks them, or at least they are meant to be such. If they fail to convey the inner consciousness of a person we do not take them seriously, e.g., when a demented person rambles on unintelligibly. When someone deliberately speaks words inconsistent with his inner awareness, we see this as contrary to the way things ought to be; this is the evil of lying. The very fact that we see a lie as evil indicates that we implicitly recognize that a man's words should convey himself. *The word is a bearer of the person.*

Experience also teaches us that the spoken word is not the only, nor necessarily the most effective, human word. At times, when no words seem sufficient to convey what we have to say, we use a significant gesture, like a shrug of the shoulders or a smile. These gestures—and we employ a wide range of them in our ordinary dealings with people—are in constant use. We can see from certain art forms, like the ballet, how powerful a bearer of meaning the human gesture can be. Very often, however, because gestures are rich in significance and we wish to clarify what is meant by a particular bodily movement, we combine spoken words with gesture. This gives to the spoken word the added richness of gesture, and to gesture the added clarity of the spoken word.

Because it is the means of personal communication between men, the word is an *instrument of self-giving.* One human who wishes to make friends with another begins the process of giving himself by speaking. As the friendship deepens, the verbal communication increases and the words spoken (by speech or gesture) become increasingly meaningful. To someone who is nothing more than a chance acquaintance we speak very little of ourselves; to a dear friend our words can often carry a great deal of our own self-awareness.

Because words carry the person, because they are such a privileged means of giving the self to another, words are our instrument for *achieving union* with others. Without language of some kind, we would remain completely isolated from one another, unable to enter into any kind of relationship. Human community is based upon communication; words make society possible. It is quite obvious that words cannot achieve this unification of men in society unless they be truly meaningful words. People must be willing to speak themselves in their words, if there is to be that sharing of ideas and objectives which lies at the heart of any society.

In every culture or language there are certain gestures, certain words that are especially rich in meaning. Some of these, like the gesture of eating a meal with a friend, seem rooted in the very nature of things and have a universal significance. Others, like signaling for a right turn when driving a car, are arrived at by common agreement and convention. Particularly significant words or gestures, which we call symbolic, acquire the added meaning they have by being related to various elements in our human experience. The word "water" as used in a poem can be quite symbolic, because it can be related to our experience of growing plants, or quenching our thirst, or washing, or drowning, and so on.

Religious ritual has always made wide use of these symbolic gestures and symbolic words. Of its very nature, liturgy is meant to be more than a purely informational kind of word. It is meant to be a word that conveys the self-giving of the worshipper. Men hope that it is a word that somehow bears the power of some good to them. Because it deals with the deepest elements of human consciousness, because it attempts to bring man into meaningful contact with the mysterious and ineffable reality of the divine, ritual always tends to be highly symbolic. In the cultural history of mankind, no use of gesture or language is more consistently and more deeply symbolic than that of liturgy.

What is true of all religious ceremonial is even truer of the sacrificial ritual of the Old Testament and the Eucharistic liturgy of the Church. The people of Israel formed a liturgy out of gesture and word, out of covenant meal and psalm. They drew from all the rich natural significance of water and light and growing things; but they had in their ritual a dimension of meaning unique among ancient religions, and still characteristic only of Jewish and Christian ritual. They are unique in their emphasis on the historical aspect of ritual. The religious ceremonies of both Old and New Testament point to actual historical happenings (e.g., the Exodus or the last supper). Such ceremonies are basically acts of commemoration. Through them the revealed significance of the key events of sacred history is retained and passed on from one generation to the next; the liturgical action communicates this significance to each generation by reenacting it.

Christian sacrament, however, goes a step further. It not only speaks the significance of the past historical event; it makes that event in some way present because it speaks the event effectively. To a limited extent this was true of Old Testament ritual; the annual commemoration of the great events of the Exodus did make the reality of the covenant a continuing event in the people's life. *But in the Christian sacraments, the very heart of the redeeming event, Christ's inner attitude of accepting death and new life for the sake of men, is actually still present.* It is Christ who performs the sacraments, in and through the action of the Christian community which is his body. Sacraments not only speak about Christ's redeeming act, not only contain the significance of that redeeming act, but actually make that event present by speaking it effectively. This is part of what we mean by saying that *sacraments cause what they signify.*

THE "WORD" OF THE EUCHARIST

SPEAKERS OF THE EUCHARISTIC WORD

RITUAL SIGNIFICANCE

In the Christian Eucharist as it is celebrated today, Christ and his Church speak an effective word in the latest stage of sacred history. This central action of Christian liturgy is a highly complex combination of ritual gesture and word. In this complexity, the spoken words of the ceremony (including the homily) provide the final specifying element; they define most clearly what the action signifies. Most prominent in the spoken words of the Mass are the passages drawn from scripture. In a special way, they serve throughout the liturgical year to highlight the various meanings of the Mass. If we reflect that many of these scripture passages originated as the apostolic sacramental catechesis it becomes clear that our understanding of the action of the Mass is still being guided by the teaching of the apostles. Thus the Mass is the word of God the Father, the word of Christ, the word of the Church in its entire historical reality, the word of the present Christian community.

THE WORD OF GOD THE FATHER

The very fact that Christ is present in the action of the Mass, offering the redeeming sacrifice, means that the Father is speaking to men in this action. It is the Father who sends Christ to do this. Not only does the Father send his Son; he sends him precisely in the speaking role, for this divine Son is his very Word. As the letter to the Hebrews tells us: "In many and various ways God spoke of old to our fathers by the prophets; but in these last days he has spoken to us by a Son" (Heb 1:1-2). God the Father tells us how he is Father by making his Son manifest to us.

This action of the Father speaking to us in his Son, his own infinite Word, is the latest stage in that process of continuing sacred history. The word of Old Testament prophet and liturgy and sacred writing, even the human words of Jesus in his own life on this earth, are continued and fulfilled in this on-going word of the Father in the Eucharistic liturgy. It helps to understand the fact that the Mass is the word of the Father if we ponder the saying of Christ at the last supper: "He who has seen me has seen the Father" (Jn 14:9). Whatever Christ speaks to us in the Eucharist the Father also speaks, for Christ is literally the Word of the Father.

From all eternity the Father has spoken his divine Word in the incomprehensible mystery of the procession of the Son. But with the inception of creation, and in a special way with the supernatural vocation of man, the Father speaks his Word creatively: The Father's giving of his entire being and life to this Son whom he speaks, extends somehow to the men whom he also makes his sons. His eternal Son, his Word, is sent into the world to speak creatively to men, transforming them by his power as Word into sons of the Father. The word of the Father in the Eucharist is, then, the creative Word; it is the intrinsically effective Word; it is the life-giving Word; for the Father is speaking his Son in the mystery of the Son's life-giving and redemptive incarnation. This is the most radical reason why these actions we call sacraments, and in a special way the Eucharist, cause what they signify.

No more meaningful catechesis of the Eucharist as word of the Father has ever been written than that contained in the sixth chapter of St. John's gospel. As John describes it, the discourse of Jesus on the bread of life took place in the synagogue of Capharnaum on the day following the miraculous multiplication of the loaves. Jesus reproved the people because they had not seen the deeper significance of this miracle of the loaves, and he pointed out the meaningful link between his action and the giving of the manna in the desert. He also pointed out the great difference between the manna and the bread that he would give: those who ate the manna were not kept from eventual death; he who eats the new bread from heaven will live forever (Jn 6:48-51).

To grasp the full meaning of the parallel between manna and the bread of life, we must recall how one element of revelation developed in the Old Testament. The giving of manna to the people in their desert sojourn showed that Yahweh provided for their life, even if this required some special intervention. The manna was the sign of this life-giving concern of God. When the people settled in the promised land and manna was no longer necessary, the prophets had to help the Israelites see that the life-giving rain that watered the earth and brought forth the wheat was also a sign of the providential concern of Yahweh. Then, as the people's insight deepened and they could be led to a more profound understanding of life, the prophets were inspired to reveal that the word of God—in Law, in liturgy, in prophetic utterance—is the source of life. Perhaps the Old Testament passage that most comprehensively reflects this theology of the word is contained in the book of Isaiah:

> For as the rain and the snow come down from heaven, and return not thither but water the earth, making it bring forth and sprout, giving seed to the sower and bread to eater, so shall my word be that goes forth from my mouth; it shall not return to me empty, but it shall accomplish that which I purpose, and prosper in the thing for which I sent it (55:10-11).

In the discourse at Capharnaum, Jesus, the Word sent forth from the Father, tells the people that he is the true manna, the true bread from heaven. He is the true source of life given by his Father to men, the source of the unending life that comes with resurrection. And the passage in St. John's gospel goes on to point out that Jesus is bread from heaven in terms of the mystery of the Eucharist, i.e., Jesus gives himself as life-giving food. So that his Eucharistic gift of himself may be seen as source of human life, Christ uses the external sign of bread.

In the Eucharist, the heavenly Father, who gave life to the Israelites through manna and rain and the prophetic word, effectively speaks his life-giving intent by sending his eternal Word to provide life for men through the sacramental sign of bread. The Eucharist is the final stage in this progressive unfolding of the Father's intent to provide men with unending life. It speaks more fully and more effectively than did the Old Testament revelation, because it speaks the Father's own creative Word, Christ.

THE WORD OF THE CHURCH

At the same time that it is the word of God the Father, the Eucharistic action is also the word of the Christian community, the Church. It is the word about Christ, the Father and the Spirit that the Church speaks out of the whole of her historical heritage. It is the word that the present-day Christian community speaks. Not only does the Church in this action speak about Christ who is her Lord, about the Father and the Spirit, but also about her own reality as the body and bride of Christ, as a community of faith and love. Any being or any society most fully expresses its inner reality by performing its proper and distinguishing activity. An apple tree expresses itself as such by producing apples, a man manifests himself as man by communicating with other men. The proper and distinguishing activity of the Church is the action of the Eucharistic sacrifice. In performing this action the Church most fully expresses and manifests the internal reality that is uniquely hers.

The Eucharist is the word of faith. From the earliest days of the Christian community this fact was recognized. It was, above all, in the fellowship of the breaking of bread that the early Christians expressed their belief that Jesus was Messiah and Lord. It was in this context, when they were gathered together in his name, that they were most sharply aware of his risen presence. For Christians of the early centuries, the Eucharist was a very important profession of their faith in Christ. It is interesting, for example, to study the liturgical texts contained in the *Apostolic Tradition* of Hippolytus (written at the beginning of the third century), and to notice how the Eucharistic prayer from which our canon of the Mass developed is in large part a creed. In the Christian tradition, sacrament and faith are inseparable, and the greatest of the sacraments professes Christian faith most fully.

Because it is a word of faith, the Eucharist is a word of commitment. Faith in Christ does not mean mere assent to certain facts about his identity as God and savior. It means an uncompromising acceptance of him as a person. For a Christian to have faith means that he accepts Christ on Christ's own terms, as a savior who achieved his power to give new life by passing through suffering and death for us. Christ offers himself to the Christian in friendship; he offers to transform man by his redeeming love. And so the acceptance of Christ by the Christian means the acceptance of this offer of friendship. It is impossible to have genuine Christian faith without a personal commitment in love to Christ and to all he stands for. In performing the action of the Mass, the Christian community makes public this commitment to its Lord. This is especially signified when the assembled Christians receive the living Christ at the communion of the Mass.

Finally, the Eucharist is a word of witness and revelation. St. Paul spoke of this centuries ago when, in writing to the Corinthian community, he said: "For as often as you eat this bread and drink the cup, you proclaim the Lord's death until he comes" (I Cor 11:26). Because the action of the Mass makes Christ present in his continuing redemptive act of sacrifice, it bears witness to the redemption of mankind by the death and resurrection of Jesus. Through the Eucharistic action the Christian community brings mankind into contact not only with graphic teaching about the risen Christ but also with the reality of Christ in his present living humanity. Since the Christ who is present here is sent from the Father as his Word, the Church is in the Eucharist also witnessing to the Father and revealing him to men. And since the Eucharist is the action that most properly translates into external and visible form the Church's own internal reality, the Eucharist is the most important revelation about the Church itself. Unless we understand the Eucharist, we cannot understand the Church, for the Church is most basically the community which performs the Eucharist.

THE WORD OF CHRIST

Since it is the word of the Church, the Eucharist could not be other than the word of Christ; for the Church is the body of Christ through which he still continues to speak and work in the world of men. Were it not for the fact that Christ so lives in its midst, the Church's word of faith and witness in the Eucharist could not be sacramentally effective, could not be life-giving. The Christian community's word has this power in the Eucharistic context only because the Father's own creative Word is present to the Church as her head. Christ, then, is the one who speaks in the Eucharist, which is his word in the Church—a word of revelation, of consolation, of transformation.

All the truth that Christ had taught by what he said and did during the years of his public life was a preparation for the redemptive event of the last supper, crucifixion and resurrection. This final redeeming action caught up into itself all the "words" that Jesus had spoken during the previous years of his earthly life. This action spoke with a depth of meaning that the Church will never be able to fathom entirely. Moreover, this action continues unceasingly. In its essential elements, as redemptive and as significant, it is still present in the Eucharistic action insofar as this is Christ's own act.

As the continuance of the redemptive act, the Eucharist reveals the fact of man's redemption by Christ. Not only that, it also indicates the way in which redemption is achieved: by Christ's giving men his own risen life, gained by his passage through suffering and death. It reveals the fact that the act of redemption is continued through the life of the Christian community, that Christians share in redeeming as well as in being redeemed. In short, it reveals the entirety of the Christ-mystery, from the sending of the Word by the Father to the fulfillment of the entire mystery in final glory. We could, if space and time permitted, see how the entirety of Christian revelation is contained in the Eucharistic liturgy. The Eucharist makes present to us the fullness of the Father's utterance.

Not only does Christ in the Eucharist speak a word of revelation to the faith of Christians, he also speaks a word of consolation as the basis of our hope. His very presence, of course, is the most basic source of hope, for it is his reality as the risen Lord that promises to the Christian community its own share in the triumph over evil and death. This does not mean merely that his own resurrection proves that risen life is possible. It does this, too. But more is involved. Christ is risen and present in the Eucharist *for men*; he is risen in order to share risen life with men. What is involved in his Eucharistic presence is this personal fidelity in love to those whom he has made his brethren. Christians not only trust the fact of Christ's resurrection; they trust this person who is man and risen for their sake.

Thirdly, Christ speaks a word of transformation. The fact that the most significant moment of the Eucharistic action, the moment of the Consecration, is one of transformation of bread and wine into Christ himself points to the important place transformation plays in the significance of the Eucharist. Actually, many of the miracles of Christ's public life that prepared for the understanding of the last supper (and therefore of the Christian Eucharist) were extraordinary transformations, e.g., the changing of water into wine at Cana. In the Eucharist, through the action that the community is placing as his body, Christ speaks creatively and effectively of transformation. He thereby changes mankind, and especially Christians participating in a given Eucharistic action, by the new life of sanctifying grace and charity.

Love is the most deeply transforming element in human experience. Even though its presence may not be so keenly felt in sensible experience, divine love can be and is meant to be the most transforming of all love. That is why God has been revealing to men over the centuries the reality of his unlimited love for mankind, a love that is utterly gratuitous and creative of life. In the Eucharist this revelation of divine love comes to fullest utterance, for it fulfills two key scriptural statements about Christ's and the Father's love: "God [the Father] so loved the world that he gave his only Son, that whoever believes in him should not perish, but have eternal life" (Jn 3:16), and "Greater love has no man than this, that a man lay down his life for his friends" (Jn 15:13). In the Eucharistic action Christ speaks his love for men by the continuing action of giving himself to them to be the source of their own risen life. Christ speaks this word of love in order to win from his followers the response of love, for he knows that their own response of love is exactly what is needed in them to effect internally their redemption.

We can see, then, how Christ in the Eucharist speaks to man's supernatural life of faith, hope and charity. The Mass provides an unparalleled situation for the development of these powers by which we participate in the divine way of being. Without an awareness of the Eucharist, without sincere participation in it, it is impossible for a Christian to develop adequately the divine life of grace planted in him at his Baptism.

CONTENT OF THE EUCHARISTIC WORD

WHAT THE MASS SAYS

Though we have described the function of the Eucharist as word, it will be profitable to examine in greater detail the message that this action speaks to men of faith. The significance of this central Christian act of sacrament is so various and complex that we can do little more than touch upon the surface of its meaning, even during a lifetime of theological study about the Mass. Yet as Christians we must strive to comprehend what we can of this significance, because only in terms of our understanding of the Eucharist can we obtain an accurate and personal understanding of ourselves, of the Church and of Christ.

In the course of his discussion of the Eucharist in the *Summa Theologiae* (ST 3. 60. 3c), St. Thomas Aquinas indicates that the Mass has a triple reference: it speaks of the past, of the present and of the future. Its significance is commemorative, contemporary and eschatological. This triple division provides an arrangement for our discussion.

THE MASS SPEAKS THE PAST

We have already indicated the way in which the events of Old Testament times as well as the events of Christ's own historical life are recalled in the Eucharistic action. There is no element of the positive supernatural significance of previous sacred history that is not somehow contained in the word that the Eucharist speaks. Moreover, this "gathered-together" significance, forming part of what the Eucharistic action expresses, has its influence on the effect of the Eucharist in men's lives because the Eucharist as sacrament has its effectiveness through its significance.

Actually, what we are dealing with in the Eucharist as commemorative of Old Testament and Christian history is the process we call *tradition*. We can use the word "tradition" to refer to the body of truths revealed by Christ and handed down by the Church through the centuries. Or we can use the word in a more inclusive sense to express the living process by which the Church preserves and transmits these truths. It is in this latter sense that we will use the word here.

The clearest and most noticeable element in this process of transmitting revelation from generation to generation is the official teaching of bishops, popes and ecumenical councils of the Church. Along with this, we can include all the other teaching activities: Catholic schools, catechizing, and so on. But if we study the process of tradition carefully, we begin to see that all the aspects of the Christian community's life—Christian family life, Christian art, Christian influence on culture and society—contribute to the complex process of retaining and clarifying the heritage of faith. In this integrated process of tradition (which, in a sense, is equatable with the living Church) the action of the Eucharist plays a privileged role. It, and it alone, bears the entirety of Christian revelation; for it alone *is* the mystery of the redeeming Christ. Any other speaking about the mystery of Christ must be done in human words. Even though they be the words of a Church council issuing a formal definition of a revealed truth, these words can never express the totality of the Christian mystery. Only in the Mass does the word of the Church speak the entirety of revelation, for the Mass does not speak by words alone, but by an action carried on both by the Church and by Christ himself. Because it plays this unique role in the whole process of tradition, the Mass speaks the centuries-long heritage of the Church's life of faith. In a sense, it is not just the Church of the present day that speaks to us in the Mass; here the Church of all the ages speaks, for in the Mass we hear that all-embracing word that these previous ages also spoke. We can see, then, why the Church is so careful about the preservation of the ritual of the Mass. While this ritual requires modifications in accidentals from time to time (like the liturgical changes now taking place), its essential meanings must be safeguarded, so that it continues to bear with authenticity and integrity the deposit of Christian faith.

The Mass Speaks the Present

As sacramental sign effecting *what* it signifies, the Mass indicates the changes it is bringing about. It speaks the fact that the sacrificial prayer of the assembled community is united with and transformed by Christ's own act of sacrifice. It speaks the transformation of the assembled Christians by the new life of sanctifying grace. It declares the present significance of the Church's existence, and thereby the meaning of the present moment of human history, in terms of the past from which it has come and the future into which it is moving. It speaks the transforming presence of the risen Christ, the fact that he is so present as sent by the Father, and the fact that as the risen Lord he continuously sends his Spirit into the Christian community to unify it in love.

The ritual of the Mass tells us that Christ is present as word. His Eucharistic presence under the appearances of bread and wine is sometimes explained as if it were merely a static being-there. Even worse, it is sometimes understood as if he were bodily contained within the confines of the accidents of bread and wine. Actually, Christ is present to the external appearances of bread and wine (to the "accidents") precisely so that they can be "word" for him. Had he wished merely to make himself present to a certain place or places, he could have chosen any physical element and changed it into himself. He purposely took food and drink so that the external aspects (color, size, taste, etc.) which signify the presence of a life-sustaining reality (food and drink) could point to the Eucharistic presence of Christ himself as life-sustaining reality. By using the external appearances of bread and wine as the signs of his Eucharistic presence, Christ expresses his intention to share his own life with the Christians who receive him in Communion.

Christ bespeaks in the action of the Mass the presence of his own risen body beneath the appearance of food and drink. He effects this by changing the inner reality (the "substance") of the bread and wine into his risen humanity. This is the unique change that the Church has for centuries called transubstantiation— the change of the substance of the bread into the substance of Christ's risen body. Before the transubstantiation in the Mass, the inner reality (the substance) of bread and wine is what sustains the external appearances in existence. These appearances tell us of the presence of the inner reality of bread and wine (which itself is not visible). After the transubstantiation, the risen humanity of Christ is what sustains these external appearances in existence. Consequently, they now tell us of the presence of Christ.

The Eucharistic action also speaks of the presence in the world of Christ's mystical body, his Church. The assembly of any group of Christians for the celebration of the Eucharist clearly witnesses to the existence of the community of Christian faith we call the Church. As the action of the Mass progresses, each step indicates the union between the assembled Christians and Christ. It reaches its climax in the Communion when those present share in Christ's own body and blood. The Mass expresses the fact that Christians participate in Christ's own priesthood, for they are exercising it. It expresses the fact that they participate in the life of grace that Christ is communicating to them, and that they share Christ's own vision of life through faith.

THE MASS SPEAKS THE FUTURE

By the very fact that the *risen* Christ is present in the Eucharistic action, this action speaks of the future toward which men are directed. Christ is already in that state of final fulfillment toward which Christians in this life are striving. Moreover, the unending life of glory that is the hope of mankind will be given to men by the risen Christ, as a share in his own life of resurrection. So, truly, the future of mankind is present in the Mass, and the Mass as word speaks this fact.

However, the Eucharist does not speak about the future in a purely theoretical fashion, telling us in faith something of what the life beyond will be. Because it contains a revelation of the values which a Christian should cherish in his practical living, because it presents an ideal of what human life should become, the Mass provides practical guidelines to direct the Christian community in its task of shaping human society according to the image of Christ. All Christian apostolate is grounded in the Eucharistic action; Christians are meant to take the vision and the hope and the love which the Mass provides and with these transform the world in which they live. In this way, the Eucharist should be in principle that pattern of the future, both for this life and for the life of glory.

BIBLIOGRAPHY FOR CHAPTER 9

SCRIPTURAL AND THEOLOGICAL BACKGROUND

A. Jones, *God's Living Word,* New York, Sheed and Ward, 1961. Scholarly explanation of the biblical development of the notion of "word," written in a clear and interesting fashion.

J. McKenzie, *Myths and Realities: Studies in Biblical Theology,* Milwaukee, Bruce, 1963. Chap. 3 (pp. 37-58), "The Word of God in the Old Testament," is an excellent summation of the growth of this key idea in OT times.

H. Urs von Balthazar, *Word and Revelation,* New York, Herder and Herder, 1964. Reflective theological essay on the role of word in the process of God revealing to men and in the transmission of this revelation.

———— "Christ, the Norm of History," pp. 427-439 in Caponigri, *Modern Catholic Thinkers.* Interesting essay describing the action of the Word in human history.

WORKS ON WORD IN EUCHARIST

Liturgy and the Word of God, Collegeville, Liturgical Press, 1959. A collection of essays by prominent biblical, theological and liturgical scholars, dealing with various aspects of liturgy as word and with the relation between scripture and liturgy.

K. Rahner, *The Church and the Sacraments,* New York, Herder and Herder, 1963. Very good in clarifying the way in which sacraments are external expressions of the Church's basic sacramental nature. This book and E. Schillebeeckx's *Christ the Sacrament of the Encounter with God* together form an excellent introduction to the relation between word and sacrament.

———— "Wort und Eucharistie." Though this essay, published in vol. 4 of Rahner's *Schriften zur Theologie* (Einsiedeln, Benziger) has not yet been translated into English, it is mentioned here because it will most likely appear soon in Helicon's translation of the *Schriften,* two volumes of which have already been printed under the title *Theological Investigations.* This essay is probably the best thing written to date on the relation between word and Eucharist.

─── 10 ───

THE EUCHARIST AS REDEMPTION

•

DELIVERANCE FROM EVIL

•

SALVATION, DEDICATION AND TRANSFORMATION

CHRIST'S CONTINUING REDEMPTION

In the last two chapters we have seen that the Mass is the combined sacrifice of Christ and the Church, based upon the presence in this action of Christ's continuing sacrificial attitude. We have studied the manner in which the Eucharist is the word of the Father, of Christ and of the Church, a word that effects what it says. In the present chapter, we shall investigate in greater detail how the action of the Mass affects men, how it enters into the continuing work of Christ in redeeming the world.

Redemption carries the implication that men need liberation from some influence of evil. We know from revelation that what is at issue is man's enslavement by sin—original sin and personal sin—and his dependence upon the grace of Christ for his freedom and fulfillment. Christ's grace acts not only to transform human beings and make them capable of the personal living that is a share in the life of the Trinity; because of the reality of sin in human existence, Christ's grace must also act to counter the effects of evil in men's lives. Sin is basically disorder; redemption in grace must therefore be a process of reordering men and human society.

PRESENCE OF CHRIST'S REDEMPTIVE ACT

The central tenet of Christian faith is that the redemption of mankind was achieved by the death and resurrection of Jesus. This action of Christ, because of his identity as the Son of God and because of his human possession of the "grace of headship," is absolutely unique as the source and cause of men's liberation from evil. It is accurate to say that once Christ has accomplished his "Passover" to the Father in his death and resurrection, the work of redemption is achieved. Nothing can be added by men, even within the mystery of the Church, to the *intrinsic efficacy* of this redemptive action.

There is a tendency among many Christians to look upon the redemption as something purely of the past, something that *was* done. Yet, it is accurate to say that the redeeming work of Christ still goes on. He is operative in human history, liberating men of each succeeding generation from their particular enslavements. The Church, while it does not add anything intrinsic to Christ's redeeming power, does function as the instrument for this continuing reordering of men.

The resolution of this apparent conflict of beliefs lies in the presence in the Eucharistic action of Christ's own redeeming act. Since the Mass is the continuing sacrificial action of Christ, it is Christ himself who places the Eucharistic act, though he does so through the words and gestures of a given Christian community. Present in this act of Eucharistic sacrifice, Christ still has the attitude of accepting passage through death into risen life. It is this attitude that effects reconciliation between man and God; Christ's own individual human action of accepting the sovereignty of his Father provides a human act of obedience unique in its personal worth. And this human act also functions as a real cause of reestablishing the link between other men and the heavenly Father.

Man is meant to fulfill the finality of his human nature by directing his consciousness and love to the God from whom he comes and to whom he is oriented by his personal being. Once man had rejected the divine offer of love (through original sin), the capacity so to order the self to God no longer belonged to the human race. Man had alienated himself from the divine Persons who alone constitute the destiny of man. Christ's entry into human history in the mystery of the incarnation reintroduces into humanity a power capable of ordering man's thought and love to the Father. This power is Christ's "grace of headship." Capable of reordering all possible men to their supernatural destiny, the grace of Christ was given his humanity in order that *as man* he might function in the redemptive role of reconciling men to the Father.

However, it was not sufficient that this all-powerful grace of Christ reside in him as a potential for redemption. Human potential can only be effective in the lives of others if it is expressed through human actions. Unless, for example, a sculptor were to give outward expression to his artistic insights, the men of his day would in no way be affected by his artistic gift. So also in the case of Christ. His "grace of headship" had to find expression in that supreme act of submission in love and freedom which is the redemptive act, the event that unfolds from the last supper through the cross and into the resurrection, the event of Christ's passover. *This event, then, as the expression of his special redeeming grace, is the source of all human redemption.* Obviously, all redemption of man begins with the Father, who works along with the Son as God and with the Spirit. But all redemption is achieved through the instrumentality of Christ's grace and redeeming act.

Christ's presence in our sacraments, continuing this redeeming action, explains why these sacraments are effective—"ex opere operato." By this we mean that whenever there is a genuine sacramental action, there is always present in it a power effective of sanctification. However, this effectiveness in the lives of men is conditioned by whether or not those men accept sanctification of their own free choice. Unless they freely accept sanctification from Christ and cooperate with his work on their behalf, he will not sanctify them in *automatic* fashion. The power of sanctification that is always present in a sacrament is the power of Christ's own redeeming attitude, expressing his redeeming grace. Christ continues to express his obedience to the Father so that this inner attitude of his may flow effectively into the lives of men and reorder them to his Father.

Continuation of salvation history. Christ's action of redemption fulfilled the entire process by which God had gradually been leading the Old Testament people to salvation. The divine action during the centuries of Israel's life had been one of deliverance, liberating the people from their political, social and personal bondage. It had been one of gradually redirecting their thinking and their affective life. Jesus in his life, death and resurrection brought all this to completion. Yet, the mystery of the Christian Church is this: though redemption is fully realized in the risen Christ himself, it is still in the process of being expressed in the lives of men. The present-day life of the Church is still part of salvation history, a history that will go on to the end of the world.

This continuing process of God working in history for the redemption of the human race finds its focus in the Mass. In this Eucharistic action, Christ's own redeeming attitude, which is the key to this continuing process, comes into contact with our present context of space and time. It is in the Mass that the redeeming Christ is present to contemporary history, continuing to take his part in the developing story of mankind.

Because this Eucharistic action is such a focal element in the continuance of salvation history, it provides for the Christian community its opportunity to contribute to this history. It is not as though the Church were only the "place" in which Christ continued to perform his work of redemption, as though the Mass were merely a context into which Christ's action was placed so that it might contact the present world. This action of the Mass, which is the key to the present-day redemption of men, is simultaneously the act of Christ and of the Church. Christ's own community actually shares in his redemptive work.

Effecting of reconciliation. Sin is essentially an alienation of men originally destined to be sons, an alienation from the heavenly Father. Redemption must consist, then, in a return to the position and role of sons. That this is effected in the Mass can be seen from the externals of the ceremony. The Eucharist is an action of reconciliation, one which fulfills Christ's parable about the prodigal son. Just as the prodigal was met by a father who went out to seek him, so in the Mass the sinful community of men is met by Christ as the sacrament of his Father. This Father has sent Christ as the good shepherd to search out and find those who had strayed from the Father. Just as the recovery of his prodigal son was celebrated with a great family feast by the father in the parable, so, too, the reconciliation of men to the heavenly Father is celebrated in the Paschal feast of the Eucharist itself.

Because it is a sacrament, an effective word, the Eucharist not only speaks of men's return to the status of sons of the Father; it actually effects that return. The Church has always recognized this fact by making the "Our Father" an integral part of the Eucharistic liturgy. Moreover, this prayer, which "we dare to say" only because of Christ's own directive that we do so, is placed in the liturgy of the Mass as the introduction to the Communion ceremony. This seems to explain quite clearly the meaning of Communion itself as an act proper to sons. Reconciled to the Father in and through his Son, we are once more welcome at the table of God.

The effecting of reconciliation in the Mass is also symbolized and caused by the exchange of gifts. As the Mass begins, the Christian community, with the risen Christ in its midst, approaches the altar of God and lays on the sacred table its gifts of food and drink. For a sinful people to do this is clearly a gesture that signifies a desire to be reconciled with the Father. And if the gift of man in this gesture of sacrifice be accepted by God, it is a sign that reconciliation has been effected.

Acceptance of the community's gift takes place in the consecration of the Mass. At this moment, by transforming the bread and wine into the body and blood of Christ, the Father makes our human gift his own. In a true sense, he has removed it definitively from our possession. But he has also prepared it as a gift in return, thus sealing in unexpected fashion the reconciliation. He accepts us back into sonship by giving us, under the Eucharistic species, his own Son, so that we can once more find identification with that Son and so share in divine sonship. Thus the ceremony of reconciliation in the Mass is not only a matter of God's acceptance of man's appeasing gift; it is a familial exchange of gifts. The Father once more recognizes us as sons by the very action of making us sons.

EUCHARISTIC DEDICATION

When the New Testament literature describes the actual process of mankind's redemption, it speaks of it as a rededication of a people to the Father. This categorizing of redemption in terms of dedication is inseparably linked with the idea and reality of covenant. Both in the Old Testament and in the early Christian community, the covenant meant that a people had been set aside to establish God's kingly rule. The people's own choice to offer themselves to God enters into the establishment of this covenant dedication, but the actual effecting of the covenant is the work of God himself. It is God who sets a people apart as his own, as a dedicated community.

This dedication of the people was aptly symbolized in Old Testament sacrificial ceremonial. Bringing gifts to Yahweh, and dedicating these gifts by placing them on the altar of sacrifice, was calculated to indicate the people's own desire to set themselves aside as belonging to Yahweh. However, the final sealing of this dedication required Yahweh's action in accepting and setting aside the gift. This was effected through the sacrificial fire which, acting as Yahweh's instrument, changed the gift.

Not only was the community as a whole considered to be a dedicated people, but the individuals within the community were also set apart for Yahweh. This was particularly true of such men as the kings or priests, who played a special role in the life of the people. This was not merely an external or ritualistic dedication; in their lives and their behavior these men were to be truly "Yahweh's men," given over to his service, consciously dedicated to the fulfillment of Yahweh's will for his people. This Old Testament ideal of full personal dedication to the service of Yahweh and his people finds its highest expression in the passages of the book of Isaiah that describe the Servant of Yahweh (the famous "Servant songs"). These passages tell us about one who will come as a mediator of God's salvation, one who will be totally given over to fulfilling God's will and whose dedication will be so complete that he will accept suffering and death in order to establish the covenant between God and man.

In the New Testament sacrifice of the Eucharist this notion of dedication is even more prominent. Christ, who is the principal agent of the Eucharistic offering, is himself the Servant—for example, at his baptism and transfiguration. The narrative of his passion and death makes it perfectly clear that the early Church saw, as did Jesus himself, his sacrificial death as fulfilling the Servant songs. Though from the first moment of his earthly existence Jesus was fully dedicated to accomplishing the Father's work of redemption, it is in his death and resurrection that he is definitively set apart from the profane world.

Christ set himself apart as a dedicated victim, in order to extend this priestly action into the lives of men. He entered completely into the realm of the sacred, i.e., into risen life, so that he might lead others to this same situation. At the last supper, as he was already beginning this solemn dedication of himself, he prayed to his Father: . . . "that they also, whom you have given me, may be with me where I am" (Jn 17:24). Earlier he had said of his brethren, "and for their sake I consecrate myself" (Jn 17:19). We can see, then, that Christ's own sacrificial dedication to the Father lies at the very heart of his redeeming activity.

In the Mass, Christ is present as continuing this self-dedication, inviting the assembled Christians to join their own dedication to his, and making it possible for them to do so by sharing with them his own priestly office and power. This priestly office had come to each of them in their Baptism, when they received the participation in Christ's priesthood that we call the sacramental character. Now in the Eucharistic action they exercise this sacramental character by dedicating themselves as a community whose head is the one high priest, Christ.

If we examine the attitude Christians should have as they perform this act of Eucharistic self-dedication, we can see how it coincides with the very process of redemption being accomplished in them. Such an act of dedication is a conscious ordering of oneself, in acknowledgement and love and freedom, to the Father. This conscious act is the very opposite of sin. Therefore, in performing this Eucharistic act, the Christian community is reordering itself to the Father, in union with Christ and by his power. Consistent and intelligent participation in the sacrifice of the Mass is meant to overcome gradually that disorder of human personality which is sin and concupiscence. Not that the assembled Christians can by themselves redeem themselves. The very attitude they are meant to have is one of admitting their need to be redeemed by the Father. This Father, who will not impose his saving love on those who do not freely wish it, then redeems them by drawing them to himself.

EUCHARISTIC TRANSFORMATION

Probably the most basic symbolism that runs through the Christian sacraments is that of transformation. In his public life, in the first of the signs he worked in preparation for the understanding of the sacraments, Christ at Cana transformed the water into wine. At the high point of sacramental life, at the consecration of the Mass, the symbolism is still that of transformation.

Closer scrutiny shows that what is signified and effected by this symbolism is the reality we call sanctifying grace. Grace is a radical transformation of the human person. It is this transformation in grace that constitutes the most basic reality of man's redemption. What man needs from a redeeming God is a reorientation of his being. This is precisely what the reality of sanctifying grace is: the reorientation of man to the heavenly Father. The effecting of grace is the effecting of redemption.

The Eucharist, more than any other form of sacramental action, speaks clearly and effectively of this Christian transformation. As the continuing mystery of human life and death, centering around the Passover of Christ from this earthly life to the life of resurrection, the Eucharist communicates to God's people the life that Christ himself possesses. Giving himself in Communion under the external signs most appropriate to signifying life, bread and wine, the living Christ not only gives life to men, he also gives his own risen life. His action is not merely one of vivifying; the very act of vivifying is one of Christianizing. To be a Christian means more than belonging to a particular religious organization; it means more than following the teaching and example of Christ. In its full sense, it means really living the Christ-life; it means *sharing a new way of human existing in and with Christ*. This is what the Eucharistic action reveals to us, for the bread and wine are Christianized by having their very inner reality transformed into the risen Christ. So, too, the assembled Christians who are represented by the bread and wine that they have offered are Christianized by the grace-life that comes from Christ.

Though this new life consists, most fundamentally, in the sanctifying grace that transforms the very roots of our personal being, its full scope embraces also the new activity that comes to us in this transformation. To live out the Christ-life means to live with the new vision of faith and the new motivation of charity that come from Christ. Nowhere else can the Christian community live this Christian faith and love so intensely as in the Eucharist itself. In the action of the Mass, the assembled Christians share a consciousness and love of Christ, as well as a consciousness and love of the Father.

This means that the highest powers of Christians at Mass, their intellects and their wills, their imaginations and emotions, are being directed in faith and love to the Persons of the Trinity. Again we can note that this is the very opposite of the attitude of one who sins, that the entire psychological life of man is being reoriented in faith and love, and so redeemed. No force in the internal life of man is more redemptive than true and deep love; no situation in a Christian's life is meant to foster such love more than the Eucharist. So it is that the Eucharist continues Christ's redeeming work throughout all the generations of mankind's existence on this earth.

COMMUNITY, FREEDOM AND FINALITY

SOCIAL ASPECT OF EUCHARISTIC REDEMPTION

Christians who are being redeemed in and by the Eucharist are engaged in a common action. We mean more than this, however, when we say that the redeeming action of the Eucharist is social in nature. What we mean is that society itself is being redeemed, the society of the Church primarily, but also the wider society of mankind.

When Christians gather for the celebration of the Eucharist, they already form a community that shares in Christ's redemption. But this community requires further redemption. The Church is never as fully a community of love, a community of living faith, as it is meant to be. Because its members still harbor animosities, prejudices, jealousies—even toward other members of the Church—the unity and peace that Christ wishes his Church to have are never fully realized. Because its members are sinful men, the Church is never fully faithful to Christ. Its purpose of achieving Christ's kingdom is always somewhat associated with other, less lofty objectives.

St. Paul's letter to the Ephesians tells us that Christ, in the course of human history, is preparing the Church for himself as a bride without stain or blemish (Eph 5). This action of Christ takes place in all the sacraments, but most specially in the Eucharist whose very symbolism points to the bridal union between the Church and Christ. Throughout its history, the Church is being slowly drawn more closely to Christ; Christ is patiently working by his love to shape the Church to greater maturity.

As we reflect on the various elements in the act of the Mass, we can see how they are designed to form the assembled Christians into an ever deeper community. All listen to one word of God in scripture and liturgy, and so they should more and more come to share one vision of life. All profess their acceptance of one heavenly Father, and so should become increasingly aware of their common sonship and of their brotherhood with one another. All receive the very same Eucharistic body of Christ, and so share life together, even more intimately than do the members of a human family.

In one of his parables, Christ described the Church as leaven placed in a mass of dough. This description points to the historical role of the Church. It exists in the world of men in order to gradually transform human society according to the vision and love of Christ. In this process, the Eucharist is intended to play the pivotal role. From the Mass, Christians are meant to derive the vision of Christian faith so as to transmit it to their contemporaries, and thus gradually change the patterns of human life. From that same action of the Eucharist they are meant to share ever more deeply in Christ's love for men and bear that love out to men as a redeeming force. As human history unfolds, all the truth of men and their world and all the goodness of created reality is meant to be transformed by being related to this action of the Mass.

EUCHARIST AS THE ROOT OF APOSTOLATE

If the Eucharist continues Christ's redeeming activity in human history, it must be the principle of all genuine Christian apostolic effort. This does not mean that all who exercise a role in bringing mankind closer to Christ and through him to the Father must do so in constant consciousness of dependence on the Mass. But, in fact, the Christian love that is the heart of all true apostolic work flows from Christ's own love present in the Eucharist.

True Christian love impels a person to work against any form of evil he finds oppressing the men of his day. In his own public life, Christ exerted his ministry by attacking evil on every front. His teaching was directed against the error, dishonesty, prejudice and hypocrisy of the men he encountered. His acts of healing were opposed to the evils that afflict man in his body. He spoke out fearlessly against the social injustices of his time. He overcame death in his own passage through it into risen life. And he struck at the very roots of evil by his own rejection of sin and his forgiveness of the sins of other men. This opposition to evil, this liberation of mankind from the shackles of evil, came to its climax in the redemptive passover of Christ to his Father. This mystery is still operative in Christ's Eucharistic action.

Any implementation of the Eucharistic activity of Christ must, then, be a continuation of this same opposition to evil. Christians who in the course of the sacrifice of the Mass truly enter into Christ's own attitude are thereby committing themselves to a life of *effective* charity. They must remain restless until Christ's transforming charity touches men's lives and makes them free and meaningful.

The Christian apostolate must find its motivation in the Eucharist; it is in this action that the community of faith should constantly be dedicating itself to the task of Christianizing the world. But apostolate is also meant to be the "translation" of the Eucharist. This sacrificial action of Christ and of the Church contains *in germ* the meaning of human life, the directions for wise human behavior. But these basic principles of insight must be spelled out in differing detail for different historical situations. This spelling out is the task of the Church. As individuals and in society, Christians must judge which applications of Christ's wisdom are pertinent to a given historical and geographical situation.

Obviously, the "spelling out" aspect of the Christian apostolate is largely the function of lay people in the Church, and necessarily so. They are the ones who are actually involved in the everyday life of mankind, engaged in business and the professions, confronted with the demands and challenges of family life. For the vast majority of men, the lay person is the only point of contact with the mystery of Christianity. He and he alone can act as a sacrament of Christ. Hence it is vitally important that lay people participate in the Eucharist with understanding, so that they can bring the word that the Mass speaks into the lives of men.

EUCHARIST AS SOURCE OF FREEDOM

From its inception, God's activity in human history has been a liberating activity; God has always revealed himself as one who frees men from enslavement. Christ stated explicitly that his purpose in becoming man was to bring freedom to the human race (Jn 8). This is an essential element of his redeeming action.

Yet Christ said something about his freeing action that is not easily understood: he makes men free by bringing them truth (". . . and the truth will make you free"; Jn 8:32). The difficulty is increased because law expresses what true human behavior should be; and our superficial human judgments tend to oppose law and freedom. Actually, the opposite is true: without law man's life on this earth, which is unavoidably social, would be sheer chaos; and in the midst of this lawless chaos no one would be free. True law, the expression and norm of order, is the foundation of free society.

Though this relation of law to freedom is correct in principle, there is at times an application of law to human lives that is excessively limiting, narrowly restrictive, inhuman. While law is a blessing (one of the most basic and important blessings Yahweh gave the people of Israel), legalism loads men "with burdens hard to bear" (Lk 11:46). Aware of this potential problem, Christ provided for it in most basic fashion by *being* the new law: "Come, follow me" (Mt 4:19). In other words, Christ offered himself as an ideal of human behavior. This was evident in his own inner attitude of honesty and love, his straightforward acceptance of life, his openness to other persons and genuine esteem for them. He could summarize much of this in his command: "Love one another as I have loved you" (Jn 13:34). Above all, in the redemptive act that extended from the last supper to the resurrection, he lived out a most sublime example of human greatness. It is very seldom noticed that this was also a unique instance of human free behavior. Christ did nothing that he did not wish to do. As he told the scribes and pharisees: "No one takes [my life] from me, but I lay it down of my own accord. I have power to lay it down, and I have power to take it again" (Jn 10:18).

The Eucharist is the law of Christianity because Christ is still freely and totally expressing his love. This redeeming action of Christ liberates men from evil; it is also the supreme example to men of the way in which they themselves are to attain freedom by his help. Ultimately, love is the force that works in our own internal life to liberate us; he who knows how to love genuinely is a truly free man. Jesus commanded his followers to love, because he knew that this would be the very thing that would bring about the deep freedom that he wished them to possess. The most basic law, then, of Christianity—and this the Eucharist should teach us—is that men should strive for freedom by loving.

Again, the Eucharist is a source of freedom because it is a source of hope. The presence of the risen Christ, giving himself in risen life so that we may share with him his fulfilled way of being, is the basis of our Christian hope. Because we have this hope, we possess a counter-agent to the many deep-seated fears that confine us. Few things are so radically opposed to true human freedom as is fear. Because of fear, whether of physical suffering and death, or of rejection by one's fellow men, or of failure, we all do many things we do not really wish to do. Because of fear, we leave undone many things we really wish to do. If such fears can be banished, we are much freer to act as authentic persons, much freer to be our own true selves. If it be understood for what it is, the Eucharist can powerfully help to free us from these dispiriting fears.

ESCHATOLOGICAL NATURE OF THE EUCHARIST

During Old Testament times, particularly during the period of the great prophets, there developed a mentality that is sometimes called "eschatological." By this is meant the expectancy of some future situation in which God would realize his plans for Israel. This future situation, the "day of the Lord" when Yahweh himself would come to save his people, would not however be something totally new; it would be, at least to some extent, the outgrowth of the centuries-long process by which he was guiding and saving Israel.

Christianity, too, is eschatology. Though Christ in his historical coming was an absolutely unparelleled instance of human existing, a man whose human greatness will never be equalled, still what he did in his human life among us was the beginning of something that looks toward a future fulfillment. Only through the course of the Church's history will the full expression of Christ's redemptive work be achieved. For this reason, the presence of Christ's action in the Eucharist is always the source of a Christianization yet to be obtained in the lives of men. The Eucharist points to a "day of the Lord" yet to come, the final realization of Christ's plan for his Church and for mankind. Until the end of human history the Church will always be a community "on the way"; and the celebration of the Eucharist will be the sign that the community is truly being led by Christ to eventual fulfillment—for he himself in his risen life is already in possession of that goal.

The history of the Church is the process of the risen Christ gradually leading the Christian community to the condition of maturity in faith and love which will be its full reflection of him. Over the centuries, as he leads his Church toward the unending glory he has prepared for it by his own Passover, Christ carries on his redeeming work in and through the action of the Eucharist. It is in the Mass that redemption is revealed to us. It is by the Mass that this redemption is actually achieved in us.

BIBLIOGRAPHY FOR CHAPTER 10

BACKGROUND READING

Y. Congar, *Mystery of the Temple,* Westminster, Newman, 1962. Excellent synthesis of the revelation on God's dwelling with men, the basis for Jewish and Christian worship. Fundamental to the understanding of the Church and its life of worship.

J. Gaillard, "Faith and the Sacraments," *Theology Digest* 9(1961), pp. 161-164. One of the finest presentations of the way faith is meant to function in sacramental worship.

J. Jungmann, *The Early Liturgy,* Notre Dame University Press, 1961. In its clear description of the early developments of sacramental ritual, this book gives a valuable insight into the way in which early liturgy influenced the development of Christian creeds.

H. McCabe, *The People of God,* New York, Sheed and Ward, 1964. More than a book on the Eucharist alone, this volume is an interesting discussion of sacraments in the life of the Church.

WORKS ON EUCHARIST AS WORSHIP

C. Davis, *Theology for Today,* New York, Sheed and Ward, 1962. Chap. 17, "The Mass as the Assembly of Christians" (pp. 232-247), helps to point to the intrinsic function of the Christian community in the significance and action of the Mass.

G. Diekmann, *Come Let Us Worship,* Baltimore, Helicon, 1961. Popular in style, this book contains excellent insights and orientations from the thought and experience of one of the world's leading liturgical scholars.

H. Küng, *That the World May Believe,* New York, Sheed and Ward, 1963. His chapters, "Was it always like this?" (pp. 47-59) and "Our liturgy" (pp. 61-73) give simple yet provocative suggestion as to what Eucharistic worship should be.

THE EUCHARIST AS WORSHIP

•

WITH CHRIST TO THE FATHER

•

WORSHIP IN HISTORY AND SCRIPTURE

THE NATURE OF WORSHIP

One of the most common ways in which people think of the Eucharist is as an act of worship. Catholics are aware that they must praise God through Eucharistic participation, but the exact reason for the obligation is not always clear to them. To a large extent they do not really understand what is meant by "worship," nor the way in which the Eucharist is worship. It might be well, then, in discussing the material of this chapter to examine first the notion of worship, and then proceed to see *how* the Eucharist fulfills this idea.

No element is more basic in the notion of worship than that of "acknowledgment." In every religion, the act of worship, whether private or official, involves a recognition of some divinity. This divinity may be seen as kindly or hostile, as connected with some particular phase of life or nature or as the supreme (and perhaps only) ruler of the universe. But the humans who perform the act of worship always tend to look upon the god as having power, as being important in men's lives, as deserving some recognition. By the same act, the worshipper is admitting his own dependence upon and his own need of divine help. He is thereby acknowledging his own "creatureliness."

In a situation in which the divinity being worshipped is looked upon as benevolent, the act of worship may include the element of thanksgiving. If the worshipper believes that the god has been favorable to him, has provided him with life and happiness, then his very admission of this fact constitutes at least part of what we call thanksgiving. However, it is also possible that the admission of blessings received can imply, as it seems to have implied in some religions, an attitude of shrewdness—praising the God for his help serves the purpose of keeping him happy, so that he will continue to be favorable.

To acknowledge the sovereignty of some divinity, to express gratitude or some similar but less lofty sentiment, ritual gifts were used. These gifts were at times food or drink, which could then be used in a sacred meal ceremony that signified union with the divinity. But in themselves the gifts expressed devotedness to a god, recognition of his superiority, acknowledgment of his past blessings, petition for his continued benevolence.

Quite naturally, the public and communal recitation of prayers, the singing of hymns of praise and similar ritual uses of language are found in practically every religion. These signify the community's worship of their divinity. As we examine these forms of religious expression, we notice the same basic attitudes being manifested as in the giving of gifts. Worship need not be verbalized in this way; it can be a silent recognition of a god. However, there seems to be universal recognition that it is proper to externally express one's attitude of worship.

Worship of the True God

We can see from the first three precepts of the ten commandments (as recorded in Exodus 20:1-11) how basic a role worship played in Old Testament morality. This early part of the decalogue, which is concerned with Israel's recognition of Yahweh, controls the entire law of Israel. Even before the bulk of the people came to realize that there was no other God than Yahweh, the Law's exclusion of other divinities was an influence leading the Israelites toward conscious monotheism.

Recognition of the true god still remains the most basic demand of human behavior. Any authentic human living must be based on a straightforward acceptance of reality. To live truly as man, one must accept honestly what it means to be a man. But there is nothing more radical in the human situation than the fact that man is a creature. He finds meaning, therefore, by reference to the god who has created him and still sustains him in existence. What man thinks of his god or gods is therefore supremely important, for he finds his own self-identification in terms of this god. To refuse such acknowledgment of relation to the divine, to deny worship to the god who is the source and goal of human existing, is to deny a most important aspect of reality. Worship is an acceptance of reality, a reality that comes from God, is created by him and is therefore essentially good.

Israel expressed its acceptance of this one God, Yahweh, by entering into the Mosaic covenant. Acknowledging the fact that their existence as a people came from this divinity who had delivered them from Egypt, they began a centuries-long process of expressing this in acts of ritual worship. Gradually, as their religious insight deepened, they incorporated into their worship the recognition of Yahweh's supreme and unique cosmic rule. But this comparatively philosophical approach to the oneness of Yahweh as their God was always secondary; Yahweh was first of all "the god who brought our fathers out of Egypt." The Israelites were not primarily concerned with acknowledging a first cause of existence; they committed themselves by covenant to acknowledging their dependence as a people upon this God who had acted in history on their behalf.

It is important to note that the Israelites did not direct themselves in their worship to the "god of the philosophers." It is true, of course that Yahweh, whom they adored, did possess all the attributes—infinity, eternity, simplicity, and so forth—that metaphysical analysis can ascribe to the first cause of creation. In later centuries Old Testament thought actually came to this realization. But when the Israelites worshipped their God, it was a definite personal being to whom they directed themselves, someone who had spoken to them through Moses and who continued to speak through the prophets. There was a directness in their contact with him; he was not some supreme good at which they arrived by a process of reasoning.

Thus Jesus spoke of his Father as "he whom you call your God" (Jn 8:54); the Jews of his day found it perfectly normal to think of God in this very direct fashion. Christ did not in any way have to deny the validity of the Old Testament worship of God, nor for that matter the value of the worship offered by "natural religions." He had only to point out its inadequacy. If we are to recognize the full reality of God, then we must know that he is "Father"; not just "fatherly" in general, but the Father of our Lord Jesus Christ. And we must know also that this Father shares the fullness of his divinity with Christ and with the Spirit. In other words, full and genuine worship must be directed to three divine Persons, each of whom is fully God. True worship must be an acknowledgment of the reality of the blessed Trinity.

If all honest worship is an acceptance of reality, then Christian worship must be an acceptance of the Christian revelation about reality. It must acknowledge that God the Father "so loved the world that he gave his only Son"; that this Son, sent by the Father, works through the mystery of his redemptive incarnation for the salvation and transformation of human life; that this Son as risen Lord sends his Spirit into the Church to make it the living instrument of his continuous redeeming love. In other words, Christian worship must be a profession of faith in the revelation brought to us in Christ.

In sending into our midst his Son, who is his Word, the heavenly Father is offering men an invitation to divine friendship. This is the mystery of mankind's "vocation." Any honest acknowledgment of the Christian dimension of reality demands, then, far more than abstract acceptance of the facts of Christianity.

It calls for a personal response in love. One cannot truly say "yes" to an offer of friendship without giving his own love in return. In Old Testament times God had already stressed this affective aspect of worship when he spoke through prophets like Hosea, saying "I desire steadfast love and not sacrifice, the knowledge of God, rather than burnt offerings" (Hos 6:6).

CHRIST'S WORSHIP OF THE FATHER

Discussion of Christian worship must center on Christ's own act of worshipping the Father. Only he is the high priest. Only he of himself offers effective recognition to the Father. We Christians share in his unique priestly act, share in his acknowledgment of the Father. "No one knows the Father except the Son and anyone to whom the Son chooses to reveal him" (Mt 11:27). Christian worship of the Father in the Mass has validity and adequacy only because Christ himself is the principal agent in this action. If we can say "Our Father," it is only because he has so instructed us, and because he says it in union with us. Our first effort, then, must be to examine Christ's worship of his Father.

First of all, we must remember that it is *as man* that Christ worships his Father. In his divine being as the second Person of the blessed Trinity, Christ cannot profess any dependence upon the Father, for they are absolutely and entirely equal. Once incarnated, however, Christ as man can and must admit the dependence of his humanity upon the loving providence of his Father. In his human consciousness he knows that he has been sent into human history because of his Father's love for man. He knows that he has his redeeming mission and his unique grace and priesthood from this same loving Father. He knows that the ultimate explanation of all created reality is the love of his Father. And in his human awareness, Christ remains utterly open to this reality of his Father. We can see this by reading carefully the pages of the gospels. The consciousness of Jesus is continuously dominated by awareness of his Father. This is evident from Christ's constant mention of the Father.

There never was a moment when Jesus did not wish to open himself utterly to the reality of his Father. Yet, it must still be stressed that his acknowledgment of the Father was a free human act; it was his own deliberate choice. This is the same act of human choice we examined when we studied Christ's act of sacrifice. Throughout his human life on this earth, Jesus was totally in agreement with the concrete life-situation as given him by the Father. This agreement carried through the crucial experience of passing through death into new life. Christ's entire life-experience was an act of worship, which came to fulfillment and focus in the final event of Christian redemption.

No human experience more sharply reminds us of our dependence and creatureliness than the experience of death. We are hesitant and fearful at the prospect of death precisely because it is not something under human control; man does not even know with clarity or in detail what awaits him in the next life.

And so trustful acceptance of that death is a supreme acknowledgment that God is truly Father. This was true also in the case of Christ: in his human experiential knowing (though this was not his only way of knowing), he did not know what it meant to pass through death until he actually experienced it. For him, it was truly a passage into the unknown, even though he went with utter trust in the Father. In dying, Christ experienced how completely a man is dependent for his very existence upon the sustaining love of the Father; for in his human consciousness and freedom Christ admitted this fact gladly and gratefully.

In this way, Christ's acceptance of the need to face death in order to pass into new life was a radical act of worship, one that necessarily involved his total humanity. As we have already seen, the death of Christ is placed in a solemn ritual context by the last supper; for it was in the supper that he publicly and liturgically consecrated himself to his passover. The supper and crucifixion (along with the resurrection) constitute together the most total action of worship ever performed by man.

Knowing his Father as no other man possibly could, faced with the most demanding situation in human existence (the imminence of death), Christ remained totally open to his Father. At the moment that he passed into new life, Christ accepted his Father without reserve, accepted also his utter dependence as man upon the love of his Father as giver of this new life. However, as he did this, Christ was acting not simply as an individual man, but precisely as the new Adam, the new head of the human race, whose own acknowledgment of the Father redirected the entire race back to God in worship. The first Adam's refusal to acknowledge the sovereignty of God had resulted in the alienation of men from God. Christ's supreme act of worship reverses the state of man, reorientating him to the Father.

At the moment of his passage through death, the very core of Christ's act of worship was his inner attitude. Since this attitude of acceptance remains forever unchanged in the human consciousness of Christ, he has never ceased so to worship the Father—and he worships this way today. Abiding with his Father in the fullness of his risen glory, Christ unendingly praises the Father for his life-giving love of mankind. This is the center of that heavenly liturgy in which we are all meant one day to share, and which is symbolically described in the book of the Apocalypse.

There is only one risen Christ. If today he continues his unique worship of the Father, he does this as present in his Church and particularly in the action of the Eucharist. When the Christian community in its life in the world praises the Father for his providential goodness, when it sees the truth and goodness and beauty of creation as a gift from this Father and thanks him for it, when it uses these gifts of the Father with reverent gratitude, it does so in and through Christ who abides in the Church as its Lord and Savior. When the Christian community gathers to formalize this praise in the action of Eucharist, of thanksgiving, it does so as the body of Christ. Christian worship of the Father in the Eucharist is a sacrament of Christ's own worship which is expressed through the words and gestures of the faithful.

The purpose of the Mass is, then, that the incarnated Son of God may, in and through his brethren, speak his praise of the Father throughout the entire course of human history. Not only does he continue in his risen life to acknowledge by his human consciousness and love the goodness of his Father, he is also able to express that attitude of worship in visible form through the medium of the Church's Eucharistic act. The Mass is the ultimate act of worship because it is Christ's own act of worship.

OUR WORSHIP

WORSHIP BY THE PRIESTLY COMMUNITY

When we say that the Eucharistic action of the Mass is the worship given by Christ himself as man, this does not imply that the participation of the Church in this act is without its own meaning or value. All the value of this worship derives from Christ, but what Christians themselves do has its intrinsic value. Our acknowledgement of the Father in the Mass is valid and redeeming worship, precisely because Christ in this action joins us to himself and allows us to share in his own relationship to the Father. We really worship, but we do so as Christians.

Each of us received the capacity to express praise of the Father in this effective manner when we were baptized. In that ceremony of initiation, we were introduced into a priestly people, into a community whose primary purpose is to perform this act of worship. We were given an official delegation to participate in this public act of Christian praise. This delegation is not a mere external appointment to a position; God has directed us toward a definite role by giving us that orientation to priestly function we call the sacramental character.

This sacramental character points the new Christian toward the fulfillment of his Baptism by participation in the Eucharist. Without such participation, our Baptism would, in a sense, be frustrated. Baptism is a first profession of faith, a first acknowledgment of the heavenly Father who sends his Son in the mystery of death and resurrection to give us life. But in itself it is only the promise of a covenant with God, a pledge to go on to the fullness of Christian living, to the exercise of the priesthood conferred in Baptism.

Baptism inducts new members into the Church, the community of faith and worship. In the Eucharist this community of faith assembles, in union with Christ who is its head, to express its faith in the act of sacrificial worship. Gathered together, the Christian community celebrates the new covenant enacted in and through Christ. As a continuing covenant action, the Mass is a constant acknowl-

edgment of the God of the covenant, the Father of our Lo'
in the Old and in the New Testament, what is primarily *?*
munity is its liturgical service of God. In Israel this was
ficial ritual; in the Church through the unique sacrifice o.
which Christians participate.

At this point in our discussion it might be good to advert briefly to the
of the Holy Spirit in the Christian act of worship. In the liturgies of Eastern
Christianity, there is much clearer recognition in the rite of the Mass itself of
the crucial importance of the Spirit. In our Latin liturgy this role is less accentu-
ated; yet it is of capital importance. The Mass is essentially a "word" that Christ
and the community speak together; and that word is "Father." We recognize
not some abstract and detached infinite being, but a person who is the Father of
Christ and (because of our identity with Christ) our Father. Yet St. Paul assures
us that we are incapable of saying "Father" except through the power of the
Spirit who dwells in our midst and who speaks for us (Gal 4:6).

In the mystery of the Trinity, the second Person, the Son, expresses his love
for the Father through the procession of the Spirit. Only this equally infinite
Person, whose very personality is the expression of infinite love, suffices to express
the Son's love for his Father. Become incarnate, the Son does not cease to
express his love for the Father in this way. The Spirit is for Christ, even in his
human love for the Father, the expression of his total openness to his Father.
We who are joined to Christ, we with whom he identifies himself, possess what
is his—including his Spirit. And so, for us also, the Spirit expresses our sonship,
speaks to the Father in adequate fashion that word which we of ourselves so
feebly say, "Our Father."

This is not to say that the Holy Spirit substitutes for us in acknowledging the
Father. As the community of the Church, we are the ones who speak our sonship,
for we are the ones who are sons, the Holy Spirit is not. But it is by the transforming ("son-making") power of the Spirit that we are rendered capable of
recognizing the Father as ours, as related to us in mysterious familiarity. Christ
expresses his love for his Father, gives glory to him, by sending the Spirit into
us to make us sons; for the glory of a father as father is to have sons. This glory
of the Father we bring to fulfillment, under the Spirit's urging, when we
acknowledge that sonship in the action of the Eucharist.

As far back as we can trace the history of the Eucharistic liturgy (to St. Paul's
first letter to the Corinthians), we find that the Mass has been a profession of
faith in the redemptive mission of Christ. The very notion of ritually com-
memorating Christ's Passover involved belief in the unique significance of this
event. And the very early utilization of the "Our Father" as a part of Eucharistic
liturgy reflects that mentality of praising the Father which the gospels incessantly
attribute to Jesus himself.

In the very early document on liturgy, the *Apostolic Tradition* of St. Hippolytus (c. 215), we have the ceremony of the Eucharist detailed for us. We

find here a form of the canon of the Mass which undoubtedly was already in use in the second century. As we read through this canon, which is really just one continuous Eucharistic prayer, we see that it is a combined creed and hymn of praise. It is worship precisely in that it expresses the faith of the Christian Church in the goodness of this Father who sent his beloved Servant, Jesus, to carry out our redemption by death and resurrection.

We can see how intimately sacrament and profession of faith were linked in the early Church if we reflect upon the fact that the earliest creeds originated in the sacramental rites. When the first of the great conciliar creeds, that of Nicea-Constantinople, came into existence somewhat later, it was very logically incorporated into the Eucharistic liturgy, where we still have it today.

Christian faith consists in two elements: intellectual assent to the truth of the Father's self-revelation in Christ, and practical acceptance of Christ and Christian life. Both of these elements of faith are able to come to their fullest realization in the Eucharist, for the Eucharist is the situation in which the Christian community is confronted with the totality of divine revelation in a living and present form. It is the supreme challenge to human love to respond to the divine invitation of friendship.

ASSENT TO REVELATION

As an intellectual assent, faith is not a saying "Yes" to some abstract and impersonal truth. It is not an insight into the logic of some reasoning process (though there definitely is reasonableness in a mature acceptance of the evidence for Christ and Christianity). Faith is saying "Yes" to the reality of three Persons who are "for us." It is an intellectual understanding, but of an experiential kind. It is knowing that Christ is savior "for us"; it is having the conscious experience of being a Christian and a son of the Father.

It is above all in the Eucharist, when Christ is clearly speaking his identity with us by giving himself to us in Communion, that we are able to experience the reality of redemption. It is in the very activity of offering sacrifice in union with Christ that we are meant to discover what it means to be Christians. And it is in the very act of placing the significant action of the Mass that we admit publicly that we accept its significance, the redemption of mankind through the redemptive mystery of Christ.

Gathered together for the Eucharist, the Christian community encounters the gift of friendship offered by the three divine Persons. If the sacramentality of the Mass says anything, it says that the Father loves men to the extent of sending for their sakes his Son and his Spirit. He does this in the Mass. It says that the Son so loves us that he passed through death into new life, so that he might share this new life with us. This is precisely what he does in the Mass. It says that the Spirit so loves us that he dwells in our midst, giving us divine life and

sonship, enabling us to associate personally with Father and
understands what is happening in the Mass, it is a situat
intimacy. It is a situation in which the three divine Person/
to draw men into the circle of their own transcendent happn.

In response to this divine offer of love, the Christian community a.
the action of the Eucharist. Listening to the word of epistle and gospc.,
responds with the creed. It brings its gifts to show its desire to establish union
with God, gifts that will make possible a sacred covenant meal. Above all, at
the moment of the Communion, the assembled Christians receive the body of
Christ as the pledge of their union with him and through him with the Father.
This entire reception of the divine love and responsive self-giving on the part
of Christians at Mass is done in a spirit of rejoicing and gratitude. This is
Eucharist, an act of giving thanks.

Before leaving this topic of the Mass as a profession of the community's faith,
we might mention that the other sacraments are, in analogous fashion, professions of faith. In Baptism, Confirmation, Orders and Matrimony the Christian
publicly professes belief in the mystery of Christ and Christianity by accepting
a function in the community of faith. In Penance and Anointing of the Sick
he states his need for healing and his belief that such healing comes to him in
the Church through the redeeming power of the risen Christ. But it is in the
Eucharist that the Church most fully states its faith, most deeply enters into union
with Christ, most clearly commits itself to sharing with Christ his own redeeming
mission and his own worship of the Father.

THE GLORY OF GOD

Since they are God, the three divine Persons can have no other final goal than
themselves in creating the world and man. Being infinite, there could not be
something or someone other than themselves to which their activity would ultimately be ordered. Somehow, then, all creation and the entire process of human
history is meant to terminate at the Father through the Son and Spirit.

This is not an attitude of selfishness on the part of the three divine Persons.
Actually, nothing is added to them, no benefit comes to them. Only man is the
beneficiary of their creation—if he does not reject its ultimate blessing of divine
life by his own sinful abuse of freedom. Humanly, we tend to think that the
Father "gets something" from our praise and acknowledgment and that this is
his glory. But what is really involved in the glory of God is the fact that the
divine love is manifested in the achievements of his human creatures. The
Fatherhood of God is manifested in men being sons. The higher the level of
true personal achievement on men's part, the greater the manifestation of divine
love.

This highest achievement of man comes precisely in the act of Eucharistic
worship. This action most completley fulfills the human person. Human fulfill-

..ient can only come through the perfecting of man's highest and most truly personal powers of being and action: his intellect and will. But these powers are most fully engaged and developed only when they are in contact with their most perfect object: ultimate truth and ultimate goodness. And the conjunction of these two powers in the power of choice can find its realization only when a man engages himself totally in the most radical of choices, the choice of his own identification and destiny. This is the Eucharistic situation—a man's power of understanding comes face to face with infinite divine truth personally revealing itself to him. A man's power of love is challenged to its depths by the infinite good confronting him as the three divine Persons offer him their friendship. A man chooses identification in terms of Christ and merges his own destiny with Christ's. The very act, then, by which a man worships the Father in the Mass is the act by which he reaches his fullest human development. Personal realization deepens progressively through participation in the Mass, until it reaches its complete fulfillment in risen life.

Not only the individual Christian, but the community of faith as a whole finds fulfillment in this Eucharistic action. The Church has a corporate "intellectual life," a corporate life of charity. As a community, the Church searches for ever deeper understanding of the mystery of Christian salvation, searches for clearer identification of itself, searches for a more exact knowledge of its destiny in this world and beyond. As a community it has a responsibility to acknowledge its dependence upon the love of the Father, its identification with Christ, its dependence upon the life-giving Spirit who is its "soul." All of this it is able to accomplish in the Eucharistic action. At the same time, it is enabled to fulfill its role as bride of Christ by loving acceptance of Christ as its Lord and spouse.

As the supreme and fulfilling action of the community that is of its very nature meant to be catholic, the Eucharist plays the key role in directing all human history and all created reality back to the Father. Catholic by essence, the Church is meant to be found in every period of history, in every culture and language and people. Its members, drawn from all these diverse situations, catch up into their own lives and experiences all the truth of created things (as known by common experience or as known more deeply by scientific research and artistic creation) and all the goodness of creatures. Then, when these Christians, with their diversified life-experience, acknowledge the Father in the Eucharist as source of truth and goodness and beauty, they make it possible for all this created truth and goodness to contact through human consciousness the creator to which their being points. Even more importantly, each generation of Christians lives in the midst of human achievement and experience and absorbs into its own awareness and values the human life of its day. As Christians celebrate the Eucharist they refer all this to the Father in and through Christ. Only Christian faith is able to discover the basic thread of meaning that runs through all the happenings in the universe and in human history—the Father's love for us, manifested in Christ's saving death and resurrection. Only the supreme act of Christian faith is able to acknowledge this meaning of the universe and of human history, and praise the Father for it.

It is because the Eucharist thus channels all creation, natural and supernatural, back to the Father of all gifts, that the solemn central prayer of the Mass, the canon, ends with the doxology: "Through him, and with him, and in him, is to you God the Father almighty, in the unity of the Holy Spirit, all honor and glory."

BIBLIOGRAPHY FOR CHAPTER 11

WORKS ON GENERAL TOPIC OF REDEMPTION

J. Bonsirven, *Theology of the New Testament*, Westminster, Newman, 1963. Written by one of the most competent NT scholars of our day, this book is really a NT theology of redemption. Part 3 (pp. 193-370), which treats of Christ's redemptive mediation, is particularly good.

F. X. Durrwell, *In the Redeeming Christ*, New York, Sheed and Ward, 1963. Though its style is more meditative than theological, this book contains many excellent insights into the concrete process of a Christian's redemption.

——— *The Resurrection*, New York, Sheed and Ward, 1960. This book, one of the most important to appear in the past decade, has been a major influence in drawing attention to the role of Christ's resurrection in the process of redemption.

M. Schmaus, *The Essence of Christianity*, Chicago, Scepter, 1961. This book treats of many of the basic elements of Christian faith, relating them to redemption as a central theme. The author is one of today's leading theologians.

WORKS ON SACRAMENTS AND REDEMPTION

J. Danielou, "Symbolism and History," pp. 417-426 in Caponigri, *Modern Catholic Thinkers.* Stimulating study of the role of sacraments in the redemption of history.

E. Mersch, *Theology of the Mystical Body*, St. Louis, Herder, 1951. Two chapters are particularly pertinent: chap. 11 (pp. 271-322), "Nature of the Redemption" and chap. 18 (pp. 546-593), "Sanctifying Office of the Church: The Sacraments." This book still remains one of the most challenging pieces of theological writing available.

K. Rahner, "Personal and Sacramental Piety," pp. 109-133 in vol. 2 of *Theological Investigations.* An excellent study of the manner in which Christian sacraments enter into the actual process of redeeming a person.

INDEX

Eucharist
  as redemption, 155 ff.
  as sacrifice, 31, 87 ff., 135 ff.
  as word, 140 ff.
  institution of, 15, 108, 123, 125
  promise of, 15, 23-24, 27
  significance of, 151-53
Exodus, 3-5, 7-8, 10, 24, 118, 121 ff.
Expiation, 119

Faith, 1-3, 17 ff., 31 ff., 65, 70 ff., 81, 112,
  137, 141, 148 ff., 161-62, 169 ff.
Father, God the, 10, 13-14, 24, 30, 39, 42,
  47, 55, 59-60, 62, 72-73, 97, 102,
  105 ff., 126 ff., 158, 169 ff.
Fatherhood, 9, 113-14, 126 ff., 137, 175
Forgiveness of sins, 64-66, 84 ff.
Freedom, 21-22, 70, 82-84, 129-30, 163-64
Friendship, 37 ff., 67, 144, 148, 169 ff.

Gesture, 92-94, 144-46, 158, 172
Gift, 37 ff., 55-56, 60, 62, 81-82, 86, 90 ff.,
  95, 112-13, 119, 158, 168
Glory, 10, 80, 127, 149, 153, 165, 171 ff.
Grace
  actual, 80-81
  as new birth, 53-54
  as regeneration, 54-56, 58-59, 63
  as union, 62-64
  necessity of, 77 ff.
  sanctifying, 27, 32, 37, 40-41, 49, 52 ff.,
  70, 81, 95-96, 108, 113, 134, 150
  uncreated 37-38, 42

Holy Orders, Sacrament of, 31-32, 109 ff.

Imposition of hands, 86, 91-94, 111-12
Incarnation, 39, 44, 62, 65, 71, 102, 105 ff.,
  128-30, 146, 156
Incorporation, 16-17, 31-35, 84, 90
Indwelling, 42 ff., 62-63, 95-96, 174-75
Inheritance, 59-60

Israel, 3 ff., 28, 38-39, 43-44, 61-62, 73, 77,
  98-99, 106, 168-69
Israel, New, 7 ff., 17, 21, 24, 27-28

John the Baptist, 2, 5-7, 12-13, 99
Justification, 64-66, 80

Language, 33, 144-45, 168
Last Supper, 14-15, 24, 30, 46, 87, 99,
  120 ff., 131-32, 149-50
Law, Eucharist as, 123, 163-64
Law, Old Testament, 43-44, 99, 141-42,
  168
Layman, role in church, 30-31, 34, 163
Liberation, 82-83, 87, 157, 164
Life
  new, 16 ff., 37, 53-55, 62, 127-28, 170
  supernatural, 1, 32, 34, 46, 55-56, 60-63,
  68, 78, 81, 95
Liturgy, 23, 66, 89, 110, 123-24, 134 ff.
Love
  divine, 38-39, 41-42, 47, 71, 97-98,
  102-3, 156
  human, 41-42, 71 ff., 83, 97, 101-3
  of Christ, 14, 30, 48, 101, 113-14, 133-34,
  162 ff.

Manna, 8-9, 122, 147
Mass (see Eucharist)
Matrimony, 31-32, 90, 95 ff., 101-3, 114
Maturity, 22-23, 72 ff., 90, 97, 165
Merit, 60-61, 64-66, 83, 125, 128
Messiah, 2 ff., 20, 53, 72-73, 132, 148
Metanoia, 6
Ministry, 7, 13, 88, 111-12, 161-62
Miracles, 13, 45, 96, 124-25, 147, 150, 160
Mission, 4-5, 42 ff., 95-96, 109, 170, 173
Mystical Body, 17, 21-22, 33-35, 45-46, 48,
  53, 62, 100-101, 130-31, 134, 153

Obedience, 30, 73, 125-26, 156-57
Oblation, 113, 123, 125-27, 131-32

Date Due

DEMCO NO. 295

		DEC 1 '68	MAY 1 2
APR 10 '67			
JUL 1 3 '67			
JUL 3 1 '67	CANISIUS		
DEC 19 '67	CANISIUS		
FEB 1 '68			
SEP 8 '69	CANISIUS		
DEC 13 '69	CANISIUS		
MAR 8 '70	CANISIUS		
APR 19 '71	CANISIUS		
FEB 25 '74 PAID	CANISIUS		
DEC 1 2 '74	CANISIUS		
FEB 18 '75	MAR 16 '76 CANISIUS		